D1413000

THE EQUALITY ILLUSION

KAT BANYARD

THE EQUALITY ILLUSION

The truth about women and men today

faber and faber

First published in 2010
by Faber and Faber Limited
Bloomsbury House, 74–77 Great Russell Street,
London WC1B 3DA

Typeset by Faber and Faber
Printed in England by Mackays of Chatham, Chatham, Kent

All rights reserved
© Kat Banyard, 2010

The right of Kat Banyard to be identified as author of this
work has been asserted in accordance with Section 77 of the
Copyright, Designs and Patents Act 1988

The opinions expressed in this book are solely those of the author

A CIP record for this book
is available from the British Library

ISBN 978-0-571-24626-7

LIBRARIES NI	
C700301222	
RONDO	12/03/2010
305.42	£ 12.99
CLL	

2 4 6 8 10 9 7 5 3 1

For Mum, Dad, Sarah and Tom

Contents

Acknowledgements

This book is built around interviews with over one hundred individual women and girls – each of whom so generously chose to share with me what were often very painful experiences. Their hope – and mine – was that, by speaking out, society could learn from what they've had to go through and prevent it happening again. I am hugely grateful to them all, and sincerely hope this book does some justice to that aim.

I have been privileged to have Sarah Savitt as my editor, whose fierce intelligence, skill, and passion for feminism have taken this book further than I could have hoped. The whole team at Faber and Faber has been wonderfully supportive of *The Equality Illusion*. Sincere thanks also to my agent Claire Patterson at Janklow and Nesbit – who recognised the acute need for a new book on feminism, and believed in a rather bewildered-looking twenty-five-year-old.

Campaigning alongside Sandrine Leveque to reform lap-dancing club licensing during the year of writing *The Equality Illusion* was a source of constant inspiration. Her courage and commitment to gender equality are awe-inspiring, and her support and insights on the book were invaluable. She is truly a superstar activist.

I am hugely grateful to my friends, family and colleagues

at the Fawcett Society who supported me throughout the process, including those who read through the manuscript and provided input: Sam Lyle, Rosie Downes, and Tamsin Clay, as well as Dorothy, Stephen, Sarah, and Phil Banyard.

Countless individuals and organisations assisted me in my research, and in addition to all those quoted or mentioned in the text, I'd like to thank the following: Anne Quesney at Marie Stopes International, Bronwyn McKenna at UNISON, Campaign for Equality (Iran), Caroline Hames, Cath Elliott, CROP, Debs Reynolds, Education for Choice, Family Planning Association, Jess Baily, Julia Long at Anti-Porn London, Kate Law, Laura Woodhouse at The F-Word, Malcolm Anderson, Marion Moulton, Melissa Farley at Prostitution Research & Education, Refuge, Tender, Toynbee Hall, UK Resource Centre for Women in Science, Engineering and Technology, and Women in Science and Engineering Leadership Institute.

Introduction | An Alarm Call

Today it is widely believed that feminism has achieved its aims and that the struggle for equality between women and men is over. Some even worry that feminism might have gone too far. Nobel Prize winner Doris Lessing, author of *The Golden Notebook* – considered by many to be a key feminist novel – suggests there is now 'an unconscious bias in our society: girls are wonderful; boys are terrible', and says that she has 'nothing in common with feminists'.[1] Sir Stuart Rose, Chairman of Marks & Spencer, has insisted that 'there really are no glass ceilings despite the fact that some of you moan about it all the time . . . You've got a woman fighter pilot who went on to join the Red Arrows . . . I mean what else do you want, for God's sake? Women astronauts. Women miners. Women dentists. Women doctors. Women managing directors. What is it you haven't got?'[2] And when Conservative Party leader David Cameron was asked in public whether or not he was a feminist he replied, 'Er, I don't really know what it means any more,' then venturing, 'But I suspect probably not.'[3] The general consensus seems to be that feminism has had its day. But what does our apparently equal society actually look like?

- Women in the UK are paid 22.6 per cent less per hour than men.
- Women do two-thirds of the world's work, yet receive 10 per cent of the world's income and own 1 per cent of the means of production.[4]
- At least 100,000 women are raped each year in the UK and the rape conviction rate is 6.5 per cent.
- Only 18.3 per cent of the world's members of parliament are women[5] (the UK figure is under 20 per cent).
- During the 1990s the number of men paying for sex acts in the UK doubled.

These are not statistics from a bygone age – this is our world. The equality that so many people see existing between women and men is an illusion. Proclamations that we are 'there' now, that equality has been achieved, have chased feminism from the mainstream. It is time to find the way back – to recognise feminism for what it is: one of the most vital social justice movements of our age.

Insidiously, the problems that remain seem to have become an accepted part of the landscape of our every-day lives – normal and inevitable. Rape happens; women hate their bodies; world leaders are usually male – that's just the way it is. Having spent our lives in a society with these attributes, we have grown accustomed to them. And with so many people asserting that feminism has achieved all it can, it is tempting to conclude that the remaining gaps between women and men are mere by-products of natural physiological difference. But this would be a mis-take. The majority of human beings are, of course, born with a chromosomal structure, reproductive system, and sexual characteristics that are either distinctly male or female,* but although our sex is the result of a biological lottery, the inequality gaps that remain between women and men are not. Rather, they are constructed by society and assigned to us at birth. 'Gender', and all that word implies today, is the net result of the decisions, debates, accidents, and battles played out amongst our 100 billion forebears. It is what it means to be a boy/man or girl/woman in today's society: what constitutes 'masculinity' and 'femininity'. But – crucially – the two genders are not alike in value or status. Throughout the world, men still hold a higher status in society than women. In fact, gender itself pivots on a power relation: the height of masculinity – a 'real man' – is when it is furthest away from the 'depths' of femininity. While the level and forms vary, women and girls in every society on earth have less access to opportunities, resources, and political power than men and boys[6] – not because of sex, but because of gender – something we create.

There have undoubtedly been huge gains for women's rights over the past century. The three periods of most intense activity – often referred to as the three waves of feminism – have helped deliver monumental reforms: equal voting rights for women and men; the legal right for a woman not to be denied employment because of her sex or fired because she becomes pregnant or gets married; and – though only as recently as 1991 – the right not to be subject to rape in marriage. There have also been huge cultural shifts, with issues such as domestic violence now seen as a serious crime rather than a private dispute, and a network of refuges established to support the victims. From

*The Intersex Society of North America report that one in a hundred people's bodies differ from standard male or female.

Mary Wollstonecraft to Germaine Greer to Ariel Levy – activists and theorists throughout the years have created a rich body of feminist thought and together brought about historic gains for women.

Yet despite all this, in reality the struggle for gender equality has only just begun. We are still very early on in the process of unpicking from our society the laws, decrees, practices, and cultures that have accumulated over millennia to enshrine women's subordination. So many legal victories, such as the right to equal pay won in 1970, remain abstract pledges that are yet to translate into reality. Hard-fought gains, such as the right to a legal, safe abortion, are under continual attack: in 2008 all but one of the Conservative Party front bench voted (unsuccessfully) to reduce the upper time limit for women to have an abortion,[7] and routine abortion remains illegal in Northern Ireland. The constantly evolving economic and political world order means the ground we are working on for gender equality is constantly shifting, and new technological developments present challenges unique to this age. To top this all off the route to gender equality is, metaphorically speaking, badly signposted, littered with dead-ends, and beset with traps. Nowhere is this better illustrated than in the present-day normalisation of the sex industry, widely proclaimed as an empowering choice leading towards women's sexual liberation, yet ending in a scale of commercial sexual exploitation never witnessed before in human history, and leaving feminist campaigners in uncharted territory.

Current progress in tackling gender inequalities is glacially slow. Between 1995 and 2008 the worldwide proportion of women in parliament increased by just seven percentage points, from 11.3 to 18.3.[8] The Equality and Human Rights Commission have calculated that at the current rate of change it will take 200 years to achieve gender parity in the UK Parliament – only slightly less than the 212 years it would take for a snail to crawl the entire length of the Great Wall of China.[9] In some areas progress isn't just slow or even stalled – it is actually in reverse. In 2008 the World Economic Forum analysed how much progress countries had made on tackling various gender gaps and found that overall the situation had got worse over the previous year in 41 of the 128 countries they had data for. Similarly, over that same period the gender pay gap in the UK widened.

The ease with which feminism is currently dismissed becomes particularly perplexing, however, in light of the fact that discrimination against women is never far from the surface in many other social-justice problems about which the world is more vocal. Take poverty for example: a fifth of the world's population live on less than US $1 a day[10] and the campaign to end poverty has become one of the biggest social movements of our time. In 2007 a Guinness World Record was set when 43.7 million people demonstrated their commitment to 'Stand Up Against Poverty'.[11] Make Poverty History, the UK arm of the Global Campaign Against Poverty, succeeded in mobilising one in four members of the British public to take action.[12] Hundreds of thousands took to the streets in marches, protests, and vigils, and over three billion people watched Live 8 – a series of concerts across the globe staged in July 2005 to draw the world's attention to those living in poverty.[13] What was less well understood and talked about, however, was the fact that poverty has a female face: 70 per cent of those living on $1 or less a day are women[14] and two-thirds of the 780 million people who are illiterate are also women.[15] It is they who own just 1 per cent of the world's land and property, and where there is a lack of healthcare it is predominantly women who, very often forgoing their education, care for the sick.[16] These facts are not incidental. An international research institute has demonstrated that the number of South Asian children under three years old who are underweight would decrease by 13.4 million if women and men had an equal hand in decision making.[17] Why? Because when resources are thin on the ground, women are generally found to prioritise family nutrition. In Africa children are 40 per cent more likely to live beyond their fifth birthday if their mother has spent five years in primary education. Discrimination against women is not only a consequence, but a cause of poverty. Yet the international community has been largely quiet about this.

If we look to the devastating pandemic of HIV and AIDS we see here too that gender inequality plays a pivotal role and actively fuels the spread of the disease. The United Nations Population Fund reports that across the world, young women are the most affected group. In developing countries fifteen- to twenty-four-year-old women are up to six times more likely to be infected than men their age.[18] Women's lower status means they often lack control over their sex lives. In order to avoid confronting their husbands about infidelity many women would rather risk contracting HIV than request he use a condom. The overwhelming majority of women newly infected by HIV are married or in a long-term relationship with one man, yet a study of two Ugandan districts found 74 per cent of the women thought it unacceptable for a married woman to ask her husband to use a condom.[19] The widespread myth that sexual intercourse with a virgin can cure AIDS has led to an increase in sexual violence in some countries. When it comes to dealing with the consequences of HIV and AIDS we see gender inequality rearing its head yet again. Women and girls do the vast majority of caring work for those living with HIV and so they are disproportionately hampered in their efforts to earn a living.

Look also at climate change: as the majority of the world's poor, women disproportionately suffer the consequences and find it most difficult to adapt.[20] In some parts of Africa lack of developed water resources means that water has to be fetched manually – and it is almost always women who perform this role. When water supplies are affected by global warming it is women who have to spend more of their time and energy sourcing and transporting it. And an analysis of natural disasters, the frequency of which is increasing under climate change, shows more women than men die as a result. But there is nothing 'natural' about this differing mortality rate; it is not because women aren't as physically strong or that their immune systems are weaker. When Bangladesh was hit by a cyclone in 1991 90 per cent of the 140,000 people killed were women. The clothes women wore hampered their efforts to run and swim to safety, and some were not permitted to leave their house without a male relative.[21] Similarly in the 2004 Asian tsunami disaster three times more women than men died.[22] Women's greater vulnerability to natural disasters is the result of societal rules and social mores that stem from gender inequality.[23] Despite this, initiatives addressing the impact of climate change that incorporate the role of gender are rare.

At times the matter of gender inequality is not just

ignored in other movements for social justice but actively dismissed. The role of outsourced, sweatshop labour in the rise of global capitalism has been well documented, and a social movement to challenge the exploitative underbelly of capitalism has blossomed in recent years. Yet one of its most high-profile proponents, Naomi Klein, offered this explanation when accounting for the failure of universities to stem the increasing corporate influence on themselves in her bestseller *No Logo*: '[Academics were] too preoccupied with defending themselves against their own "McCarthyite" students. So there they all were, fighting about women's studies and the latest backlash book while their campuses were being sold out from under their feet. It wasn't until the politics of personal representation were themselves co-opted by branding that students and professors alike began to turn away from their quarrels with each other, realising they had a more powerful foe.'[24] Gender inequality is painted as a distraction, a petty dispute deviating from the 'real' cause of society's ills. It is true that unequal gender relations are intimately connected with capitalism. Yet gender inequality cannot simply be designated an unfortunate by-product. It predates capitalism, and no economic revolution alone will knock the scourge of gender inequality down like a row of dominoes, because at some point in human history the concept of female inferiority was woven into the very fabric of how we see ourselves, how we treat each other, and how we organise society.

There is just too much at stake for us to allow society to continue denying that gender inequality is a problem or ridiculing efforts to draw attention to it. This book has been written as a wake-up call: feminism is one of the most important movements for social justice of our age – and we need it now more than ever.

And yet few girls and boys growing up today are taught that gender inequalities even exist. It wasn't until I got to university that I discovered feminism was still relevant. I had gone to an all-girls comprehensive school and grew up simply assuming that women were now equal citizens. It seemed so obvious that it would have been mildly embarrassing at the time to suggest any different. Yet when I started university I couldn't make sense of some of the things that were happening – from feeling uncomfortable when my psychology lecturer used images in his PowerPoint presentation of Anna Kournikova in a bikini ('to illustrate the workings of memory') to finding out that female graduates were paid less than male graduates for doing equal work. It was only when my mum lent me a book called *The Descent of Woman* by Elaine Morgan that things started to make sense. First published in 1972, it was a pioneering polemic that challenged the sidelining of women in accounts of human evolution. As I started to read more about feminism it felt like I was cracking a code. But as it dawned on me that sexism still ran like a thread through everyday life, I started to feel gripped by a growing sense of indignation: Why did no one seem to be talking about this? Where were the mass protests? How was this not headline news?

I was convinced that if gender inequality became more widely reported and more people simply knew about it then things would start to change. So in 2004 I established FEM Conferences – a volunteer-run series of national feminist conferences – to help raise awareness of the issues. That first year ninety people attended. The next year four hundred came. At the last conference, FEM o8, there were over five hundred people packed into the auditorium at Sheffield University Students' Union, plus a very long reserve list. And FEM Conferences was just one small part of a much wider pattern of grassroots activism developing across the country. Over the past five years hundreds of feminist blogs have appeared online, new feminist magazines have started up, and grassroots activist groups have been forming. It is clear that there are a lot of people out there who, like me, are frustrated that the sexist practices and cultures wreaking so much havoc in people's daily lives are receiving such scant mainstream attention – and are doing what they can to draw attention to it.

After university I went on to work with women refugees and asylum seekers at the Northern Refugee Centre in Sheffield, setting up women's groups where they could go to learn English and make friends. The many women I had the great fortune to get to know through these groups came from a diverse array of countries, yet their experiences frequently were depressingly similar – from early marriage and denial of an education to rape and domestic violence. And for many, their lives were being made even tougher by a brutal asylum determination system that failed to take into account the differing needs and experiences of male and female asylum seekers. In my current work at the Fawcett Society, the UK's leading campaign for women's rights, I continue to meet countless women whose experiences bear testament to the existence of deep-rooted inequalities: women who have been sexually abused, exploited and harassed; women who have been denied promotions at work because of their gender, paid less than men for doing equivalent work or trapped in poverty because of their childcare responsibilities.

These women are the reason that none of us can afford to be silent or complacent about the realities of sexism any longer. And their stories are therefore central to this book, which is the culmination of over a hundred interviews I have conducted to discover how gender inequalities are playing out in people's everyday lives. All the quotations used from the interviews are real and direct, although individuals' names and certain other details have been changed to protect their identities. The women I interviewed came from diverse backgrounds in terms of class, race, age, sexuality, and disability. The experiences they share demonstrate how differing aspects of people's identities influence how gender inequality manifests itself in day-to-day life – but also how all women's experiences of that inequality are interlinked. The book also includes interviews with men and boys who are involved in trailblazing anti-sexism work. Because, while women bear the brunt of harm from patriarchal forces and structures, men too are restricted by them. In the final chapter, 'A New Day', I look in particular at how men are both crucial to the success of feminism and beneficiaries of it.

Each chapter focuses on a particular time of day and begins with a snapshot of individual girls' and women's lives as they successively get up, go to school, return home from work and go to bed. This structure stems from the reality that when we talk about feminism or gender inequalities we are not talking about abstract concepts – we are talking about people's actual, everyday lives. Each of these women's stories reveals the impact that gender inequality has on them: from the time a young girl spends applying make-up before school because she knows she will be judged on how attractive she looks to the terror a woman experiences travelling home to a violent partner. These moments by no means represent an exhaustive list of how sexism plays out in daily life, but instead are a selection of what I consider to be key issues. Of course, sexism is a worldwide problem, and although the main focus of the book is on Western society, I also explore additional issues facing women and girls in other countries – from the risk of being denied an education in sub-Saharan Africa to the high rates of clandestine abortion in Latin America.

By looking at both cultural trends and individual women's experiences, I also aim to join the dots between widespread societal beliefs and specific acts. Incidents of domestic violence, for example, don't spring out of nowhere. When a man hits his girlfriend, he of course has his own personal history and experiences, but he is also part of a cultural pattern – a pattern of men being encouraged to demonstrate their masculinity through violence and control. While the links are hidden in the equality illusion, violence against women – and the many other manifestations of inequality featured in this book – are in fact tragically logical products of images we see, words we hear and things we do from day to day.

This book has also been written as a call to action, and integral to each chapter is the notion that change is possible. None of the problems you will read about are inevitable. The final chapter features interviews with grassroots activists and members of feminist organisations that are managing to bring about change. There is also a resources section to help you get involved. Every individual, woman or man, has a crucial role to play in shattering the equality illusion and ending gender inequality. The challenges may be great, but you are more powerful than you know.

Part 1

TODAY

06:56 | Mirror, Mirror on the Wall

Waking Up to Body Image

Ellen rolls over and peers at the alarm clock: 06:56. Still four minutes to go. Her hands and feet are always numb in the morning so she cuddles up to Mark. Ellen often spends the unclaimed time before the alarm goes off contemplating what she has eaten the day before. Had the peas, broccoli, and dissolved Oxo cubes come to fewer than 100 calories? Had the three water biscuits she'd eaten at 9 p.m. pushed her over the 200 limit? She watches quietly as Mark's shoulders rise and fall. He had asked her to eat potatoes during dinner last night, despite knowing that they are not one of her safe foods. The alarm goes off, so Ellen quickly reaches over, switches it to snooze, and pulls back the duvet. She sits up and waits for the dizziness to pass before walking downstairs – an act that feels especially painful today as every muscle in her body seems to ache.

Ellen agreed to share her experiences with me after I was put in touch with her by beat, a British charity that offers support to thousands of women just like her. Ellen is just one of the 1.5 million people in the UK who wake up every morning to an eating disorder – 90 per cent of them women and girls.[1]

While waiting for the kettle to boil Ellen opens the fridge

door and contemplates what to eat today. 'I feel uncomfortable eating before 5 p.m., and only drink black coffee or fruit tea up to this time. I think about food all the time. I frequently dream about it, often waking up in a cold sweat, convinced that the dream was real and that I have actually eaten the food I dreamt about.' After finishing her coffee Ellen makes her way to the bathroom. As she gets in the shower she catches her reflection in the mirror, and what she sees disgusts her: 'I hate the fatness, the flesh, the excess. I can't see myself ever liking it.' While brushing her teeth, Ellen can clearly notice the scars of her efforts to gain control over her body. 'I have had to have dental work because of the bulimia (the stomach acid in the vomit eroding my teeth) – one tooth had to be reconstructed as it collapsed entirely. I've recently just had my front teeth filled due to erosion.' Before leaving the bathroom she collects up the clumps of hair that have fallen out in the shower and over the floor. It worries Mark when he sees them so she always tries to remember to remove them before he uses the bathroom. Once dressed, Ellen sits down at her desk and tries to get a few hours done on her essay.

Ellen has suffered from anorexia nervosa and bulimia nervosa since she was ten years old. Now twenty-five, she is studying for her history degree through the Open University, having had to drop out twice previously from university owing to her eating disorders. She tells me by email that 'my old school notes have sums scribbled in all the margins – working out what I could eat so as not to have too many calories, or working out how many calories I have had over the past day, week, month . . .' Now weighing 6 stone 10 pounds, Ellen suffers from extremely painful acid reflux each day as the top valve in her stomach is damaged from years of vomiting. As a result of the eating disorders Ellen's eyesight has also deteriorated significantly, and doctors have informed her that, because her bone mass is lower than it should be, she could face osteoporosis at an early age. Ellen has tried to commit suicide on numerous occasions during the last fifteen years. 'The most serious overdose I took was in 2004. I had relapsed with anorexia and just couldn't be bothered fighting it any more. I hated myself, I hated my weight, I hated the fact that rationally I knew that I'd hate myself and body regardless of whether I weighed four stone or nine, and I had had enough. I ended up in hospital with heart failure.'

Shocking as the consequences may be, Ellen's feelings about her body are far from abnormal amongst women and girls today. Despite decades of feminist critique of the tyranny of beauty, monitoring and manipulating their appearance remains a daily feature of women's lives. Today it is 'normal' for women to worry about their looks when they get up each morning, to religiously check their appearance in the mirror throughout the day, to not want to leave the house without make-up on, or to feel fat or disgusted at the sight of their thighs. None of the anxieties Ellen described to me would be unfamiliar to most women: a fear of overeating, of getting fat, of feeling her body needs controlling. Women and girls have consistently been found to be more dissatisfied with their bodies than men and boys,[2] and studies show girls have a starkly different relationship with their bodies from boys. A girl will place far greater emphasis on how attractive her body looks to others, while what his body can actively achieve – his physical capabilities – is far more important to a boy's sense of self.[3] And while a boy's concerns about his body image decrease during adolescence, a girl's spiral. A survey conducted by the cosmetics manufacturer Dove amongst over three thousand women and girls in ten different countries* found that 90 per cent wanted to change some aspect of themselves, with body weight and shape being the main concerns.[4] Although financially out of reach to many, a staggering one in four women has considered having cosmetic surgery.[5]

Susan Bordo, Professor of Philosophy at the University of Kentucky, points out that anorexia was barely heard of a century ago, and describes eating disorders as a 'crystallisation of culture' – logically and devastatingly embodying ideals dominant in today's society.[6] How the day begins for Ellen – and others who suffer from eating disorders – differs from the majority of women's mornings only in the extent to which she proceeds to pursue a solution to the perceived failings of her body. Eating disorders are no freak occurrence. A range of factors influence whether an individual develops an eating disorder – including family relationships and even genetics – and particular events such as bereavement or abuse can act as triggers. But the uncomfortable reality is that eating disorders have their roots in the humdrum of our everyday lives, in the things we take for granted and accept as normal in the equality illusion.

The focus of women and girls on their physical appearance is the result of neither free expression nor gullible duping by the beauty industry. They have correctly discerned the female body ideals our culture treasures most and which shape the perceptions of their friends, potential partners,

---

*Countries included in Dove's survey were the United States, Canada, Mexico, Brazil, United Kingdom, Italy, Germany, Japan, China, and Saudi Arabia.

family, employers, and even the strangers they pass on the street. These people will all be able to judge how near or far a particular woman is from the ideal; how vigilant she has been, how disciplined she is and how committed she is to providing it. The Western female beauty ideal itself has morphed over the past century. In the 1920s Joan Crawford embodied the thin, flat-chested flapper ideal; in the 1940s Lana Turner exemplified the ideal voluptuous 'sweater girl'; by the 1970s Twiggy's nearly emaciated appearance was the order of the day; while the slim yet curvy shape of models like Cindy Crawford and Naomi Campbell became the look of the 1990s. Today the ideal woman is thin, large-breasted, free of body hair, white, and young. She has changed, but she has also remained.

There is much media coverage about the harmfulness of these ideals: who they preclude, how hard they are to achieve, and what consequences they have for those aspiring to them. Yet the existence of a suffocating ideal has stubbornly persisted – and it has remained an overwhelmingly gendered phenomenon. Cultural debates and initiatives that simply seek to reform or diversify the range of beauty ideals on offer to women fall short because they fail to challenge the fundamental notion that a woman's worth could and should be located in her appearance. The foundations of a beauty ideal – however it is constituted – lie in one of the most powerful and enduring forces operating on women and girls today: objectification (treating a person as an object, not a human being). Bodies are important; they are what enable us to function and survive in the world and are an integral part of our identity and sense of self. Yet today, women's and girls' bodies are widely denigrated as inanimate objects to be publicly scrutinised, judged, maintained, and manipulated for the benefit of others; they are shared public property. A female body is deemed an object that could and should be made beautiful – at almost any cost – for the benefit of those looking at it. And the troubling reality is that objectification itself bypasses the inherent worth of a human being and has women's and girls' self-esteem locked in a stranglehold from the moment they wake up each morning.

This is obviously not a new phenomenon. The inherent harm of objectification was amongst the motivations for the protest by feminist activists at the Miss America beauty pageant in 1968 – an event that has almost become synonymous with feminism in the popular imagination because of the mythical presence of women burning their bras at this event. (The reality was that bras, along with other feminine accoutrements such as corsets and stilettos, were thrown into a trash can as a symbolic trashing of beauty ideals. The burning bra is just one of the many myths about feminism and feminists.) And the following decades were punctuated by radical critiques of beauty. In 1974 feminist activist and author Andrea Dworkin wrote in *Woman Hating*: 'Standards of beauty describe in precise terms the relationship that an individual will have to her own body. They prescribe her mobility, spontaneity, posture, gait, the uses to which she can put her body. They define precisely the dimensions of her physical freedom.'[7] Sixteen years later, Naomi Wolf declared in *The Beauty Myth*: 'We are in the midst of a violent backlash against feminism that uses images of female beauty as a political weapon against women's advancement.'[8] Yet despite these alarm calls, the objectification of women's bodies is today at an all-time zenith: the pressures on women and girls to manipulate their appearance have never been greater, the range of methods on hand to achieve this never more extreme, the profits garnered from it never higher, and the consequences for women's and girls' lives also more destructive than ever.

An unattractive choice

Women's and girls' bodies continue to be stigmatised on an unprecedented scale partly because scrutiny of 'beauty' withered away during the 1990s and early 2000s, only to be replaced by a rhetorical smokescreen of 'choice' and 'agency' supported not only by the beauty industry but by some active in and writing on feminism. In 1998 Natasha Walter declared in *The New Feminism* that 'the strings that once tied women's decoration to women's lack of power have been cut'. Walter was adamant that 'times have changed' and insisted 'women's feelings about their clothes and bodies are easier now than at any time in the recent past'. She maintained that women's increasing equality enabled them to freely choose whether or not to labour on their appearance and, as such, 'the new feminism must unpick the tight link that feminism in the seventies made between our personal and political lives'.[9] This emphasis on individual choice was also reflected by Jennifer Baumgardner and Amy Richards, authors of *Manifesta: Young Women, Feminism, and the Future*, when they wrote in 2003 that 'feminism isn't about what choice you make, but the freedom to make that choice'.[10] Looked at in this way it is apparent that no one is holding a gun to her head when a woman applies lipstick before leaving the house, and she isn't dragged into the plastic surgeon's operating theatre kicking and screaming.

However, an approach like this fails to take account of

the coercive forces in Western society that mean a girl's appearance can dictate how she feels and what she thinks on any given day. It fails to recognise that her 'choices' and actions reflect gender inequality. While Naomi Wolf recognised the pressures on women to focus on their beauty, even she ultimately concludes in *The Beauty Myth*: 'The real issue has nothing to do with whether women wear make-up or don't, gain weight or lose it, have surgery or shun it, dress up or down, make our clothing and faces and bodies into works of art or ignore adornment altogether. *The real problem is our lack of choice.*'[11]

But feminism isn't defined by a process (choice) but by an aim (ending the subordination of women). Simply basing feminism on the individual act of choosing fails to take into account how practices such as dieting and plastic surgery are connected with gender inequality and what impact they have on other women and gender relations as a whole. And it fails to question whether any woman would genuinely want to continue with the practices of objectification if true gender equality were achieved. Would women seriously still want invasive surgery? Would they still want to apply wax to their legs and have it ripped off? Sheila Jeffreys, a professor at the University of Melbourne, has written about the intimate connection between beauty practices and gender inequality. She argues that beauty regimes show 'that women are not simply "different" but, most importantly, 'deferential'. The difference that women must embody is deference [to the higher status class of men].' Beauty practices function as one way of demarcating or creating femininity on women's bodies and, Jeffreys suggests, showing deference: 'In western societies [deference] is expressed in the requirement that women create "beauty" through clothing which should show large areas of their body for male excitement, through skirts . . . through fig-ure-hugging clothing, through make-up, hairstyles, depila-tion, prominent display of secondary sexual characteristics or creation of them by surgery and through "feminine" body language.'[12] It can be difficult to contemplate that mundane beauty practices could have such profound polit-ical implications. But perhaps here lies an indication of why gender inequality has persisted so long – because it is sup-ported by cultures and practices embedded in the minutiae of everyday life.

While the dominance of arguments around choice has made it difficult to resist the notion that women's value lies in their appearance, it has become nigh-on impossible in the context of a global beauty industry that has co-opted lan-guage associated with feminism. Reflecting this trend, UK-based cosmetic surgery provider The Cosmetic Clinic has as its brand slogan 'Your body, your choice'. Cosmetics firm L'Oréal declares on its website that its products offer women 'the opportunity to improve their well-being and self-esteem' and that L'Oréal 'make a difference by offering everyone the right to beauty'. Similarly, Maybelline New York – whose cosmetics products are sold in over ninety countries – explain that they are 'focused on helping women feel more beauti-ful and recognizing their individuality and potential through education and empowerment'. Christian Emile, founder of the Miss University London beauty pageants which have been running since 2006, insists, 'If you talk to any of the contestants, they will tell you it is actually empowering.'[13] Choice, rights, empowerment – such apparently feminist proclamations adeptly assuage critics and reassure con-sumers, enabling the beauty industry to flourish. Indeed, the beauty market is estimated to be worth £3.7 billion in the UK alone.[14] As long as the beauty ideal remains, business will keep on picking the scab and selling us a plaster.

There have, however, been a number of media debates and initiatives over recent years challenging beauty ideals, the most high-profile of which has been the 'Campaign for Real Beauty' conducted by Dove. Devised by advertising agency Ogilvy & Mather, the campaign was launched in 2003 with ads featuring six ordinary (or 'real') women in their underwear and marketed as a challenge to the stick-thin, airbrushed models usually featured in the media. To accompany the campaign Dove also commissioned the international survey of how women rate their body image mentioned above. Adding extra credibility and legitimacy was the fact that one of the partners in this research was Dr Susie Orbach, psychotherapist and author of *Fat Is a Feminist Issue*. The campaign hit a societal nerve and created an extensive media debate about beauty ideals and the pressures placed on women to achieve them. However, the campaign had two major flaws. The first was plain, old-fashioned hypocrisy. The original advertisements featuring six 'real' women were for a Dove skin-firming lotion. Yet if real women have cellulite, and these same women should be seen as beautiful, why would they need this cream? The second, more fundamental flaw is that, despite critiquing particular beauty ideals, the campaign still endorses the objectification of women's bodies; in fact, it is based on it. Instead of saying, 'The beauty worth celebrating and commending is on the inside', the campaign said, 'Don't worry – you are physically beautiful after all, and we can make you even more so!' Of course, if they had challenged the cultural notion of beauty Dove's sales figures probably wouldn't have rocketed 700 per cent, making it the fastest-growing beauty brand in Western Europe.[15] Millions of women's and girls' days still begin with a series of rituals necessary only because their sense of self hinges on the gaze of others. But few questions are asked – because apparently they freely choose to practise them.

Beauty school

One of the reasons the problems surrounding female body image have proved so intractable is that girls are taught from a very early age that their physical appearance is a reflection of their worth and value, and are treated accordingly. The fact that physical appearance is the result of a 'body lottery' is rarely acknowledged – instead it is always a matter of trying, striving, succeeding, and failing. A girl will likely receive praise along the lines of 'Who's a pretty little girl, then?' (as a sign of 'achievement') long before she learns how to write or ride a bike. An analysis of animated cartoons produced by the major studios, including Bugs Bunny, Mighty Mouse and Yogi Bear, showed that female characters were far more likely than males to be portrayed as physically attractive, and those attractive characters were significantly more likely to be portrayed as intelligent, employed, happy, loving, and participating in affectionate romantic acts such as kissing and hugging.[16] The result is that girls internalise this third-person perspective of their bodies and become as proficient as anyone else at treating themselves like objects ('self-objectification'). As part of some research in 2007 into young girls' feelings about self-esteem and body image a group of Brownies aged seven to ten, members of Girlguiding UK, were asked to describe 'Planet Sad': they spoke of its inhabitants as being fat and bullied because of their weight and appearance.[17] A survey conducted in the UK in 2009 by YoungPoll.com also found that a quarter of the 3,000 teenage girls they questioned believed it was more important to be beautiful than clever.

The importance of attractiveness for girls is something Dhatri, Chitra, and Asha, three fifteen-year-old girls I spoke to during my research, attest to. 'We spend about twenty minutes putting on our make-up before school. If you didn't look good people from school would look at you in a different way. Sometimes it's a lot of effort – appearance. But I will never go out with my hair not done. I hate people looking at me weirdly. They'd laugh.' Their morning routines – straightening their hair and applying blusher, eyeliner, concealer, and eyeshadow – differ little from those of millions of other women and girls across the world, whose primary concerns when they wake up every day include how their body looks to other people. 'I don't like a lot of things about me. I don't like my face. I've got a big nose,' Dhatri pitched in. 'I don't like my knees; they're knobbly.' 'And I don't like my hips,' interjected Chitra. The three girls were sitting together at Dhatri's mother's house in East London, eagerly sharing their thoughts about their bodies. Asha assessed why they cared so much about their looks: 'It's important for girls to look good. People don't like you otherwise. If you're slim and pretty it transforms your life. You become popular.' The others agreed. 'When people compliment you it makes you feel really good. Pretty girls get it all the time; with us it's a rarity. We're just not that pretty.'

Advertisers are acutely aware of how concerned girls like Dhatri, Chitra, and Asha are about their appearance. Nestlé advertised its new 'low calorie' Kit-Kat Senses bar in the run-up to Christmas 2008 using billboard posters emblazoned with the slogan 'Goodwill to all Women'. Health professionals too are aware: a recent government-funded anti-smoking campaign in the UK targeted female smokers with posters that showed how it affected their appearance and attractiveness. The campaign's slogans, including 'Minging teeth' and 'Cat's bum mouth', were accompanied by an 'Ugly Smoking' website. (Ironically, research by the American Psychological Association has shown that many young women start smoking in the first place as a method of controlling their weight – precisely because of concerns about their body image.)[18] Similar campaigns targeted specifically at men very rarely hinge on their desire to lose weight or look sexually attractive – because they wouldn't work. When corporations and even the NHS capitalise on women's body insecurities they reinforce them as being valid concerns.

The American Psychological Association also reveal that the more mainstream media high school students consume, the more they believe sexiness and beauty are important. Dhatri, Chitra, and Asha, my three fifteen-year-old interviewees, are all avid media consumers. *Teen Vogue* and *Elle* rank amongst the favourite magazines, and on TV it's *MTV* and *The Hills*. Asha explained, '*The Hills* features blonde girls with blue eyes. They've got jobs in fashion. The main character works for *Vogue* but she hardly goes to work. I would love to have her lifestyle. There's no people of colour in the programme. We don't care, though, we still watch it.' Chitra added, 'I'd most like to look like Aishwarya [actress and former Miss World]. She's the prettiest Indian we know.' Dhatri, Chitra, and Asha are all fully aware that the dominant Western beauty ideal is white. Indeed, as Susan Bordo notes, the specific beauty regimes required of women are shaped by issues such as race, class, and age. Research suggests black girls do not tend to compare themselves to images of white women in the media and don't tend to believe that other people are evaluating them in relation to these either. However, that doesn't mean they are protected from the beauty ideal. Maya Gordon at the University of Michigan found that the more African-American girls consume and identify with black women in television sitcoms, music and music videos, the more they believe it is important for themselves and other girls to be physically attractive.[19] And researchers at Millikin University and the University of California have found that African-American women are just as dissatisfied with their bodies as other ethnic groups.[20]

Whether it be TV, films, computer games, toys, music videos, advertising or magazines, the message is clear: female physical attractiveness matters. Nowhere is this better illustrated than in the punishments dished out to women who fail to meet or even attempt to meet prescribed standards of beauty. When Susan Boyle walked on to the stage of the ITV show *Britain's Got Talent* in April 2009 she was met with sarcastic wolf-whistling, giggling, and smirking. When she began to sing the derision turned to astonishment: 'You didn't expect that, did ya? Did ya? No,' insisted presenter Ant McPartlin. 'Without a doubt that was the biggest surprise I have had in three years of this show,' claimed judge Piers Morgan. It was the kind of incredulity that wouldn't have been amiss if an elephant had appeared on stage riding a bicycle. Such amazement was occasioned only because Boyle wasn't wearing make-up, wasn't thin, and had untidy hair and crooked teeth. She met all the requisite conventional, pernicious criteria to be labelled an 'ugly woman', and the fact that she had dared to present herself before a national audience while apparently 'failing' to meet even basic standards of female beauty was deemed delusional or, at best, incompetent. Susan Boyle proceeded to become an overnight global media phenomenon, with her audition watched over 100 million times on YouTube. Amid the countless newspaper articles and online forum discussions about Boyle there was one recurring description of her appearance that illustrates one of beauty's major functions. Responding to the news that she had received a 'makeover', one commenter on Us Magazine.com wrote, 'she still looks like a man'. Beauty is a prerequisite for femininity. Boyle was deemed to have failed the 'pretty test', so she had therefore failed the 'femininity test' – and she was derided for it. Indeed, researchers in the US found that the more sexist and hostile people are towards women, the more important they think it is for women to be beautiful.[21] Overall, the media furore surrounding Boyle was like a twenty-first-century freak show, and no one witnessing any of this could be in any doubt as to how society views females who don't meet required standards of physical attractiveness.

It's not only cultural cues that inform women that their physical appearance must meet certain standards: the demand has also been institutionalised, with some employers conveying (sometimes explicitly) that beauty is an integral part of a woman's professional performance. In February 2009 it emerged that the Bank of England had held a seminar for its female employees called 'Dress for Success', at which they were advised to 'always wear a heel of some sort – maximum two inches; always wear some sort of make-up, even if it's just lipstick'.[22] Ankle chains were discouraged, apparently because they look 'professional, but not the one you want to be associated with'. Ernst & Young similarly held sessions for female employees at the end of 2008 on how to dress appropriately. The firm's Head of Diversity, Fleur Bothwick, stressed, 'You don't want to be remembered as the woman with red lips,' and the sessions advised women not to wear low-cut tops or carry evening bags to daytime meetings, and to make sure the colours they wear 'bring out the best in your skin tone and hair colour'. Anne Freden, chair of Ernst & Young's women's network, insisted: 'There is a huge number of capable and talented women at Ernst & Young looking to maximise their achievement in the firm and in their career, and looking for the skills and tips and tools to do that . . . The firm doesn't view this as something that is nice to have, but as an integral part of the business strategy.'[23] The 'Professional Beauty Qualification' – identified twenty years ago by Naomi Wolf as the conditioning of women's progression on their appearance – appears to remain a feature of the modern-day workplace. According to reports, these sessions were not deemed necessary for male employees – and one can assume that even if they had the men would not have been advised to wear make-up so they appeared more desirable to onlookers. The message sent by employers (overtly in the case of Ernst & Young) to women by holding these sessions is that their physical appearance is as important as their skills and abilities.

What, then, is so wrong about women being taught that their self-esteem is located in their physical appearance? It's not just that women are using up valuable time and money by manipulating their appearance, rather the problem is that viewing one's own body as an inanimate object to be made pleasing to onlookers is inherently harmful. It has been revealed that the more a girl views herself in this way, the lower her self-esteem will be,[24] and a study by researchers at the University of Wisconsin of eleven- and thirteen-year-olds found that the extent to which girls surveyed and monitored their appearance predicted how likely it was they felt depressed and ashamed about their bodies.[25] Researchers at Flinders University in South Australia found that, for women who view their bodies as objects, even complimenting them about their physical appearance can have negative consequences. This apparently counter-intuitive conclusion followed upon the discovery that the compliment focused these women's attention on their body and led them to feel more ashamed of it.[26] Body image is also a crucial risk factor in suicide – the third most common cause of death for people aged between fifteen and twenty-four in the US. Researchers found that the extent to which individuals – male or female – feel negatively about their bodies helps predict how likely it is they are currently considering suicide.[27] Why? Because a person who views their body as an inanimate object, and one that may have failed to meet particular standards, feels less inclined to protect it from harm. This also helps to explain the finding that the more dissatisfied a person is with her body the greater their propensity for self-harm. Self-objectification also prevents women and girls from participating in basic, everyday activities. Two-thirds of women report having avoided an activity such as swimming, or going to a party or club, because they felt bad about their appearance,[28] while 16 per cent of fifteen- to seventeen-year-olds have avoided going to school and 20 per cent have avoided giving an opinion in public because of it. An experiment by

Barbara Fredrickson (from the University of Michigan) and colleagues also found that mental functioning is impaired by body image concerns. Female college students performed worse in a maths test while wearing a swimsuit than when wearing a sweater, yet this pattern wasn't found for boys.[29] This finding has also been replicated in spatial skills and logical-reasoning tests.

Before Asha, Dhatri, Chitra, and I ended our interview, I asked one final question: 'Would you like not to be concerned about your appearance?' Asha was incredulous: 'The day when that comes – God knows how far away that is!' The schooling women receive in the need for them to be beautiful starts at a young age, and will continue to be delivered throughout their lifetime by a range of instructors, from magazines to managers.

Slim pickings

'SLIM IN SECONDS' / 'LBD diet: lose 7lb fast' / 'YOUR BEST BODY IN 4 WEEKS!' / 'DRESS SLIM'

Simply walking past a supermarket magazine display will quickly reveal that one of today's most pervasive body ideals is thinness. As a result the front covers of women's magazines vary very little. An analysis of sixty-nine American women's magazines in 1999 found 94 per cent of them had a model or celebrity on the cover who conformed to the the thin ideal.[30] The magazines focus on how readers can improve their lives through changing their appearance, with cover images and text implying that being thin means being more lovable, sexier, and happier.[31] The body shapes of the women pictured in these magazines bear little resemblance to most women's. At 5' 11" and 117lb the average model is now thinner than 98 per cent of American women, and most models are clinically underweight.[32] In the UK the average adult woman is a size 16, yet at size 12 Britain's Tarryn Meaker models 'plus-size' ranges.[33] The consequences are unsurprisingly gendered: women are up to ten times more likely to worry about their weight than men,[34] and are significantly more likely to go on crash diets, abuse laxatives and engage in compulsive exercising.[35] Fifty per cent of young women in the UK report having skipped a meal to lose weight[36] and the UK population spends over £11 billion a year on books, magazines, special foods, classes and other aids to weight loss.[37] In the US, that figure is put somewhere between $40 and $100 billion.[38] (This is despite the fact that 95 per cent of dieters regain the weight lost.)

And media images of the thin ideal have a huge impact. Researchers in Australia found that women who viewed magazine adverts featuring images of thin women felt more dissatisfied and anxious about their own bodies and viewed themselves in a more objectified way.[39] In fact, studies show that just five minutes of exposure to thin and beautiful images of women leads viewers to feel more negatively about their body image in comparison to viewing neutral objects.[40] The same effects have been replicated in studies using music videos and TV commercials.[41] Disturbingly, five- to seven-year-olds have been found to have a greater desire to be thinner after exposure to Barbie dolls.[42] The overwhelming influence of the media on young girls' perceptions about their weight was also dramatically demonstrated in Fiji – a country where dieting has traditionally been discouraged, disordered eating thought rare, and where Western TV has only recently been introduced. Researchers questioned indigenous adolescent girls within one month of TV being introduced to their area, and then again three years later. The researchers uncovered a significant increase in disordered eating amongst girls in the interim.[43] The percentage of girls scoring high on tests of disordered eating increased from 12.7 to 29.2, while the proportion of girls who reported they made themselves vomit in order to control their weight increased from 0 to 11.3 per cent.

In recent years the fashion industry has been engulfed in a debate about size-0 models – the US equivalent to a UK size 4 – and the effects this culture has on women and girls. It was ignited by the deaths of two catwalk models, Luisel Ramos and Ana Carolina Reston, from complications caused by anorexia. In response the Italian fashion industry vowed to get tough on the issue of skinny models, and in Spain those with a body mass index of less than 18 were banned from shows in Madrid fashion week. However, an independent inquiry backed by the British Fashion Council into model health held in the UK came to nothing after its recommendations to introduce model health certificates and ban models under sixteen were never implemented.[44] Despite the many column inches and industry postulations, size-0 models are still very much in fashion. This has even spurred British *Vogue* editor Alexandra Shulman to write to designers and fashion houses including Prada, Versace, and Yves Saint Laurent, criticising the 'minuscule' garments they provide for photo shoots which compel the magazine to hire seriously underweight models. Shulman even revealed that the magazine has felt obliged to retouch photographs to make models look less thin than they really are.[45]

Reinforcement of the thin ideal can also stem from a source closer to home. I recently received some photos from a family celebration. (We rarely get our whole family together in one room at the same time, much less in the same camera shot, so the photos were pretty special.) But when I looked at them all I could focus on was the bulge around my lower stomach. I had thought I was thinner than I looked in the photos. Rationally, as an active feminist campaigner and someone who was researching body-image issues at the time, I knew I shouldn't be thinking like this, but I still kept dwelling on my stomach. I emailed my sister about it and she quickly wrote back saying I must be joking because I looked 'fab'. She finished with: 'But my hair's awful. And I need to go on a diet. Ugh.' My sister is a UK size 8.

Aside from revealing how hard I find it to stop scrutinising my body, this exchange was also an unwitting demonstration of 'fat talk' – conversations between friends, family etc. focused on negative self-assessments of the body – which plays an important role in reinforcing the thin ideal. Research in the US showed that women feel worse about their bodies after hearing a thin woman talk negatively about her own.[46] Social comparison with less benign intent also perpetuates the thin ideal. Direct suggestions or teasing from their peers drive adolescent girls to lose weight, and experiments in which girls had their weight guessed heavier than it actually was felt fatter and more depressed when the person doing the 'guessing' was a peer.[47] The message from contemporary Western culture is clear: curves (in the wrong place) and fat (in any place) are not welcome on the female body. The result? A daily epidemic amongst women of harmful body surveillance, crash dieting, compulsive exercising and anxiety and depression about their weight and shape. And this 'ordinary' epidemic has also laid the groundwork for one of the most deadly psychiatric disorders of our age.

At war with hunger

Up to seventy million people across the globe suffer, as Ellen does, from an eating disorder,[48] and the overwhelming majority of them are female. Worldwide, such disorders are among the top four causes of premature death, illness and disability amongst women aged between fifteen and twenty-four. Ten per cent of women with anorexia die from it.[49] While researching eating disorders I received email after email from women outlining how their disorder had devastated their life, and very frequently I would read things, written almost as asides, such as 'I got more and more depressed, leading to me attempting to take my life on a few occasions', or 'I did attempt suicide quite a few times,' Sadly, this isn't surprising given that anorexia has the highest suicide rate of any psychiatric disorder.

The daily physical symptoms experienced by Ellen from the minute she gets up in the morning are typical of eating disorder sufferers. As the body is starved during anorexia, periods often stop and bone mass drops. Michelle, who has had anorexia for seven years, now has a compression fracture in her spine resulting from the reduction in her bone density. In addition to the physical and psychological damage, eating disorders also make everyday activities a struggle. 'It can be tiring as everything feels like a battle in my head – what to eat? How can I avoid a meal out? Can I cope with meeting up with someone? Should I stay at home? Should I go to the gym? Everything feels like a negotiation between myself and the eating disorder. Sometimes I am able to fight back and do what I know is good and healthy, at others the eating disorder wins.' Alexandra, now thirty-one, developed an eating disorder aged sixteen, and as it escalated it proceeded to put all stop to normality. 'I gave up work, I gave up the gym, I gave up college, I gave up my friends, my social life, everything . . . my life was just about sleeping, eating and puking. I would only go out for an appointment (counselling or hospital) and to buy food to binge on.'

Despite the prevalence of eating disorders amongst women today, their history is short. They have largely arisen within the last century, accelerated during the 1980s and 90s, and are found predominantly in advanced industrial societies.[50] It is no coincidence that during this time the culture of objectifying women's bodies has gathered pace and that same culture is infused with the notion that a woman's body needs to be controlled and contained and, increasingly, thin. Research shows that the increasing dominance of the thin ideal has preceded the highest rates of anorexia.[51] In contemporary Western society a woman who loses weight has 'achieved'. This is a common theme that emerged from my interviews with eating-disorder sufferers. Elizabeth recalled that before she developed her eating disorder, 'I always felt physical appearance was important, perhaps because I had always been told I was "slim" and "attractive", and so I placed value on these as my "achievements" in a way. From a young age I had a strong idea of thin being beautiful and to be desired.' Michelle's childhood was also heavily influenced by this ideal: 'I felt like a failure, and I can remember thinking it was very important I wasn't fat. I remember feeling that my thinness was like a badge of honour – as if it was something I had achieved.'

So if culture is at the heart of eating disorders, why

don't all women develop eating disorders? Susan Bordo
points out that everyone's life is configured differently.
When the cultural current of the thin ideal meets the surface of an individual woman it is refracted by dimensions
such as family structure, experiences, genetics, education,
class, and ethnicity.[52] Such dimensions influence the like-
lihood that an eating disorder will consequently develop.
Natalie's disability, for example, influenced the development of her anorexia. 'As a female with a disability some
people within society do view you differently or have their
own misunderstandings about your abilities as a capable,
independent person. As an individual I want to portray
myself to others in the best possible way . . . I'd always
thought I was very plain and ordinary looking and felt
others were more attractive than me.' Natalie dropped
out of college after failures to provide her with accessible
work caused her self-esteem to plummet. 'I always strived
for high academic standards and was a real perfectionist.
For the first time in my life – due to feeling very depressed
and not being given accessible course material – I began
to fall behind with my work . . . I was quite a people
pleaser so felt dreadful requesting the work in the format
they'd promised me and was made to feel like a nuisance.
I left the course and everything spiralled out of control.'
Being a perfectionist, as Natalie was, is a key risk factor
in developing an eating disorder.[53] Experiences like
Natalie's are a tragic testament to the illusory nature of
gender equality today. As long as 'thin' remains an ideal
and control over hunger is deemed an achievement there
will be women and girls who continue to 'excel' – with
devastating effect.

Under the knife

As technologies have advanced in recent decades, the severity of the procedures available to help women sculpt their bodies to fit the ideals of beauty has been ratcheted up. Slicing, pulling, sucking, grinding and cutting have all become commonly applied adjectives when discussing common methods of achieving beauty. Between 1992 and 2002 the number of people undergoing elective cosmetic surgical and non-surgical treatment in the US increased by 1,600 per cent. Nearly 6.6 million Americans paid for cosmetic medical treatment in 2002,[54] and in 2007 almost 1,600 cosmetic surgery procedures were carried out each day in the UK.[55] The menu of available options for the face alone includes Botox, face lift, nose reshaping, facial implants, neck lift, eye lift, brow lift, collagen injections, and eye-bag removal. Clare Chambers, a Fellow of Jesus College Cambridge, reports that one particularly popular procedure amongst Asian women 'involves inserting a crease in the eyelid to replicate Western facial features'.[56] It is no surprise then that cosmetic surgery is big business.

Who are the people mainly having surgery? A survey by the British Association of Aesthetic Plastic Surgeons found that 91 per cent of cosmetic surgery patients in 2007 were female.[57] In Western cultures, cosmetic surgery is being offered to those women who can afford it as a valid and even 'empowering' solution to dissatisfaction with their bodies. Millions are making the 'choice' to have this surgery – but gender inequality, not empowerment, is again at the heart of this story.

Surgery is the route through which many women try to meet another dominant beauty ideal – youth. Nicky Hambleton-Jones recently spoke out about her substitution by Myleene Klass – a woman seven years her junior – as the presenter of the British reality TV show *10 Years Younger*: 'It does seem to me like a classic case of replacing any woman over thirty-five, regardless of how suitable she is for the role, with a younger face . . . I want to tackle what I see as ageist attitudes.'[58] It would seem that Hambleton-Jones doesn't see any contradiction between this statement and her old job. Her sacking elicited an attack on the prejudice in favour of a 'younger face', yet as the front woman of the first mainstream TV show in the UK to normalise cosmetic surgery, Hambleton-Jones spent five years enabling women to change their face to avoid, and so sustain, that same prejudice. Indeed, the media have been a major catalyst for the expansion and mainstream acceptance of cosmetic surgery. Aside from the direct advertising by cosmetic practitioners themselves, indirect promotion has been offered by cosmetic surgery makeover shows like *10 Years Younger*, as well as *The Swan, I Want a Famous Face, Cosmetic Surgery Live*, and *Extreme Makeover* – which in 2003 was the second most-watched programme in the US amongst adults under fifty.[59] Critiques of the practice of cosmetic surgery have notably diminished over recent years[60] and public approval of the practice has soared. In 2007 Liverpool's 107.6 Juice FM ran a competition for female listeners in which the prize was breast enlargement. Listeners were requested to post online messages detailing why they deserved 'enhanced fun bags'.[61]

The procedures sought and on offer increasingly bear testament to the growth of a separate commercial enterprise. The 1980s and 90s witnessed an unprecedented expansion of the international sex industry, and by the beginning of the new millennium pornography and prostitution had become both available and respectable to an unprecedented degree. This tidal wave continues to influence what goes on in the operating theatre. The overwhelming demand by pornography consumers is for large-breasted women, so it is common for women working in pornography to have breast implants. And with the normalisation of pornography, which influences mainstream advertising and fashion, it is no coincidence that the majority of women today now want bigger breasts,[62] or that in 2008 breast implants were the number one cosmetic surgery procedure in both the US and the UK.[63] In 2007, the yearly US spend on breast augmentation alone amounted to over $1.3 billion.[64]

Pubic hair removal is also de rigueur for women in pornography. One particular result of this is that the labia are more visible, so in order to provide pornography consumers with small and uniform labia, airbrushing and cosmetic surgery are increasingly employed in the industry. And again this has spilled over into wider society. 'Designer vaginas' are becoming increasingly common cosmetic surgery choices for women. The surgical options include vaginal tightening, liposuction and lifting of lips, clipping of elongated inner lips and 'repair' of the hymen.[65] Between 2002 and 2007 the number of 'labial reductions' performed on the UK's National Health Service doubled. Authors of a British Medical Journal article reported that women commonly took pictures from advertisements or pornography to illustrate to surgeons what they wanted their genitals to look like.[66] Some doctors have compared this surgery to female genital mutilation,[67] a practice defined by the World Health Organisation as 'procedures that involve partial or total removal of the external female genitalia, or other injury to the female genital organs for non-medical reasons',[68] and recognised internationally as a human rights violation.

Elective cosmetic surgery is, by definition, not medically required. Yet, as with any form of invasive surgery, it carries severe health risks including internal bleeding, post-operative infection, blood clots and heart attack. In order for such surgery to flourish, therefore, justification and explanation are necessary. The language commonly deployed for this is familiar: 'fulfilment', 'control', 'empowerment'. The California Center for Plastic Surgery, which describes its website as 'educational', insists that 'plastic surgery has truly become a way to better ourselves. It allows us to take control of our lives, and to give ourselves the body and look we always wanted, and truly deserve. Why not! We deserve the best.'[69] Echoing that statement, UK-based SurgiCare encourages website visitors to 'Take control of your life' with weight loss surgery, amongst other procedures.[70] Surgery is commonly portrayed as a way for an individual to express her 'true self'. Yet what is the starting point from which women are making these decisions to 'take control'? It's rather obvious, but well worth remembering, that women who are less satisfied with their appearance are significantly more likely to consider cosmetic surgery,[71] and those who are more ashamed about not meeting cultural bodily ideals are more accepting of the practice.[72] Indeed, a central narrative in episodes of television's *Extreme Makeover* is that the individuals seeking surgery are unhappy with their looks and have suffered as a result. In one episode a woman named Michele has a nose job, eye lift, fat removed from her cheeks, a chin implant, brow lift and lip augmentation. Her motivation for this?

She wants her face to look more feminine because she believes her looks have prevented her from attracting men: 'I feel as though there is a lot more potential in me. Maybe I want a kid. Maybe I want a husband.'[73] The programme locates the source of suffering as being the individual's physical appearance, plain and simple. Cultural prejudice is never subject to an examination. Similarly, the 'before and after patient stories' on the website of cosmetic surgery provider The Hospital Group tell a similar tale of women's bodies being stigmatised by others and the women then resorting to surgery as the solution: 'Unhappy with her appearance and bullied at university, Lowri decided it was time for action . . . Kelly saw herself as a real life ugly duckling and was bullied at school for the way she looked . . . Liz overheard someone criticising the shape of her nose, then cried after seeing her wedding photos and decided it was time to save up for a new nose!'[74] And so, individuals have their flesh cut and pulled, surgery companies proclaim it as an empowering choice, and the stifling cultural ideals about women's appearance are left unscathed.

Women's and girls' bodies are objectified and stigmatised on a scale as never before, and the culture of objectifying and 'beautying' women's bodies is intimately linked with gender inequality. The spectrum of behaviours it inspires is wide – from the mundane to the life-threatening – but it is a spectrum on which having your flesh cut, sucked and sliced for non-medical purposes is a logical act. And all the while, this state of affairs is insulated by the rhetoric of individual choice and empowerment. But that notion of free choice is a pure fantasy, and neither are women deluded or duped. When they

43

wake up each morning women know that their appearance will be crucial currency for getting through the day.
Women know their performance at work may be judged
according to their make-up choices, and girls are aware
that they may get laughed at in the playground for being
perceived as overweight. And so girls and women attempt
to match their bodies to the ideals. As long as some
women and girls begin their day in the same way as Ellen,
we will know that equality is still an illusion.

08:40 | Hands Up for . . .

A Gendered Education

As her mother straps her little brother into the car, Jena stands by the front door, unable to move. She's starting to feel dizzy. Why won't her mum listen when she brings up her problems with Alec? It's not going to stop. This was made clear at the end of last week when she had approached Mrs Evans, the deputy head, about the problem. 'She listened to me carefully and then said, "Well, you know, you're all growing up and boys do this sort of thing, because boys will be boys."'

Hearing the car engine start, Jena finally picks up her rucksack and walks down the path. In the car, she puts her head back and starts counting her breaths, determined not to have another panic attack like last week. As the houses and streets shoot past the window all she can think about is Geography at 11:40, because Alec will be there. Alec is not in the same tutor group as Jena, but on four days out of five she has lessons with him. His typical behaviours towards her include: 'grabbing my breasts in the school corridors. Sitting opposite me in class and making obscene gestures and threatening comments ("I'm going to fuck you"; "Are you going to sit on my cock?"). Jumping on me in the playground and rubbing against me. Swearing at me loudly in front of other pupils ('fucking bitch'). He refers

45

to me as "tits", "fucking massive tits", and "fucking bitch".'

Jena is fifteen. She has experienced sexual harassment from boys since she was nine, and thinks it's related to the fact she is 'developed' for her age. But it has never been this bad before and over the past five months school has become unbearable. 'On one occasion I fainted in class because I was so terrified of going to the next lesson which he shared with me.' Jena has recently started refusing to go to school. But with her grades slipping, and GCSEs next year, her mum has been getting stricter about it. Jena can understand this, but given that she can't concentrate when she's at school – and the deputy head has now refused to do anything – what's the point? All too quickly, her mum pulls up behind a row of parked cars opposite the school. Saying nothing, Jena gets out of the car and walks towards the main entrance. By the time she reaches her locker the registration bell is ringing. She has a sickly feeling in her stomach. Only two hours and forty minutes to go.

Jena got in touch with me after I sent out an email through several feminist e-networks asking to interview girls who were experiencing sexual harassment at school. Hers was one of many responses I received, and she is just one of many millions of girls throughout the world who are sexually harassed at school every year. According to the World Health Organisation, school is the most common setting for sexual harassment and coercion.[1] Researchers have found girls experience more harassment by adult school personnel and peers than boys do, and their experiences are also more severe.[2] A US study in 2008 found that of the 34 per cent of middle- and high-school students who had been sexually harassed during that school year, girls suffered significantly more trauma symptoms and experienced a greater toll on their self-esteem and their mental and physical health.[3] Lesbian and disabled girls are found to be particularly at risk of harassment.[4]

A couple of months after the harassment began Jena started to binge eat in the evenings, as it made her feel better for a short period. But afterwards she would invariably feel so disgusted with herself that she would make herself sick. Recently, however, the bingeing has stopped and she is now obsessively regulating her calorie intake, and becomes distressed if she consumes more than 500 calories a day. 'I initially started to diet in the hope that doing so would reduce the size of my breasts,' Jena explained, telling me quite frankly that the sexual harassment is making her hate her body, and that she wants to reverse her physical development. She described her dieting as 'a way to regain control of my life'. Unsurprisingly, she is also experiencing a slump in her academic performance.

Despite sexual harassment being rampant in schools, society often turns a blind eye to it, frequently writing it off as 'natural' behaviour as Jena's teacher had. The truth is that sexual harassment of girls by boys isn't natural and certainly isn't inevitable. On the contrary, it is part of an institutionalised system of gender inequality found in schools throughout the world. And the system both reflects and then informs inequality in wider society. Sexual harassment is only one of the problems for girls as they arrive at school each morning: they also learn stereotyped behaviours, are discouraged from maths and science, and are steered away from physical education. To ignore this hidden curriculum, or to ascribe differences between girls and boys at school to biology, is to perpetuate the equality illusion.

The common perception today is that it is boys who are

being systematically disadvantaged at school. Their much-touted academic underperformance is hailed as proof that 'feminised' lessons are failing them. Tony Sewell, a former board director of The Learning Trust – which runs all education services in the London borough of Hackney – said in 2006, 'We have challenged the 1950s patriarchy and, rightly said, this is not a man's world. But we have thrown the boy out with the bathwater . . . I believe it has gone too far the other way.'[5] I asked Dr Becky Francis, Professor of Education at Roehampton University, how accurate messages like these are. 'I would never use the phrase, "girls are outperforming boys". The class gap is far greater than the gender gap: middle-class boys outperform working-class girls.' Francis points to the influence of one subject area in which girls are indeed vastly outperforming boys: literacy and language. 'This skews the whole debate.' But even the literacy gap is not the result of a school system inherently biased against boys. Instead, 'boys don't see the skills necessary for [literacy and language] as appropriate for their production of masculinities'. In other words, reading and writing are seen as un-masculine, and therefore unnecessary and undesirable. Francis also feels that 'issues facing girls have been marginalised'. Behind the headlines and the equality illusion, we find girls struggling every day in school, whether against stereotypes, discrimination or violence.

In developing countries, being a girl puts you at risk of never making it to school at all. There are 10 million more girls out of school than boys. This amounts to 41 million girls currently not receiving a primary education. The anti-poverty campaign group ActionAid have shown that, despite an international target to achieve gender parity in school enrolment by 2005, the gap still persists in sixty-two countries and is particularly acute in sub-Saharan Africa and south and west Asia.[6] And enrolment figures are just one small part of the picture. The UN reports that one in five girls in developing countries who do enrol at primary school fail to complete it, much less go on to the next stage in education. It's sadly no surprise then that of the 137 million young people in the world today who are illiterate, two-thirds are female.[7] While poverty is the overriding barrier to receiving an education, poverty alone can't explain the disproportionate absence of girls on school registers. The Forum for African Women Educationalists, a pan-African NGO founded in 1992 by five women ministers of education, point to a range of factors: 'Gender discriminatory practices and attitudes remain prevalent within schools. Curricula and teaching and learning materials are gender biased and do not provide equal opportunities for girls and boys. Discriminatory attitudes and practices such as early marriage amongst local communities aggravate the situation.'[8] The disproportionate burden of domestic work placed on girls' shoulders and the risk of gender-based violence en route to school also contribute to girls' lower enrolment rates. A survey of girls in Zimbabwean junior schools in 2000 reported by Amnesty International found 92 per cent had been sexually propositioned by an older man on their way to school, and half of them had experienced unsolicited sexual contact by strangers.[9] Factors such as these mean that, simply by virtue of being born female, millions of children across the world are denied their right to an education. In fact, according to the charity Childline, in South Africa a girl actually has a higher chance of being raped than of learning to read.[10]

While equal access to schooling has been achieved in

developed countries, the hidden curriculum of gender inequality still makes itself felt in devastating ways for girls in these countries. Classrooms have become breeding grounds for segregation, sexist stereotyping and violence against girls. A hidden curriculum, imparted by teachers, parents, and the media, directs children into the 'gender trenches' – the crude dugouts of masculinity and femininity, reproducing and maintaining gender inequality amongst the newest generation. It is time to expose the curriculum that divides girls and boys every day in the classroom and sustains inequality between them in later life.

Learning to be boys and girls

In early 2009 I went to visit a nursery in West London. I watched as the three-and-a-half-year-olds started to trickle into the classroom at 8:55, weaving around the tables and proceeding to congregate in small, same-sex groups at opposite ends of the classroom. A head count I conducted shortly after revealed three boys at work round the Lego table, five girls scribbling away at the art table, three boys crafting structures with a modelling kit, an unfortunate collection of dolls being bathed in icy-cold water by three girls, and four boys and a girl eagerly lined up at the door to the playground with their coats on. This kind of segregation between male and female children is a firmly established feature of classrooms by the time they are five years old,[11] and it only strengthens with age. By six and a half years old the ratio of same-sex to cross-sex play is a staggering 11:1. And when children do play with someone of the opposite sex, they play differently. They are more likely to play in parallel, watching each other without interacting.

The nursery I was visiting is connected to a junior school,

and during lunchtime I wandered out into the playground where the older children were playing. Here, the divide was particularly clear. A group of boys playing football dominated a large section of the playground, while a few girls playing hula-hoop were positioned on the sidelines. I asked seven-year-old Alika why no girls were joining in the football game: 'They just push us off the pitch, saying, "No, go away", calling us names.' I asked why she thought they did this. 'Maybe they don't like girls,' she suggested. Lauren, a classmate, added, 'Girls always play football on Fridays. Boys join in and we have to tell them not to join in. Sometimes when other girls are skipping boys step on the rope.' Lauren's not the only one to notice this. Researchers in the US found boys more frequently and overtly exclude girls from their games than vice versa.[12] Girls are more comfortable in crossing gender boundaries and vary their behaviour more after being read stories that challenge gender stereotypes.[13] Boys, however, are much more reluctant to play with toys deemed feminine, more rigid in their gender-stereotyped play, and more resistant to change.

Boys and girls in segregated groups also commonly play differently. Boys are more likely to enjoy 'rough and tumble' play, and are more openly competitive and frequently aggressive. I saw many examples of this at the nursery as boys rolled around on the carpet and sent ladybird cushions flying through the air, while teachers made desperate pleas to them to use their 'walking feet'. Girls, on the other hand, are found to prefer 'pro-social play'; that is, cooperating and negotiating with others.[14] The toys the two groups like to play with differ along similar lines. Even by the age of three, children prefer toys deemed appropriate for their gender – crudely speaking, trucks or Barbies. While sat at the Lego table I asked three-year-old Hasan, who was busy building a castle, if he ever liked to play with dolls. He seemed somewhat incredulous. 'Boys are not girls! They can't play with dolls. My sister is a girl and my brother is a boy. I don't like dollies 'cause I like these [Lego].' I think he thought I was rather dim. The gendered differences are also evident in the way boys and girls interact with their peers, teachers and parents. As girls get older the strategy they increasingly use to influence those around them is by making polite suggestions, and they continue to be responsive to teachers and other girls who make suggestions to them. Boys, on the other hand, increasingly make demands if they want to influence others, and become less likely to comply with the wishes of anyone – including teachers – outside their male peer group. Indeed, researchers in Brazil have shown females seek more approval from the teacher and are more determined to obey their instructions than boys are.[15]

During the lunch break I asked one of the teachers at the nursery if she thought there were any differences in the way boys and girls behaved at the school, and whether she thought these pointed to any underlying problems. But she cheerily dismissed the suggestion. 'I don't think we have a girl/boy problem here. There is an innate thing with boys. Boys like cars. Boys like more vigorous activities.' This assumption of natural difference is still common currency in contemporary society. The fact that classrooms are segregated along sex lines, with the two groups displaying different behaviours and attitudes, and showing preference for 'their own', is seen as simply part of the natural order. This is despite years of feminist campaigning and academic research to the contrary; and it is one of the reasons the equality illusion persists. Yet a fascinating study by psychologist Beverly Fagot, of the University of Oregon and Oregon Social Learning Center, illustrates that such segregation and difference is by no means natural. Fagot looked at the behaviour of infants aged between twelve and fourteen months and found no difference in the frequency with which males and females displayed 'assertive behaviours' (such as shoving, hitting, and grabbing) and 'communicative behaviours' (such as talking, gesturing, and babbling). What she did uncover, however, were differences in the way adults responded to the infants' behaviour. When males used assertive behaviour they got a response from their caregiver (a good thing) 41 per cent of the time. But when females tried this, they got a response only 10 per cent of the time. On the flip side, when females did things like gesture and babble they got a response 65 per cent of the time, leaving males trailing with a 48 per cent success rate for the same behaviour. And, perhaps most startlingly of all, when male infants demanded attention by screaming, crying or pulling at their caregiver, they got it 55 per cent of the time, yet the very same strategy had a disappointing 18 per cent success rate for females. A year after these initial findings the researchers went back to look again at the same children's behaviour. And this time the results were different. Males and females no longer displayed equal levels of communicative and assertive behaviours. Girls spent significantly more time interacting and speaking with the caregiver, while boys were more assertive and aggressive.[16] What this suggests is that demanding and aggressive behaviour 'worked' for males – but not females. And so, they adapted. It is, of course, no coincidence that the behaviours that worked for the boys are those labelled in contemporary society as masculine while those that worked for girls are seen as feminine. The sex group differences had been socially constructed. The children had developed gender-based differences.

In a similar study, but one which looked at teachers rather than caregivers, Cambridge University Professor Diane Reay found that girls received harsh criticism from teachers when they didn't conform to stereotypical gender behaviours. Teachers described girls who misbehaved as 'bad influences', 'spiteful', and 'scheming little madams', yet when boys behaved in similar ways, they were described as just 'mucking about'.[17] Researchers at Ohio University found that teachers at a US public neighbourhood school responded differently to African-American girls than to girls of other ethnic groups and to boys. Previous research has shown that although on the whole girls get progressively more silent in class and experience an associated drop in self-esteem as they get older, African-American girls tend to maintain their assertiveness and self-esteem into adolescence. Yet this study found their outspoken and assertive behaviour in class was met with a specific form of discipline from teachers, largely directed at their femininity. They were described as 'loudies, not ladies'. In fact, the school actually ran a student club called The Proper Ladies – a group that on one occasion instructed its members to spend a week not speaking in class until spoken to first. Yet Edward Morris from Ohio University insists the active learning style of these African-American girls was just the kind of behaviour that was enabling them to thrive in their studies.[18]

The fact that African-American girls behaved differently in the classroom points to further evidence that the behavioural differences between boys and girls cannot be explained by biology. There is no universal set of behaviours that boys and girls adhere to – as might be expected if such behaviour resulted from innate biological factors. The parameters of segregation vary and shift according to social context. This was further illustrated by researchers at Indiana University who assessed groups of children from a range of backgrounds, including economically disadvantaged African-American, middle- and upper-class white American, and Italian, and who found significant variation in the communication styles and cross-sex interaction between boys and girls. For example, African-American females were more assertive in speech (as researchers in Ohio found) and less likely to avoid playing with boys than white girls were at the upper-class school.[19] And perhaps most tellingly of all, gender segregation amongst children has been found to be most rigid in societies with the highest levels of gender inequality.

Girls and boys receive very different lessons on appropriate ways to interact and behave, from reception class to graduation. And the effects of learning these gender stereotypes are long-lasting and far-reaching. As boys' and girls' behaviours begin to diverge, their play styles become less compatible, and playing with someone of the opposite sex becomes increasingly unfamiliar and difficult. And as boys become less responsive to the suggestions of anyone outside their male peer group, it becomes ever harder for girls to interact with them. In addition, children actively reinforce the hidden curriculum fed to them about gender. While sitting in the role-play room at the nursery I visited, I saw a young boy pick up a handbag from the floor and start filling it with things: pens, plastic vegetables – whatever he could find. I asked him the (somewhat loaded) question, 'Are you playing with your bag?', at which point two female voices piped up from across the room: 'He's a boy! Bags are for girls,' they explained. 'Look at mine.' The two girls came over, proudly holding out a pink Barbie bag that belonged to one of them. The boy didn't say anything. Shortly afterwards he put the bag down and wandered away. It is clear that children don't passively line up in their gender dugout. Both actively help to construct, shape, and reinforce it. They want to be 'right', and both girls and boys soon come to know what behaviours are rewarded and punished.

Jobs for the boys

On 14 January 2005 the then president of Harvard University, Lawrence Summers, was invited to speak at a conference called 'Diversifying the Science and Engineering Workforce'. In the US, women are woefully under-represented in these industries, making up just 25 per cent of architects, 26 per cent of maths and computer scientists, and 11 per cent of engineers.[20] The conference had been organised to address this shortage. But Summers chose to use this conference as an opportunity to declare publicly that women's under-representation could be explained in part by innate differences between women's and men's interests and abilities in these subjects: 'In the special case of science and engineering, there are issues of intrinsic aptitude, and particularly of the variability of aptitude, and that those considerations are reinforced by what are in fact lesser factors involving socialization and continuing discrimination.'[21] In short, while there are a lot of factors at play, boys are naturally better at maths and science than girls. In an instant, a destructive stereotype was given the seal of approval by the head of one of the world's most prestigious academic institutions. The remarks created a firestorm, and Summers eventually resigned. I asked science writer and *New York Times* columnist Natalie Angier if she thought Summers was a lone voice. 'There's no question that scientific ability is still thought to be masculine, if for no other reason than that it's still associated with machines, and we all know that boys like trucks and objects, while girls are attracted to dolls and people. I think Summers's comments were thoughtless and unnecessary, and the suggestions he made in his self-styled role as "devil's advocate" are either contradicted by existing data, or are presumptions made ahead of the data.' Yet the stereotype that boys are better than girls at maths and science remains a potent force, and every time a girl sits at her desk and opens her maths or science book, she is doing so in a society which believes she will not be as interested or as able to answer the questions as the boy sitting next to her. This is reinforced by the toys and clothes she is given, and the damage it does is profound.

As Angier says, there is currently no evidence for gender differences in children's overall aptitude for maths, and US research shows that in elementary school boys and girls perform equally well. Yet by the time they reach high school and college, performance differences have indeed crept in. In 2003 the Organisation for Economic Co-operation and Development tested children's maths literacy in forty-one countries. They found that in most industrialised countries the top performers included more boys than girls.[22] Surely this is evidence of boys' intrinsically superior aptitude, then?

Not quite. At the heart of this difference in performance is gender stereotyping. A study of female undergraduate students in France found that those who believed the stereotype that men were better at maths had less confidence in their own abilities and subsequently performed worse in statistics tests. The poorer performance kicked in when women started becoming anxious and therefore distracted from the task. The source of this anxiety was that, as the questions became more complicated, it became increasingly difficult for them to 'double-check' the accuracy of the answers they were giving – something they needed to do to assuage their lack of confidence in their ability to answer the questions.[23] Indeed, the forty-one-country report found that in most countries, fifteen-year-old girls were more anxious when doing maths and had less confidence in their abilities than boys. Similar results have been found when testing girls and boys on their spatial skills – skills seen as crucial to success in engineering and architecture.

And because girls don't think they're as good at maths, they underperform on tests and don't choose to take higher-level classes. Surveys in the US show more boys choose to enrol in maths classes, particularly advanced placement programmes, and a study of Flemish students found boys participate more actively in the classes.[24] And it doesn't require an academic study (although they exist) to tell you that students who take more maths classes and participate more score higher on maths achievement tests. This is underlined by an analysis of the forty-one-country literacy testing by Professor Paola Sapienza at Northwestern University in the US. She found that in countries that were more gender equal the gap between girls' and boys' performance in maths disappeared.[25] Women and men have an equal ability, but women's performance drops in the context of gender stereotypes.[26]

Barbie is also to blame for girls' relative underperformance in maths and science. Well, not just Barbie – in fact, gender stereotyping is utterly rampant across children's toys and clothes, and they directly influence and reinforce what children are taught about gender at school, and what subjects they expect to be good at. For the purposes of research I decided to pay a visit to the Oxford Street branch of Mothercare. The first and most obvious thing to strike me was that the entire contents of the shop are divided along gender lines. And I mean gender. There is no physical difference between male and female newborns or toddlers that requires they wear different clothes. Garments on the girls' side were of muted colours, with significantly more bows, flowers, frills, and general 'pinkness'. But what I found particularly astonishing was the difference in the 'loudness' of the clothes for girls and boys. Wandering round the boys' aisles I was confronted by row after row of T-shirts and jumpers emblazoned with phrases like 'Mummy's little explorer', 'On our travels', 'Dig dig all day long', 'I'm the boss' and '100 per cent cheeky'. Yet in comparison the girls' aisles were silent. Hardly any of the clothes had writing on them at all. All I could find were the rather lacklustre 'Daddy's little cupcake' and 'Mummy's little flower'. The lessons imparted by these clothes mirror how girls are encouraged to behave in the classroom: quieter, less outspoken – more feminine.

The boys also had a wider range of trousers and trainers – the kind of clothes one presumably needs when going adventuring and dig, dig, digging all day long. Back at the girls' side, there were considerably more clothes that are a hindrance to exactly this kind of behaviour – namely, skirts and shiny sandals. Here was the hidden gender curriculum in full flow – with very clear gendered values and expectations being imparted to the children who walked in: boys are loud and active and like 'sciencey' things such as building and constructing; girls, on the other hand, are quiet and passive, preferring to do 'caring' things and look pretty. Should a boy happen to like the look of a T-shirt with flowers on, the shop's layout loudly and publicly declares that he is 'wrong' because he has wandered into the section labelled 'girls'. This kind of gender stereotyping surrounds children every day, both in shops and at school.

These ideas about gender, science and maths are even more potent in toys. For example, the toy company Interplay have teamed up with the creators of *The Dangerous Book for Boys* to produce similarly branded 'chemistry sets for boys'. As Interplay's product manager Bob Paton explained, 'These science kits will be wonderful for boys to bond with their fathers.'[27] Dr Francis at Roehampton University has looked at the educational value of typical 'boys' toys' and 'girls' toys'. She found that very few toys for girls helped them to develop curriculum-based skills. Yet boys' toys often helped develop problem-solving skills and knowledge around technology and construction.[28] This is also backed up by research which has looked at how violent video games (a typically masculine activity) lead to the specific development of visuo-spatial skills.[29] It's no surprise then that such an early gender divide in the skills and preferences fostered amongst children is later played out in the classroom.

What happens in the classroom has far-reaching implications for what careers children go on to choose. Just 4 per cent of girls aged thirteen to eighteen want to pursue a career in engineering, while 12 per cent would like to be a housewife, and 32 per cent a model. These findings, by the UK-based organisation New Outlooks in Science and Engineering, are unsurprising given that girls are weaned from birth on a diet of gender stereotypes. Twenty per cent of girls said they were put off a career in science because they saw them as 'jobs for boys'.[30] And this is a message that appears to be coming from schools themselves. The Equal Opportunities Commission found that just 15 per cent of young people in the UK received any information or advice about work experience in a sector that is non-traditional for their gender.[31] This undoubtedly contributed to the rather shocking finding that out of 10,256 work-experience placements in 2003 that were in the mechanical, construction or engineering sectors, just 5 per cent were filled by girls. And work experience is hugely influential in children's future job choices. Evidently conferences such as the one Lawrence Summers was speaking at in 2005 are sorely needed. What are not needed are unfounded remarks about girls' 'intrinsic aptitude' that make it harder and harder for them to break free from stereotypes.

Throwing like a girl

IMUS: So, I watched the basketball game last night between— a little bit of Rutgers and Tennessee, the women's final . . . That's some rough girls from Rutgers. Man, they got tattoos and—

McGUIRK: Some hard-core hos.

IMUS: That's some nappy-headed hos there. I'm gonna tell you that now, man, that's some— woo. And the girls from Tennessee, they all look cute, you know . . .

ROSENBERG: It was a tough watch. The more I look at Rutgers, they look exactly like the Toronto Raptors.

IMUS: Well, I guess, yeah.

RUFFINO: Only tougher.

McGUIRK: The [Memphis] Grizzlies would be more appropriate.[32]

This transcript is of shock jock Don Imus and his colleagues talking about a National Collegiate Athletic Association (NCAA) Division I championship basketball game that had taken place the day before between Rutgers and Tennessee universities. Their racist derision of the female basketball players provoked a national outcry and the show was pulled from the air. But the comments also did something else. In the fifty-eight seconds Imus and colleagues spent 'discussing' a women's basketball game – by comparing the teams' sexual attractiveness – they gave voice to beliefs about gender that pervade contemporary sports, from the university championship court to the daily football game on the school playground: looking athletic isn't natural or attractive in women, and their sports are not as worthy of serious attention, aside from scrutiny of the players' appearance. In the trenches of masculinity and femininity, boys play and girls watch (or are watched for their attractiveness).

By just ten years of age, girls are increasingly less active. By age fifteen, only half achieve the government's target activity rate for children of sixty minutes a day.[33] This is in stark contrast to boys, who sustain their activity rate throughout their school life. In the UK, 1.6 million more men than women aged sixteen and over have been active in the past four weeks, and nearly double the proportion of men than women in the age bracket sixteen to twenty-four regularly take part in sports.[34] The root of this disparity is hinted at by the finding that one in five men agree that 'being sporty is not feminine'.[35] Children learn early on that a boy's body is active and functional, whereas a girl's is passive and decorative. Sporting success is how boys gain popularity, but not girls. The popularity currency girls generally trade in is material possessions and their physical appearance (the subject of the previous chapter). A study of high-school basketball players in the US by researchers at the University of Southern California found that prior to adolescence girls had to act tough and masculine to be allowed to play with boys.[36] Yet after the onset of adolescence, this behaviour led to others questioning their (hetero)sexuality. And in a context of widespread homophobia this led to every girl in the study either temporarily dropping out of sports or considering doing so. A prevalent view amongst these female basketball players was that playing sports conflicted with feminine appearance. They feared the kind of retribution dished out to women like Susan Boyle who so publicly failed to look sufficiently feminine. And they're not alone in their concern. Forty per cent of girls feel self-conscious about their bodies during PE, and 26 per cent say they 'hate the way that they look when they exercise/play sport'.[37] The straitjacket of femininity restricts girls' movements every day in the playground and discourages them from involvement in sport.

The inequalities girls face in sports are not just perpetuated by cultural influences. They also receive these messages from schools themselves. The physical development and gross motor skills of pre-pubescent girls and boys are generally comparable, yet some primary schools choose to separate them in PE, a policy adhered to by most UK secondary schools.[38] Before a girl even turns up for try-out she has been allocated to a particular team, regardless of fitness level or ability, purely on the basis of her sex. Today, compulsory sex segregation is central to the organisation of sport. However, academic Eileen McDonagh and journalist Laura Pappano argue that this hinges on the destructive myth that sex is the most salient attribute determining sporting talent and performance and that girls and women are inherently athletically inferior.[39] And this is simply not the case. In some sports attributes associated with men as a group do of course provide an advantage. This stems from their greater height, weight and upper-body strength. But these sports do not include chess, billiards, table tennis and bowling – all sports where sex segregation is prevalent. In fact, in some sports physical characteristics associated with women as a group confer an advantage, because of women's lower centre of gravity and greater proportion of body fat. And by association, male group attributes can be disadvantageous – think horse racing, sailing, or race-car driving. It all depends on the sport. There is significant overlap between the average male and average female sports competitor, and sex-linked attributes can be low on a list of individual factors such as training, individual body make-up, and social influence when it comes to determining a person's performance in a particular event. Yet the practice of dividing children on the basis of sex is institutionalised in the education system. In sport, as in so many other arenas, we accept the segregation of women and men without question.

Girls also receive very little encouragement from the sports pages. Only 4.8 per cent of the space given over to sports coverage in national and regional UK newspapers is dedicated to female sports.[40] And when women's sports do get covered, they get covered differently. To start with, they are frequently presented as the 'other'. Take the NCAA Basketball Championships. The men's tournament is typically referred to as the 'NCAA Basketball Championship Game', whereas the women's tournament is frequently termed the 'NCAA Women's Basketball Championship Game'. Spot the difference. A review of various sporting events found this kind of gendered identification occurs on average twenty-six times in a women's event, compared to zero times for a men's event.[41] This situates men's sports as the default, the regular, while women's sports are relegated to a special edition. Furthermore, the players are judged differently. For example, golf commentators are found to be more ready to forgive bad shots if they have been played by men. A study of men's tournaments showed issues such as course difficulty and 'impossible pin placements' were mentioned in relation to poor shots thirty-eight times, whereas in women's tournaments similar comments were made only three times.[42] Studies of other sports have similarly found commentators more likely to note men's strengths than women's, and conversely more likely to note women's weakness than men's.

Media coverage also tends to dwell on female athletes' physical appearance, rather than on how their game is looking. This perceived contradiction between a woman's body and an athlete's body echoes from the playground to the broadsheets and back again. Coverage of the 2008 Olympics provided ample evidence of this. When UK swimmer Rebecca Adlington won two gold medals in Beijing, the *Observer Sport Monthly* magazine celebrated this by inviting her to a photo shoot where she was dressed in a swimsuit and stilettos, heavily made-up, and asked to pose for the camera with flowers in her hair. The first 600 words of the article accompanying the pictures revolve around her appearance. 'As Adlington chats away, the stylist applies the curling tongs and there is a loud sizzle . . . In fact, the resounding verdict around the studio today is, "My God, hasn't she got great legs?" and "Doesn't she look gorgeous?" She does. Serene and beautiful, but wonderfully unaffected as, sweating under the hot photographic lamps, she asks for a tissue.'[43] The main hook of the article appears to be the 'femininity makeover' of a swimming powerhouse – someone who broke the 800m freestyle world record. The article ends by reflecting on the awards night for the BBC Sports Personality of the Year, for which she had been nominated: 'She has already chosen her dress and her shoes: all she needs now is the trophy.' And when the *Independent* previewed some of the female athletes participating in the Olympic Games, the feature was called 'World-Class Pin-Ups: Meet the Olympic Contenders for the Gold Medal in Glamour'.[44] With this in mind, the sexist comments on Imus's show don't actually seem all that surprising, nor does the lack of enthusiasm for and participation in school sports shown by girls. The relative invisibility of women's sports and an emphasis on their decorative role when featured compound the damaging messages girls receive about their respective role in exercise and sport, as well as reinforcing stifling beauty ideals.

Sticks and stones

While girls are discouraged from using their bodies on the sports field, they often find their bodies at the centre of another unwelcome kind of activity. Chloe was one of the many women and girls I heard from during the course of my research into violence at school: 'I had boys groping me en masse. It wasn't just at break times – in class as well. Sometimes they used to hold me down and take it in turns. It was universally accepted. Teachers pretended they didn't notice. I would regularly hang out in the toilets at break time. I felt pretty violated. It made me hate my body.' Having now left school, Chloe can pinpoint exactly when the sexual harassment began: 'When my breasts grew. I went from an A to an E cup when I was fourteen.' It became a regular feature of her school day, mostly happening when the boys were in groups. 'People would randomly scream "slut". One boy told me that he had a fantasy that he wanted to tie me up and viciously rape me. He was a bit of an outcast. But when he said that all the boys were high-fiving him. He got serious street-cred for saying it.' Classrooms are training grounds for boys aspiring to be 'real men', and girls like Jena and Chloe are paying the price. Humiliating and degrading girls serves to highlight just how masculine boys really are. And so, sexist bullying and sexual harassment are an integral part of daily school life for many girls.

Megan described how boys used to taunt her in the corridors at secondary school. 'Older students would say things like, "Look at those knockers!" in hushed voices. Or they would exchange looks and make breast outlines on their chests. That was particularly hurtful.' For other girls, the harassment is physical as well. Ava was just seven years old when it began. She was so far ahead academically for her age that her teacher started running out of new tasks to give her. So instead she would regularly ask Ava to go to the classroom next door and tutor some of the other pupils, and that's where she met Adam. 'At first he just sat too close . . . [Later] he would start by making excuses to bend down to look up my skirt, such as dropping his pencil. At one point, I was helping him when he suddenly declared that he loved me. While I stood there in shock, he put his hand up my skirt.' Adam also informed Ava that his dad showed him pornography. 'He used to brag about this fact.' Ava soon asked her teacher to be excused from tutoring other students. 'I told the teacher that I didn't want to, that one of the other students was being very mean to me and trying to touch me. She didn't react to my comments about him trying to touch me, and told me that I had to tutor other students because she had nothing else for me to do, and I couldn't just do nothing.' In response, Ava started intentionally falling behind in her work so she wouldn't be made to tutor Adam any more.

Hayley also described to me how some boys at her secondary school were using new technologies to harass girls. 'They try and take pictures with their camera phone up your skirt while you're sitting at your desk. Nobody knows what to say. They wouldn't want to provoke an argument.' Boys also access internet pornography on school computers. Hayley said, 'In year seven and eight it's quite common. Even the boys you wouldn't expect you see getting told off by teachers for it.' Similarly, Sarah remembers pornography being commonplace at her school: 'Every student was asked to bring in newspaper articles. Many boys saw this as a great opportunity to bring in newspapers such as the *Sun*, *Star*, *Sport* etc. and make a point of looking at, sharing and showing the countless page-three-style images. Sarah was 'extremely upset on a number of occasions when boys who sat near me in the class would push these pages in front of me and make comments. Most of the time, all forms of harassment went completely unchallenged . . . I don't think [the teachers] ever paid any attention to sexual harassment. I often made an attempt to challenge touching, porn or offensive comments, but I often struggled to find the right words to form an argument, and so often ended up shouted down or laughed at.'

The sexual harassment girls are subject to on a daily basis doesn't always come from male pupils. Alison, currently training for a PGCE, is required to do various placements in schools. When Alison contacted me she was just one week into a secondary school placement, and 'utterly shocked at what goes on in the school. I have heard one young male teacher tell a year-ten student that she is "loose, like Jade Goody" for wearing make-up and a short skirt. Today, I heard an older male teacher refer to a pupil as "an old slapper" in the staff room. There has also recently been an incident in the school where a caretaker was found to be touching girls inappropriately (on the bum) and flirting with them. No action was taken. Apparently no action is ever taken for physical/verbal inappropriate behaviour and teachers actually looked shocked at my surprise.'

Sexist bullying and harassment in schools is a worldwide problem. In Malawi, 50 per cent of schoolgirls sampled in a study said they had been touched without permission in a sexual manner by teachers or boys.[45] In Togo harassment and abuse are so prevalent that they have given rise to their own playground vocabulary, including 'Notes sexuellement transmises' (sexually transmitted marks/grades), and 'cahier de roulement' (shared exercise book or presumed to have had sex with several teachers). Ethnic minority women also face sexual harassment which is informed by or intertwined with racial stereotypes. Researchers in Australia found Asian-Australian girls had been sexually harassed by non-Asian white boys, whose comments had been infused with the stereotype that Asian women are more compliant and eager to please men with 'exotic' sexual acts.[46]

The consequences for girls who are sexually harassed or assaulted at school can be devastating. Unsurprisingly, as Jena found, it can cause victims to participate less in class, attain lower grades, and even drop out of school altogether. Depression and loss of self-esteem are common. If girls experience repeated sexual harassment, they are significantly more likely to attempt suicide.[47] In fact, the trauma symptoms reported by adolescent girls subject to sexual harassment have been found to be similar to those described by rape victims. Yet despite the fact that sexual harassment is shown to have a more damaging impact on victims than other forms of school bullying,[48] teachers are less likely to intervene in incidences of the former.[49] Why? Well, as Jena's teacher said to her, 'boys will be boys'. The sexual harassment of girls is viewed as 'normal' behaviour for boys. And it is precisely this naturalising of the act, this insidious complacency it elicits, which has enabled sexist bullying and harassment to flourish in classrooms across the world.

The daily trip to school is uncertain, frightening, and dangerous for millions of girls across the world. Those fortunate enough to make it to the school gates spend their day exposed to a hidden curriculum of gender inequality. Although not written into their timetables, the learning takes place every time they enter the classroom, go out to the playground, or walk on to the sports field. The gender trenches of masculinity and femininity produce segregation and violence. Yet the equality illusion persists under the guise that what we are witnessing are natural, biological differences. And so, school continues to be a key site where gender inequality is reflected and reproduced – with boys and girls taught lessons that will have damaging repercussions in their adult lives.

09:21 | Sexism and the City

Just Another Day's Work

Elizabeth holds the girls' hands as they step off the bus and hurry through the crowd. She doesn't usually like to rush their journey to school as this is one of the few parts of the day when she gets to spend time with her daughters. But the buses are heaving this morning and they're running late. Thankfully it's still a few minutes before nine as she's waving goodbye to the girls at the school gate. As Elizabeth turns and starts to make her way back to the bus stop she becomes aware of how heavy her legs feel. She's been on her feet for the past twelve hours, having gone straight from her office-cleaning night shift to taking the girls to school. 'It is only a 40p [an hour] difference to the day shift, but I try and do the night shift so I can do the school runs. I can't make alternative arrangements or pay someone to take the kids to school.' When Elizabeth and her daughters arrived in the UK four years ago she had high hopes of moving quickly into legal secretarial work, as this is what she had done in Nigeria, but so far she hasn't been able to find a position where the hours are flexible enough to fit around taking care of the girls. Like many women, Elizabeth faces the impossible choice of caring for her children or advancing her career.

As she gets back on the bus Elizabeth realises she's

forgotten to top up her Oyster card, so will have to pay the full fare. At the rate she's paid for cleaning she simply can't afford to make mistakes like this. 'I struggle with the money. Rent and transportation takes a lot of it. I have to do another two hours here and there whenever I can.' Elizabeth's struggles with money are only compounded by the treatment she receives at work. 'As a working mother you need respect at work. Cleaners are not respected. Employers think they are daft or nonentities, which is unfortunate.' Angered by the low pay she and her fellow cleaners receive, Elizabeth has recently become involved with her trade union and has been in negotiations with her employer to raise their pay to £7.60 an hour – the estimated income needed to support a decent standard of living, known as the London Living Wage. 'They don't believe cleaners deserve good pay. My manager said he doesn't think cleaners deserve the living wage.'

Sitting on the bus, Elizabeth mentally runs through the jobs she needs to get done today. 'After I drop the kids, sometimes I have to do studies or go shopping. My daughters finish at 3:30 p.m., I get back about 4:30 p.m., then I give them food.' Recently Elizabeth has been attending a course to refresh her secretarial skills as she's determined to break out of her current job and increase her family's income, but as a single mother it's incredibly difficult to fit the training in. 'Most times I get four hours' sleep.' But Elizabeth has few options at the moment: 'I have to work, otherwise we starve.' The bus approaches the shops and Elizabeth rings the bell. As it's 9:21 she now has a couple of hours to do the shopping and housework before going to college and then picking up the kids. The girls are usually really good at letting her sleep so she should be able to get to bed by 5:30 p.m. this evening, before heading out to work again at 9:30 p.m.

I met Elizabeth through her trade-union activity while doing research at the Fawcett Society. It is easy to see her situation as relatively normal and not deserving of further inquiry: single mother has little support with childcare so does a cleaning job and gets paid very little. But we need to start asking questions about this familiar scenario: Why do so many women have to work below their skill level because those are the only jobs with flexible hours that fit around their caring responsibilities? Why are cleaning and other forms of traditional 'women's work' (like caring and catering) paid so little – and in particular less than traditional 'men's work' (like plumbers and decorators) that requires equivalent levels of skill and effort? Because gender discrimination in the workplace is illegal and women make up nearly half the workforce it is easy to assume that all is now fair and equal. But the near-equivalent numbers of women and men in the workplace are where any 'equality' ends: 30,000 women are sacked each year in the UK simply for being pregnant, women make up only 12 per cent of FTSE 100 company directors, and women are paid on average 22.6 per cent less per hour than men.

When discussing women in the workplace a standard media refrain is to ask whether women can 'have it all', i.e. a family and a career. But women have always had to combine work and caring. For many, particularly those from working-class backgrounds, that question is redundant; if they don't work their family doesn't eat. The real question is why is it only women who have to choose between a family and maximising their career potential? And, in fact, why should anyone have to choose between these two things at all? Neither can be viewed as a luxury – they are both central aspects of society. There is also a tendency to overlook the fact that the inequalities women experience at work are not just related to their maternal status. Sexist attitudes and outdated stereotypes continue to shackle women and restrict their opportunities. Sexual harassment remains an all too common feature of daily working life, and the infiltration of the sex industry into workplace cultures poses a new and insidious threat to women's status at work.

When we look at the consequences of gender inequality at work, we are not just talking about 'high-flying' elite women failing to make it into the boardroom, we are talking about women – like Elizabeth – struggling to maintain even a basic standard of living. Women who are trapped by the sticky floor of low-paid, part-time work. And it is not only women who pay the price for this. Estimates of the full cost to the UK of discrimination against women in the workplace, including the lost tax revenue and increased welfare benefits that result, range from £15 billion to £23 billion.[1] Sexism is bad for business. While forty years of legislation outlawing gender discrimination in the workplace may give the impression that sexism no longer persists, look a little closer and it is clear that equality still largely remains an illusion in the office.

Hiring and Firing

Simply being perceived as having the potential to bear children – otherwise known as being female – can prevent a person from being hired or cause them to be fired. In the UK it has been illegal to ask women about family plans in interviews or not to employ someone simply because they might get pregnant since 1975. Legislation banning discrimination based on maternal status was a basic and fundamental step to enable women to participate in UK workplaces on an equal footing with men. But a government review found that mothers face more discrimination than any other group in the workplace.[2] The first hurdle to overcome is actually getting hired. This is a somewhat tricky business considering that 70 per cent of recruitment agencies have been asked by clients to avoid hiring women of childbearing age or those that are pregnant, and 80 per cent of human resource managers would 'think twice' before hiring a newly married woman in her twenties.[3]

Sir Alan Sugar, Britain's most high-profile businessman and 'enterprise tsar' for the British government, has argued against laws preventing employers from discriminating against women by asking about their family plans: 'If someone comes into an interview and you think to yourself there is a possibility that this woman might have a child and therefore take time off, it is a bit of a psychological negative thought . . . you're not allowed to ask, so it's easy – just don't employ them.'[4] And he is not alone in thinking this: 68 per cent of employers agree that they would like more rights to ask candidates about family plans.[5] They argue it simply makes 'business sense' to not want to employ a woman of childbearing age, or at the very least to want to ask her at interview what her plans for a family are. The minute you accept this argument, however, conversations about equality become redundant. The potential to bear children is the defining and unalterable difference between women and men, and it is a difference that is present from puberty to menopause. Not insignificantly, this broadly brackets the employment 'lifespan'. If it is acceptable for businesses to discriminate against individuals on the basis that they are or might become pregnant, then it is implicitly acceptable to deny women the right to participate in the workplace on an equal footing, to deny them the same chance at interview as equally qualified and experienced men, to deny them the same promotional opportunities as men, and to allow their careers to be cut short. Quite aside from being a complete affront to justice and equality, penalising female workers in this manner is, quite frankly, absurd. When business managers talk about wanting to discriminate against (potential) mothers, they are talking about wanting to discriminate against nearly half the total UK workforce. Take women away and the economy collapses. So it can only be assumed that such employers don't want women to leave the workplace altogether – just their company.

Women who succeed in clearing the hurdle of acquiring a job then face the task of keeping it. Statistics show 30,000 women in the UK lose their job every year simply for being pregnant.[6] In the UK a whopping 45 per cent of female employees face discrimination or unfavourable treatment in the workplace due to pregnancy. Polling by the Government Equalities Office revealed that 24 per cent of men and 17 per cent of women think pregnant women and new mothers should be first in line for redundancy. Even Rosie Boycott, co-founder of the feminist magazine *Spare Rib*, has argued against parental rights, saying '[such women] are also an immense burden on the small businesses who are expected to pick up the tab, especially at a time when the economic downturn means many are struggling simply to keep afloat'.[7] Boycott admitted having reservations about one of her own female employees: 'I would be lying if I said that I wouldn't flinch and wonder how on earth I was going to afford the maternity payments that are her right, on top of paying for a full-time replacement to take on her duties for up to a year.'[8] Boycott fails to mention, or perhaps doesn't realise, that the government reimburses employers 92 per cent of statutory maternity pay and 104.5 per cent if the employer's annual National Insurance payments are £45,000 or less.

Two years ago Helen was the most senior woman in the FTSE 100-ranked company where she had worked for the past ten years. She already had one child and was delighted when she found out she was expecting her second. She informed her employers, and within forty-eight hours of doing so they told her that if she didn't resign they would find a reason to make her redundant. Utterly shocked by what she had been told, Helen launched a formal grievance and proceeded to find herself being victimised by senior colleagues. 'There were times when it was just dreadful,' she recalled. The level of stress Helen suffered necessitated sick leave as both her health and her baby's dramatically worsened. Eventually Helen's grievance was settled out of court, but the experience had a profound effect on her life. 'My career [in my particular industry] was over. I had to accept that.'

Women who do decide to become mothers should not have to pay a penalty at work. But it is also important to ask why employers are still able to 'target' women for discrimination simply because of their potential childcare responsibilities? Why haven't the huge shifts in women's lives that have occurred over the past forty years been mirrored in men's lives – with men playing a more equal role in caring? Cultural stereotypes still persist as to women's maternal role. In 2009 the Children's Society launched a major report following the Good Childhood Inquiry about children's experiences in the UK. The report found that children's lives have become increasingly difficult, with more young people 'anxious and troubled' than in the past. The report was vast in scope, covering the effects of economic inequalities, advertising, and competition in education amongst many other things. However, one of the factors identified as contributing to the damage done to children was working mothers: 'Most women now work and their new economic independence contributes to levels of family break-up which are higher in the UK than in any other Western European country.'[9] The press then ran headlines like: 'Kids "Damaged" by Mums Who Work' (*Sun*); 'Mum's Cash "Leading to Split Home"' (*Mirror*); 'Working Women "Fuel Family Splits"' (*Daily Telegraph*).[10] The decision taken by the report's authors to frame the issue in such a way, and the subsequent enthusiasm some papers showed in highlighting this 'finding', reveal that, for large sections of the population, if there's a problem to do with caring then the buck stops with Mum, not Dad. The Equality and Human Rights Commission found that over a quarter of the general public still think the mother has primary responsibility for childcare, while over a third of people think it is fathers who are responsible for providing for the family.[11] And this is reflected in the reality of caring patterns: Over three-quarters of all mothers state they have primary responsibility for (unpaid) caring for their children; whereas nearly double the proportion of fathers work between forty and forty-nine hours outside the home than mothers. Furthermore, even women who are employed outside the home full-time spend nearly 30 per cent more time on childcare each day than men who work full-time.[12]

But the cultural expectations around motherhood are only compounded by government policy in the UK: women are entitled to up to fifty-two weeks' maternity leave, receiving statutory maternity pay for up to thirty-nine of those weeks. Compare this with the mother's partner, who is allotted just two weeks' statutory paternity leave. Unequal division of childcare has been heavily institutionalised but other countries – Iceland, for example – show how it can be done differently. There, 'parental leave' is apportioned more equally: three months are reserved exclusively for mothers, three months exclusively for her partner, and a further three months that the parents can divvy up as appropriate.[13] And in the World Economic Forum's Global Gender Gap Index 2008 (which ranks countries according to how gender equal they are on a range of measures) Iceland ranks fourth, whereas the United Kingdom ranks thirteenth.[14] Cultures around caring can only fully transform when the legal framework allows it. Until then, women will continue to pay a motherhood penalty at work, and will not be hired and fired on terms equal with men.

From the sticky floor to the glass ceiling

The term 'glass ceiling' has become common currency over the last two decades in discussions on women's participation in the workforce. Popularised in an article by Carol Hymowitz and Timothy Schellhardt in the *Wall Street Journal*,[15] it describes an invisible barrier blocking women's ascendancy into company boardrooms. When that article was written in 1986 gender discrimination in the workplace had been outlawed and ostensibly there was nothing blocking women from rising to the top of their professions, yet for some reason they were still not getting there in significant numbers.

Obviously legislation takes time to become reality, but it would be reasonable to assume that two subsequent decades of women hammering on the ceiling would have produced some major cracks at least. Yet in the fifty largest publicly traded EU corporations women make up a paltry average of 11 per cent of top executives and 4 per cent of CEOs and heads of boards.[16] In the UK, there are still twenty-two FTSE 100 companies that have no women on their boards at all,[17] and there is just one British ethnic minority woman amongst FTSE 100 directors.[18] In the US women make up just 15.2 per cent of Fortune 500 board directors, with only 3.2 per cent of these positions being held by women of colour.[19]

Women are also starkly under-represented in representational power structures. Less than 20 per cent of MPs in the UK are women, and just 0.3 per cent of MPs are ethnic minority women (despite making up 5.2 per cent of the population[20]). On the international stage the UK ranks seventieth for women's representation. In the US just 17 per cent of Senators and members of the House of Representatives are women,[21] and of course there has never been a female president. Of the world's 188 directly elected leaders, just sixteen are women. Top of the poll for female representation is Rwanda, which has a quota system that reserves twenty-four seats (out of a total of eighty) for women candidates.[22] (I look at this in more detail in 'A New Day', below.) Women's progress into positions of power has not only been glacially slow, in some areas it has been going backwards. In an analysis of companies of all sizes across the UK a research team found that the total proportion of female directors had decreased from 43 per cent in 1991 to 35 per cent in 2007.[23]

But what we are looking at here is not a single, invisible barrier quietly lying in wait outside the boardroom or at the door of the Oval Office. We are looking at the cumulative effect of women being restricted by outdated structures and attitudes at every level in the workplace. Alice Eagly, a professor at Northwestern University, and Linda Carli, associate professor at Wellesley College, point out that the term 'glass ceiling' fails to capture fully how women are excluded from power in the twenty-first century because it implies an absolute barrier at a specific level.[24] They suggest 'labyrinth' as a more accurate metaphor for what women are faced with. Right from the start the route to the top is littered with twists, turns and dead-ends as women negotiate colleagues' stereotypes and the lack of flexible working. Women have to navigate it from the minute they step into the office, not just when they are trying to open the door to the boardroom.

There are three major barriers to women's ascendancy through the workplace: the lack of flexible working, unequal division of caring, and gender stereotyping and discrimination. UK full-time employees work the longest hours in the European Union.[25] This long-working-hours culture hinges on the idea that the productivity and commitment of an employee can be gauged by how late into the night their coat lies uninhabited on the back of their chair. Because, as already discussed, women still shoulder the bulk of caring and housework at home it is very difficult for them to compete with others unencumbered by the responsibility to, for example, pick the kids up from school at 3:30 p.m., take them to a piano lesson, make dinner, and do the washing. Over recent decades, flexible working has become more common and ostensibly allows people to combine work and caring commitments. But the only people in the UK who have the right to request flexible working from their employer are parents with children under six or disabled children under eighteen. The ability to negotiate where and when you perform your tasks is seen as a special dispensation, a deviation from the norm. Flexible working has become the 'mummy track',[26] and those who do work flexibly often carry the stigma of being considered less committed to the job and less career-focused.

Lucy is a successful solicitor in the City of London but has struggled to balance caring for her four-year-old son with developing her career. 'I have found it difficult to convince the partners that I am committed to my job and worthy of promotion while I am working part-time. There is very much a long-hours culture and this is difficult to manage with a young family. While the firm supports part-time working you have to go the extra mile to prove that you are as committed as when you worked full time.' There are also very few flexible jobs available at a senior level. The higher the position, the more difficult it becomes to juggle work with duties at home. I asked Sarah Jackson – chief executive of Working Families, a charity that supports working parents and carers, if she thought it was possible for all jobs to be flexible: 'I think it's possible for almost every job to be flexible. I think people get confused and they think flexible working means reduced hours – and it doesn't. The kinds of jobs that people say can't be flexible tend to be what you could also describe as being extreme jobs – if you're running an investment bank. Actually, it's utterly flexible. You've got such power and status that you work the hours you choose to work – you're in control.'

Jackson points out that there are currently plenty of people in CEO positions working flexibly in order to balance their caring responsibilities at home. In fact, it becomes easier at this level in the sense that earning a CEO salary means you can probably afford the childcare that other people can't. Research conducted by Working Families reveals that some employers are reluctant to implement flexible working out of fear that it will be costly for the organisation. But Jackson is resolute that the only major cost comes through 'a time investment to think it through and get it right. But that is repaid over and over again because all the evidence shows that part-time and flexible workers are productive people . . . There's also plenty of evidence from managers reporting [that] people who are flexible workers are higher performers.' Unfortunately, flexible working has yet to become standard practice in UK workplaces, and as a result women are commonly faced with impossible choices; forced to pick between maximising their career opportunities and caring for a family at home. For many women this means forgoing a potentially illustrious career and getting locked into a lower-paid, lower-status job that gives them the flexibility to care for their children at home.

Recent research found motherhood led to nearly 50 per cent of all women who were managers of restaurants, salons and shops giving up their managerial responsibilities and seeking part-time work as sales assistants or in other low-paid jobs. Across the economy as a whole, women dominate the lowest-paid occupations – and in particular the five 'C's: cleaning, caring, clerical work, cashiering, and catering. These are generally low-status, low-paid positions with few opportunities for development. And this forms the sticky floor of women's work, a scenario which stops many women getting anywhere near the glass ceiling, let alone smashing it.

Gender stereotypes and prejudicial attitudes also play an active role in keeping women out of the top roles and they are the reason that it is not just mothers or women with other caring responsibilities who are unfairly treated in the workplace each day. It has been shown that employees are more resistant to women's attempts to exert influence than to men's. For example, Eagly and Carli report in the *Harvard Business Review* that in meetings at a global retail company people responded more positively to men's attempts to overtly influence than to women's, leading one of the female executives to say, 'People often had to speak up to defend their turf, but when women did so, they were vilified. They were labelled "control freaks"; men acting the same way were called "passionate"'.[27] Study after study shows that women at work are disproportionately penalised for negotiating, influencing, and self-promotion – all important skills for moving into leadership roles. These expectations about behaviour for men and women are, of course, exactly what we saw being taught in the classroom in the previous chapter. Furthermore, if a woman does reach the top at work she risks being judged not according to her actual leadership style, but by expectations about her style. In 2006 Catalyst – a leading business research organisation – teamed up with the Institute for Management Development in Switzerland to study managers' perceptions of male and female leaders.[28] When questioned, the managers, who were from ten predominantly Western European countries, all perceived significant differences between women and men leaders. But these differences didn't correlate to objective study; research has consistently failed to reveal significant differences in the style and approach of male and female leaders. What the managers' perceptions did correspond to were broad gender stereotypes about women's and men's traits. Across all cultures stereotypical feminine traits include 'emotional', 'sensitive', 'affection-ate', 'dependent', and 'weak'. Masculine traits include 'ambitious', 'strong', 'unemotional', and 'logical'. In line with these stereotypes, when the researchers asked for man-agers' perceptions about women and men leaders they heard that female leaders outperform men at supporting others while male leaders were better at influencing upwards and problem solving. They aren't.

These stereotypes directly affected some of the women I spoke to, especially around their chances of getting pro-moted. Ania, who got in touch with me at the Fawcett Society, had always been extremely ambitious. The consult-ancy where she worked had really taken off over the past few years so it was the perfect place for her to develop and gain more experience. When a more senior position became available she jumped at the chance. 'I approached my man-ager to ask if I could be considered for it . . . He told me there was no point applying because I was female. He went on to say that women have to work much harder to get such a job.' Despite knowing full well she was qualified to do this new job, Ania decided not to apply. 'I understood that I would not be taken seriously and would not be con-sidered for the role. It destroyed my enthusiasm for sub-mitting a formal application to the bank, and because of the comments I didn't feel I would have a chance anyway.'

During my research I also heard from Lisa, who had held a number of very senior roles in the banking industry. She recalled one interview for a senior position at a large bank in which one member of the all-male interview panel had said to her, 'There's no women who work in this office. You really will be the office bitch.' Lisa was, as you might expect, extremely taken aback by this, but the interview went on. Afterwards, she tried to shrug it off, and when the panel contacted her to come in for a trial period she emailed them her daily rates. 'They said, "We are astonished that you asked for money." They said it was "because you are a woman and you don't know the office".' Lisa promptly ended negotiations with them. But she was shocked by the responses from friends and colleagues when she told them what had happened. 'I was told by lots of people, "Oh, don't worry about it; that's just the way it is."' Throughout her career Lisa has become increasingly conscious of how gender has shaped her career development: 'The fight of constantly challenging that sexist crap is exhausting and I have to figure out which arguments to fight and which ones to leave – [it amounts to] another job in itself!' Lisa is by no means alone in her experiences. In July 2009 Cynthia Carroll – chief executive of the mining firm Anglo American and one of the few women to head up a large UK company – came under attack from the firm's former deputy chairman, Graham Boustred. He declared that it is difficult to find a female chief executive because 'most women are sexually frustrated. Men are not because they can fall back on call girls. If you have a CEO who is sexually frustrated, she can't act properly.'[29] Each day at work, women continue to face a myriad of obstacles that keep many trapped by the sticky floor of low-paid work and others continuing to bang their heads against the glass ceiling.

Mind the gap

There is something that all UK women in full-time paid employment should know: between the end of October and December they don't get paid. A survey by the Office of National Statistics found that women working full-time are paid on average 17 per cent less than men, which is the equivalent to men being paid all year and women working for free from the end of October.[30] This is despite the fact that the Equal Pay Act was passed forty years ago. The pay gap is even greater for some ethnic minorities, and all women working part-time earn on average 37 per cent less per hour than men working full-time. (This is an important comparison, because three-quarters of part-time workers are women.)[31] The discrepancy between women's and men's wage packets amounts to the UK having the largest gender pay gap in full-time work in the European Union, with equal pay claims accounting for one in three employment tribunal claims in the UK. Women are working at a discount price, as they have been doing since they entered the paid workforce. The reasons for this are a combination of many of the issues already touched on in this chapter, from blatant stereotyping and discrimination to the sticky floor and lack of value placed on the five 'C' categories into which many women's jobs fall.

It is commonly assumed that the reason for this stark and stubborn pay gap is the time many women take out to be a mother, but in reality it is much more complex. Catherine remembers feeling confident about her chances of promotion. She was the only woman in her team and over the previous year had outperformed all her colleagues, and was duly rewarded by being given the responsibilities of a director. But there was something missing from her 'reward package'. 'I was told I had to "prove myself" before the directorship was formalised and a pay rise given. There was no justifiable reason for this.' Catherine's frustration was only compounded when shortly afterwards another director was appointed (formally) on over double her salary, without a requirement to 'prove himself'. 'To this day I am paid substantially less than all male directors at my firm.' Discrimination such as this has been estimated to account for up to 38 per cent of the gender pay gap.

Another common explanation for the pay gap is that women are simply too timid or naive to negotiate for a higher salary. For example, a 2009 BBC online news magazine article on the subject carried the headline 'Why XX Must Think Like XY to Earn More K'.[32] And starting salaries matter: if two twenty-one-year-olds are offered £25,000 for their first job, but one negotiates that figure up to £30,000, and each receives an annual 3 per cent pay rise, the higher earner will make over £300,000 more by the time they reach the age of fifty. However, research suggests this isn't about women lacking the wherewithal to negotiate. In 2007 three researchers from Carnegie Mellon and Harvard universities divided 119 volunteers into random groups. The volunteers were asked to play the role of interviewer for a hypothetical job. They were briefed on the 'candidates', all of whom were described as exceptionally qualified and talented. The crucial variant was that some candidates had accepted the offered salary, while others had tried to negotiate a higher starting salary. When the volunteers were asked to pick the best candidates, a startling pattern emerged. They were more likely to penalise female candidates who had negotiated their salary than male candidates, perceiving the women who had asked for more money as 'less nice'. Further studies confirmed this: across all experiments male volunteers were less willing to work with women who had attempted to negotiate than women who had not. Yet it didn't matter to men whether a male candidate had negotiated or not – this didn't impact on his 'niceness'.[33] This study suggested that women's reluctance to negotiate is in fact an accurate calculation of the social costs for women involved in haggling. There are unwritten codes in the workplace about 'appropriate' gender behaviour, leaving women facing a difficult choice: don't negotiate and receive dramatically less pay over a lifetime, or negotiate and risk not getting the job at all.

Another cause of the pay gap – but one which is rarely discussed – is the fact that workers in female-dominated roles and professions are paid and valued less than workers in male-dominated roles and professions – even when the jobs demand the same level of skill, training, physical and mental effort and decision-making. When this takes place within the same organisation it is deemed illegal in the UK under the Sex Discrimination Act – violating the right to equal pay for work of equal value – but across the economy as a whole this takes place daily. The five Cs which make up the sticky floor of women's work – cleaning, caring, clerical work, cashiering and catering – are jobs which generally have traditionally been done by women at home for free, and the skills they require are seen as 'natural' for women and thus not deserving of much financial remuneration. Historically, women working in these jobs were also seen as just working for 'pin money' to supplement the male breadwinner's wage. Partly as a result of this legacy, jobs traditionally done by women are paid less than jobs traditionally done by men. And today, an individual's pay can be reduced by up to 9 per cent just by being employed in a female-dominated industry. An investigation carried out by the Equal Opportunities Commission in 2006 found that all classroom assistants in Scotland employed by local authorities (98 per cent of whom were women) were performing tasks significantly more demanding than the least demanding 'facilities-maintenance roles', yet – on annual salaries of between £7,000 and £11,000 – they were being paid significantly less than the school caretaker. There is also a historic legacy in the UK of women and men doing essentially the same work but being given different job titles and paid differently, as in chef/cook, tailor/seamstress, or administrator/secretary.

Pamela Enderby won a landmark equal-pay claim in 1997 in a test case of the legal right to equal pay for work of equal value. Enderby was able to bring this claim because the pay inequality was taking place within the same organisation. However, her experiences also illustrate what is going on across the economy as a whole – which individual women currently have no right to seek redress for. In 1986 Enderby was departmental head of speech and language therapy at Frenchay Hospital, Bristol. The profession was dominated by women and paid significantly lower than the male-dominated professions of clinical psychology and pharmacy. In fact, she was paid, respectively, £4,000 and £7,000 less than her male comparators in these two professions – both of which shared the same employer: the National Health Service.[34] Enderby spent eleven years battling through the courts to challenge this, arguing that the level of skill and training required to qualify and practise in these professions was the same – that it was work of equal value. I asked Enderby, who is now Professor of Community Rehabilitation at the University of Sheffield, how she felt when she initially found out she was being paid less than male colleagues doing equal work: 'It seemed to me that it was so obviously unfair,' she said. Enderby spent over a decade fighting her case in the courts. 'It was just tedious . . . it's like an extra job. I remember my husband being very concerned that we would be financially responsible in the end if we lost the case.' In the end, the European Court of Justice upheld her claim, and the legal system confirmed that speech and language therapists were paid less simply because they were mostly women. The ruling set a precedent, and led to the NHS implementing a programme called Agenda for Change, which is designed to ensure fair pay and rewards for all employees. It does this by evaluating jobs on the basis of attributes such as the skill and effort required and then sets the pay to reflect this (ensuring equal pay for work of equal value).

The low value attached to women's labour can stick to them as they move into male-dominated professions, with the pay and value accorded to that profession often dropping dramatically. For example, during the 1990s the post of human resources manager shifted from being male-dominated to female-dominated. Within this period, the average pay for HR managers dropped by almost 20 per cent.[35] It is an uncomfortable truth that the 'feminisation' of an occupation is linked with a decline in that occupation's pay (for both women and men). I asked Sarah Veale, Head of Equality and Employment Rights at the TUC, if she thinks the undervaluation of women's work is something that can be tackled across the workforce as a whole: 'I don't think the employers are just going to give in to it because it costs them money. They've liked having a source of cheap labour – it's been a huge advantage to them in terms of profit. Whether we can do it or not is up to us, I suspect.' As Sarah pointed out to me, some of the biggest changes to date have come after concerted efforts by women organised together in trade unions – and their role in tackling this issue is likely to remain key.

Motherhood – the factor that's usually blamed for the pay gap – does of course come into it. The time women take out of the labour market for caring is estimated to account for 14 per cent of the gender pay gap. This pattern is reflected in the fact that partnered women without dependent children earn 9 per cent less than men, whereas mothers working full-time with two dependent children earn 21.6 per cent less than men.[36] Furthermore, as mothers are also significantly more likely than fathers to take time out of the paid workforce to care for children, they can miss out on experience and skills development – thus reducing their future employment prospects. Obviously a more equal division of caring between women and men would mean mothers as a group would face a less unique penalty. But no one should pay such a high employment penalty for caring for children – women or men. Caring plays a vital role in our society and should be valued on a par with work in the paid economy. There needs to be a much greater focus by policy makers on how to reduce the impact of a parent's absence from employment while caring.

Why, then, has the Equal Pay Act of 1970 been unable to tackle all these issues effectively, despite being on the statute book for forty years? One reason is that the legislation has no teeth: employers are under no legal obligation to investigate whether their pay systems discriminate against women or to do anything about it if they do. Instead, the onus is entirely on individual women, like Pamela Enderby, to detect and challenge pay discrimination after it has taken place. Yet the secrecy surrounding pay rates and the complex nature of job evaluation schemes (required to ascertain whether work is of equal value) make it extremely difficult for women to uncover inequalities in the first place. Furthermore, pursuing an equal-pay claim often exacts a huge emotional and financial toll during the time it takes for the courts to reach a verdict (which can be as long as ten years). For that reason, the Fawcett Society is campaigning alongside the public service trade union UNISON for legislative reform that would prevent such discrimination by requiring employers to conduct pay audits and to take corrective action if necessary. Of course, this measure alone won't resolve the gender pay gap, but since discrimination is its single biggest cause, it is a crucial step.

The consequences of a workplace that financially penalises women are felt across society. It means that poverty has a female face: two-thirds of low-paid workers are women, and in London 282,000 women are low paid compared with 199,000 men.[37] The Greater London Authority report that people in part-time work (predominantly women) are four times more likely to be low paid than those in full-time work because this work is concentrated in low-paying sectors – occupations that offer few opportunities to advance. This also has another knock-on effect. Mothers' low income is the source of 70 per cent of child poverty in the UK.[38] The situation is particularly acute for children of single parents – nine out of ten of whom are women. A third of children of single parents who work part-time live in poverty, as do 16 per cent of the children of single parents who work full-time. This amounts to 393,000 children in the UK living below the poverty line. The implications of the pay gap are not just that women at the very top of their professions are failing to command commensurately huge salaries, but that many women are struggling to cover even the most basic daily expenditures.

Inappropriate behaviour

'Why is it that every time a man takes you out to lunch around here you're the dessert? . . . It's constant from every corner . . . Why can't they just leave it alone?'

These are the words of new employee Peggy Olson, exclaiming about sexual harassment at Sterling Cooper Ad Agency in the multi-award drama series *Mad Men*.

As I write, season three of *Mad Men* is about to hit TV screens in the US and has to date proved an international hit. The show is set during the 1960s in a New York advertising agency and one of the first things that becomes obvious while observing daily life there is the sexism. The 'girls' work in the typing pools while the men work in their own offices, and are uninhibited in their very public sexual harassment of the female staff. After all, this was a time when it was perfectly legal not to employ someone for a particular job because they were female, or to pay them less than male workers holding the same position. Jonathan Freedland, writing in the *Guardian*, suggests that this is actually one of the appeals of the show: 'There is both shock and comedy to be had in contemplating the world as it was before feminism . . . It's the casual, unthinking patting of female employees on the bottom, the instruction to wear their skirts shorter . . . Mad Men invites us to gaze upon the world as it was not that long ago.'[39] But is this sense of progress an illusion? We may have ditched the type-writers, but have we really left the sexual harassment behind?

While the UK Sex Discrimination Act defines sexual harassment as 'unwanted conduct on the grounds of some-one's sex; and unwanted physical, verbal or non-verbal con-duct of a sexual nature', a recurring theme in research on this issue is that some women are reluctant to label their own experiences as sexual harassment. No one knows just how prevalent sexual harassment is today, largely because few people have tried to measure it. Of those who have, estimates of its incidence vary depending on the definition of sexual harassment used. In 1999 the European Commission reported a high incidence of sexual harass-ment had been unearthed in studies in numerous European countries, including Austria, Norway, Germany, and the UK. They revealed exposure to harassment could be between 70 and 90 per cent.[40] Yet while the pernicious nature of sexual harassment means many (if not most) inci-dences go unreported, there are some things we do know about it. Sexual harassment occurs in all occupations and industries, although it is more prevalent in jobs where there is an unequal sex ratio and where there are large power differentials between women and men. Harassers have also been shown to target women who violate 'gender norms' – that is, women who display more traditionally masculine characteristics.[41] In some places sexual harassment is even officially endorsed. In 2008 a Russian woman took her male employer to court for sexually harassing her. But the judge threw out the case, stating, 'If we had no sexual harassment we would have no children,' and suggesting the man in question had behaved gallantly.[42]

One medium of 'delivering' sexual harassment at work that hasn't changed over the years is verbally; or what is often referred to as 'banter'. I received a message from Erin, who worked in the male-dominated industry of financial trading for seven years, during which time she racked up countless horror stories. 'I knew senior guys who had told HR they wanted a new junior team member and that she must be slim, blonde and pretty. One guy refused to work with me because he said my breasts were off-putting. Really! And management responded by asking me if I had done anything to provoke this, then moving the guy who complained to a separate desk.' Another message I received on the subject of office banter was from Yvonne: 'Male associates and trainees involved in recruitment events often adopt a sort of "nudge nudge, wink wink" attitude in which they focus heavily on the attractiveness of female students. This is presented as joking but strikes me as very inappropriate and certainly causes me and other female colleagues to feel excluded.' The apparently light-hearted way in which much of this is presented makes it harder for individuals to challenge it, lest they be accused of not having a sense of humour. Furthermore, women are often reluctant to acknowledge their experiences as being sexual harassment because they are uncertain whether it was 'serious' enough to qualify as such. But denying that incidences of sexual harassment have taken place has been found to be the least effective way of preventing it from occurring again.

Harassment can also be physical. One of Fawcett's partner organisations received a call from a woman called Caroline. In 2006 a senior manager from her firm had come over to the UK for a business trip. She told them, 'I was having drinks with a friend in the hotel bar in my personal time, but seeing us, the manager came over and joined us. At the end of the evening when we were in the lift going to our rooms he pressed me against the wall and whispered sexual comments in my ear. I raised a grievance with my employer – but they did not have training and policies on sexual harassment, and the issue wasn't taken any further.' Sexual harassment can have a severe impact on the victim's physical and mental health, and is linked with depression and even post-traumatic stress disorder. Not surprisingly, it can also have the effect of reducing job performance, and a study reported by the Equal Opportunities Commission found that the more incidences of sexual harassment there were within an organisation, the higher the organisation's turnover of female staff was.[43]

Over the last two decades advances in technology have been changing the face of sexual harassment in the workplace. While it is now rare to find an office that still has 'girly calendars' on the wall, a new, more advanced medium has emerged for delivering these images. I received an email from Anita that listed the litany of experiences she had while working in the City of London, including male members of her department viewing porn online. This was not a workplace diversity issue I had heard mentioned by HR professionals or policy makers before, so I gave Anita a call to find out more. She described how, having worked in the City for twenty years, she had noticed it becoming increasingly common for her younger male colleagues to huddle round each other's computers to view pornography. It had reached the point where they would be doing this daily in full view of everyone in the office. 'Some of it was explicit. It was hardcore. It wasn't pleasant by any stretch of the imagination.' On occasions the men 'would make little comments to girls walking past, like "I bet you want to be her" and "Are you jealous?"' Anita was left feeling decidedly uncomfortable by this. She describes it as 'bringing blatant sexism into the office . . . When I first started it was "Page 3". But things have escalated, especially in terms of what is available.' Internet technology research company TopTenREVIEWS reported in 2007 that 20 per cent of men admit accessing pornography at work. And the Society for Human Resource Management found that 20 per cent of employers had received complaints from employees about receiving improper or harassing emails. With the increased use of mobile devices such as laptops, video phones and Blackberries, viewing pornography at work is only getting easier.

As I'll examine further in 'The Booty Myth', increased access to pornography has gone hand in hand with increased access to other elements of the sex industry within a work context. Keen to tap the massive corporate entertainment market, many of the 300 lap-dancing clubs in the UK have developed specific marketing tailored to a corporate audience. Metropolis, a lap-dancing club in London, has a corporate page on its website which proclaims: 'Metropolis can now offer an exciting new venue for corporate entertaining, what better place to entertain your clients then the Hedonistic discrete [sic] atmosphere of the Penthouse . . . Be it an office party, a stag night or entertaining foreign clients you can guarantee an event to remember at Metropolis.'

Andrew is a lawyer in the City of London and attests to the growing normalisation amongst his colleagues of using the sex industry. 'A number of men on my street, particularly those working in the City, visit lap-dancing clubs. It is not only seen as normal, but part of client entertaining. One colleague describes how he would visit them in a limousine with two women having sex on the floor of the limousine.' But it is a culture that troubles him. 'A man in a suit paying a young woman to take her clothes off in front of him, and then placing the bill on a corporate account, is deeply shameful, in my view.' Another City employee, Sara, also relayed countless similar examples. 'Often client after-work meetings became visits to strip clubs,' she told me. 'At after-work drinks very senior managers asked around publicly if any of us knew any good brothels because they had Russian dignitaries visiting and they just wanted a couple of nice fit mature women to give them a blow job before going out to dinner. This kind of thing was just accepted.' With the continued global expansion of the sex industry, this is a workplace issue set to intensify.

Legislation can create the illusion that equality has been achieved. But just because it is officially illegal to pay women less than men for equal work, to sack them for being pregnant, or to sexually harass them, it doesn't mean these things don't go on. There is a huge gulf between policy and practice, and much current legislation – particularly around equal pay – lacks real bite. In a society where women still do the majority of unpaid caring, rigid workplace structures and the long-hours culture mean they pay a huge penalty for doing so. And on top of this a myriad of prejudicial attitudes and stereotypes still dog women's day-to-day working lives. Recent decades have witnessed crucial advances in women's status at work, but there remains a long path yet to be travelled.

18:27 | Tough Love

Coming Home to Violence

As she saves her dissertation draft and shuts down her computer, Amy's thoughts are immediately consumed by the prospect of going home. Her boyfriend, Andrew, will probably be back from work by now. He usually finishes at 5 p.m. on a Wednesday and his journey home only takes about twenty minutes. How can she possibly face Andrew after what he did last night?

'He strangled me for real, with both hands. I knew it was for real because the more I struggled the tighter he squeezed. And he used two hands. In his previous attempts, he favoured a single hand at my throat; no doubt he found it empowering and dominating in a sexual way. But this time after a few moments I just gave in and stopped struggling, letting him, which is when he stopped, I guess in surprise. I think I only struggled at first because I was horrified that I was going to die at the hands of such an ignominious asshole. Then I realised that was what I was going to do anyway, so I just gave in.'

But Amy will have to face him, there's nowhere else for her to go except home. She hasn't even been able to tell the people who are closest to her about what's been happening. 'I can't form the words. My housemate, my mom, both would erupt if I told them.'

As Amy walks home from university she gazes at groups of students as they pass her on the street. 'I see people being normal, living their lives, and I feel implacably other-worldly. They would not go home and contemplate the symbolism of their kitchen knives.' Amy isn't sure when the abuse first began. 'I can't say, because it happened slowly. Gradually. Inch by inch. We were friends first and then we got closer. He was funny, had a good sense of humour. I don't remember the first moment of physical pain, but I remember he said little things, gave out little criticisms, from the beginning. I'm an academic . . . but he used to sort of always be surprised that I knew things. He'd say things to the effect that I was blagging it all. I took it straight to heart.'

She and Andrew had met on the same course. He was popular within the department, and always the centre of attention within his group of friends. When his accommo-dation fell through he had asked if he could move into her flat for a while. Given that one of them was always sleep-ing at the other's place anyway, it seemed like a sensible idea to her. But their relationship soon soured. 'I started to feel quite owned by him, and while at first the attention was flattering it soon became consuming. One morning, because I had to go to work, he just held me down and wouldn't let me go, which meant I pretty much lost my job.' Andrew is now regularly physically abusive towards Amy. 'Sometimes he yells and yells right in my face, and backs me into a corner and just grabs my hands or my arms and squeezes and squeezes. He is a big fan of (unconsen-sual) sex, and anything that could pass for sexual, like stran-gling, so some nights he strangles me and then fucks me. I used to think, "Well, it could be worse," but I've got no idea how. Part of my head just lives in a different universe, so who knows?' Amy approaches the flat and looks up at the living-room window. The lights are on. As she fumbles around in her bag for the keys she feels like she's observing herself from a distance. She enters the flat and closes the door behind her.

Her boyfriend's violent behaviour has left Amy feeling utterly isolated. Yet, as a statistic, she is in tragically great company. One in four women living in the UK will, like Amy, experience violence at the hands of a current or former partner.[1] Amy had never told anyone about the abuse before she got in touch with me during my research for this chapter. 'I physically cannot vocalise it.' The abuse has consumed Amy's life. She has been eating very little, describing it as an attempt to 'move towards invisibility . . . at that point where I wouldn't cause offence in Andrew, because I would simply disappear'. She has also been drinking a lot. 'Alcohol is blissfully forward-looking; it's hard to remember things when one's drunk.' From an observer's perspective the emotional, physical, and sexual abuse Amy is experiencing is a classic and clear-cut case of domestic violence. It has formed a pattern of coercive and controlling behaviour. It is abuse Andrew could and should be criminally prosecuted for and for which Amy should receive extensive treatment and support. But from Amy's point of view it all seems much more confusing. She recently went on a research trip to Italy without Andrew. 'While I was struggling to maintain social norms part of my head contemplated suicide. All I could think about was maybe I'd be better off dead. All this, and I was a thousand miles away from him. Actually, that was part of the problem. I thought, "Why am I having these feelings when I'm so far away?" – which is part of the reason I sometimes think the problem is 100 per cent me.' Violence against women is a phenomenon that knows no boundaries: race, wealth, culture, nationality, economic and political systems – it cuts across them all. And it comes in many forms – domestic violence and rape being amongst the most prevalent. In total, one in three women throughout the world has been beaten, coerced into sex, or otherwise abused at some point in her life.[2]

So how is it possible that Amy can think 'it's me' when there is such a clear pattern? Because sexist violence is the Houdini of modern-day social crises – inexplicably escaping all attempts to pin it down, name it, and contain it. It is everywhere and nowhere, natural but unnatural, predictable yet without cause. Local newspapers frequently feature individual articles about women being murdered by their current or former partner – as might be expected, given that domestic violence causes more death and disability amongst women aged between sixteen and forty-four than cancer or traffic accidents.[3] Yet front-page headlines of an epidemic are nowhere to be seen. Girls and women are taught it is their daily responsibility to mitigate the threat of rape by being careful what they drink and not walking home alone at night – as if shielding their body from the natural elements. Yet when the threat materialises and the perpetrator comes into frame, he is portrayed as an unnatural being, a beast or a stranger; else the victim herself is implicated in the blame and the rape denied. And while the UK government is able to predict that 100,000 women will be raped each year in Britain – equivalent to 2,000 women a week[4] – only 6.5 per cent of those that are reported to the police end in the conviction of a perpetrator, and there is little public discussion about the aspects of our culture that encourage so many men to choose to rape women. Rape, as with most violence against women, is widely seen as a causeless problem. Our approach to violence against women is filled with contradictions, falsehoods, and illusions.

Incidents of violence against women do, of course, take place against a backdrop unique to the specific time, place, and context of personal histories and individual relationship dynamics. But the daily crimes committed against Amy and millions of women and girls like her are not random. Look beneath the surface and you find the roots of all these individual acts connected in a tangle of gender inequality that is planted firmly in the heart of normal, everyday society – in behaviours deemed 'manly', in cultures deemed 'traditional'. Rape, domestic violence, harassment, stalking: uncomfortable as it may be to acknowledge, while these are all deeply personal acts, they are also profoundly political acts drawing on a common ideology. They express and bolster the power assumed by one social group over another. The only way we will ever be able to uproot violence against women – what Amnesty International have declared as 'the greatest human rights scandal of our times' – is by changing the cultural landscape that nurtures it and dispelling the illusions which act as shelter.

In control

One of the most prevalent forms of violence against women is what Amy experiences – intimate partner violence (IPV), often referred to as 'domestic violence'. One in four women living in the UK will experience IPV at some point in her life, with two women murdered each week as a direct result.[5] In the case of IPV, the abuse is perpetrated by the victim's current or former partner. It is an overwhelmingly gendered phenomenon. Women constitute 85 per cent of the victims,[6] and women who become violent or kill their partner are significantly more likely to be responding to violence perpetrated against them, rather than instigating it.[7]

At its heart, IPV is an ongoing system of control: it has the highest rate of repeat victimisation of any crime,[8] and various different 'types' of violence are deployed in it, including physical, sexual, emotional, and financial. When abusive partners start sensing a lessening of their control, they often attempt to reaffirm their grip. Thirty per cent of domestic violence cases start when the woman becomes pregnant,[9] and correspondingly murder is the leading cause of death for pregnant women in the US. This is often attributed to the fact the partner feels threatened that he will have less of his partner's attention, that he may have less control over her. The role that control plays in IPV is also made clear by the fact that the most lethal time for a woman is at the point of separation or after she has left her violent partner.[10]

Elaine got in touch with me during my research to tell me about the abuse she experienced over a period of fourteen years at the hands of her husband, David. Her experiences exemplify the system of control integral to IPV and why it is so difficult to escape it. Elaine made repeated attempts to leave David during their relationship. 'I did separate from him but over a six-month period he ground me down emotionally using the children as a tool to gain his own way. I eventually caved in.' David instigated a pattern of sexual, physical, emotional and financial abuse that gradually eroded Elaine's sense of self. 'He used to say things like I was a sumo, fat, a witch and selfish, all things that really hurt my feelings, but to my family he was a lovely man.' He would also control which friends she could meet up with. 'He would sexually abuse me just before I went out to ensure no one else would want me and he would not let me clean myself. Once home he would sexually abuse me again. This continued for a couple of years.' Fourteen years after their relationship had begun, Elaine felt able to leave him for good.

'I decided enough was enough. My career was doing OK. I knew I could manage financially to support myself and my children. As I withdrew from [him] in the family home he became violent with me. I moved out of the marital bed into the girls' bedroom. The last week was the worst week ever. I was raped on the Monday night and my elder son came into my bedroom and witnessed this. Later that night he put nail varnish remover along the carpets and round the children's beds [so he could set the house on fire], threatening to kill us all if I did not agree to forget about tonight. On the Saturday of this week he raped me again. The next morning he got up and behaved like nothing had happened, bringing me a coffee and saying good morning and that he was going to take the kids to Scarborough.'

The following day Elaine left the house with her children to go to the sweet shop, and never went back. They moved into a refuge and she hasn't seen David since.

The two women who are murdered each week in the UK by their current or former partner represent only the tip of the iceberg of physical and mental injury caused by IPV. Approximately 40–50 per cent of women who visit a hospital emergency room in the US do so because of injuries their intimate partner inflicted on them. This amounts to over 200,000 visits every year.[11] The physical injuries women frequently endure in IPV include bruises, cuts, broken bones, lacerations, and internal injuries. The psychological consequences of being abused by a partner are also severe. Nearly half of all IPV victims suffer clinical depression,[12] and the average prevalence rate for post-traumatic stress disorder (PTSD) amongst women subjected to IPV is 64 per cent. Crucially, studies show it is the psychological abuse inflicted on a woman that is most likely to cause PTSD, rather than physical violence.

Eleanor contacted me about a three-year relationship she'd just escaped from. She had been living with her fiancé when he started to become increasingly controlling and violent. 'He'd convince me I wasn't worth anything, that I couldn't cope with the college I was at. I ended up leaving eight weeks before graduating because he'd convinced me I was worthless. I ended [up] in hospital twice from taking overdoses of paracetamol. I stopped socialising and my job suffered greatly.' Eleanor escaped from the relationship the morning after her fiancé locked her in their bedroom for five hours, during which time he beat and raped her. Since then she has been on strong antidepressants and sees a counsellor once a week. 'I have lost all trust in people around me. I have massive confidence issues and dwell on small things. However, I have now realised that nothing I did could ever make him do what he did. And I have slowly started to rebuild my life.'

It is not just individual women who bear the consequences of violence perpetrated against them. In 2003 the US Centers for Disease Control and Prevention estimated that IPV cost the country $5.8 billion per year and the UK government has estimated that the cost of domestic violence for the state, employers and victims together totals £23 billion a year.[13] IPV is a feature of everyday life for a disturbingly high proportion of women, and everyone pays a price for it.

*

In the US, one in three women will be sexually assaulted in her lifetime.[14] Up to 30 per cent of women (and up to 10 per cent of men) have been sexually abused in childhood and men make up approximately 95 per cent of the perpetrators of child sexual abuse.[15] Rape that takes place in a domestic setting is scarcely deemed newsworthy, and media coverage is consequently skewed towards those perpetrators who jump out from the bushes or follow women down secluded alleyways. Like looking both ways before crossing the road, rape has become perceived as just one of the potential 'hazards' women must be alert to, for example when coming home after a night out clubbing. The government-funded personal-safety charity the Suzy Lamplugh Trust warns women visiting its website that by going out for a drink they are putting themselves at increased risk of rape and should take common sense steps to alleviate it. In an analysis of 136 British newspaper reports about rape, British-based women's organisation Eaves found that 54.4 per cent of assaults reported in the press were carried out by strangers, almost always in a public space.[16] Thus society teaches women and girls that being vigilant and sensible will protect their bodies against the deviant stranger. In the real world, however, a woman is far more likely to be raped within the 'safety' of her own home by someone she knows. Eaves report that fewer than 17 per cent of rapes are perpetrated by strangers and only 13 per cent take place in a public space. Half of all female murder victims worldwide are killed by a current or former partner,[17] and most rape victims know their attacker.[18] Media reporting of rape is back to front.

Studies have shown that approximately 60 per cent of women who have had an experience that meets the legal definition of rape don't acknowledge their experience as such – often because it doesn't tally with the 'stranger in the alleyway' scenario.[19] Women who are unacknowledged rape victims are more likely to have been romantically involved with the rapist and to have had consensual intimate relations with him before he raped her. I recently met a woman called Selena, who was a PhD student studying in Brighton. Some months back she had gone along to her friend John's party to celebrate him passing his PhD viva voce. Selena rarely drank, so the alcohol she had that night quickly went to her head. Towards the end of the evening she passed out from it. Her friends didn't think it would be safe to take her back to her house because she would be alone there, so they helped Selena up the stairs and put her in John's bed. John told them he would sleep downstairs on the couch. The next morning Selena woke up to find herself naked in bed with John lying next to her. She immediately felt confused and panicked. 'I went to the toilet to find myself bleeding. I had never been sexually active before so I knew there was something wrong.' Medical examinations later revealed bruises and tearing and showed that intercourse had taken place. Selena had been raped not by a deviant stranger – but by a friend who was supposed to be looking after her.

It also took a long time for Louise, another ex-student,

to come to terms with the notion that she had been raped because it just didn't seem to tally with what she thought rape was supposed to be like. When Louise was nineteen she went to a nightclub with a friend and got chatting with a man she had met in the queue. He told Louise his name was Anthony and talked a bit about his job and family life and by all accounts seemed like a pretty average guy. So when he asked if he could buy Louise a drink, 'I said yes, and drank it. The next thing I remember I woke up at 6 a.m. in his house.' Louise remembers feeling extremely confused during those first few moments, seeing the man asleep next to her. 'I thought, "Who the fuck is that? Where am I? How am I going to get home?" It was a weird experience – it was if I had been teleported there.'

At the time, Louise had never heard of drug-facilitated sexual assault (otherwise known as 'drink spiking' and 'drug rape'). But the UK Government Advisory Council on the Misuse of Drugs report that it is 'a significant problem in Britain'.[20] It involves perpetrators actively drugging their victim or assaulting a woman who is profoundly intoxicated by self-administered drugs. The most frequently associated drugs are alcohol, benzodiazepines (of which Rohypnol is one) gamma-hydroxy butyrate (GHB) and ketamine. The drugs alter victims' behaviour and cause amnesia. Partly as a result of this, nobody knows just how prevalent it is. The reporting rate by victims is thought to be even lower than non-drug-assisted rape precisely because victims are often confused and uncertain about what has taken place.

While Louise didn't know what had happened to her, she did feel an overwhelming urge to leave. She had to wake the man up to unlock the front door and, still unsure about what had occurred, accepted his offer of a lift back to her parents' house. During the drive the man asked Louise if she was on the pill. 'At that moment I thought, "Oh, we must have had sex, then."' When Louise told him she wasn't on the pill, he replied: 'Why didn't you tell me that last night you stupid cow?' Louise wondered how she could have, but didn't say anything. It was only when she arrived home and went to the toilet that she knew for sure intercourse had taken place. 'In my mind I wasn't conscious. I knew something bad had happened. I wanted to tell the police. But I thought unless you've been physically damaged, nothing has happened to you. I anticipated harsh judgement from them.' It was two years before Louise told anyone what had happened, but the impact of the rape was profound. 'I had a total breakdown. I was obsessed with how this had happened. I started to cut myself. I stopped functioning, I couldn't eat, I was sick loads. I would never know what really happened – that was all I thought about. I had a morbid conviction that I was going to die all the time. It just makes you really angry, but for some reason it turns against yourself.' Since the assault Louise has received extensive counselling, but twelve years later, she is still having a recurring nightmare. 'I can't move, can't scream – a paralysis thing. I'm trying to call the police and I can't get through.'

Up to two-thirds of rape victims develop PTSD.[21] Researchers in the US found that a sexual assault usually had a more severe effect on a woman's mental health if it was committed by her partner, rather than by a non-partner.[22] When a woman is assaulted by her partner, not only does she have to cope with the sexual assault, she also has to cope with living with the abuser or seeing him regularly.

And, unsurprisingly, while stranger rape is usually a one-off incident, women raped in marriage are ten times more likely to be subjected to multiple sexual assaults. Rape is a human rights violation and has been defined as a form of torture by international criminal courts. Even amongst women whose experiences of assault amount to the legal definition of rape – but who don't themselves recognise the assault as rape – the prevalence rate of PTSD is 30 per cent.[23] The impact of sexual abuse can reverberate throughout a woman's lifetime.

*

The UN recognises some forms of violence against women as harmful cultural practices. These practices stem from the inequalities between women and men, are harmful to women's and girls' health and status, and are frequently justified according to tradition, custom or religion. Arati Rao, a feminist human rights theorist, states that 'no social group has suffered greater violation of its human rights in the name of culture than women'.[24] Cultural practices recognised as harmful to women include early marriage, dowry price, and early pregnancy. Another is female genital mutilation (FGM), which occurs predominantly in Africa and some Middle Eastern countries, but is reported to take place in all parts of the world and amongst a range of religions. It involves the removal of part or all of the female genitalia, usually when girls are between newborn and fifteen years old. It is estimated that between 100 and 140 million of the world's female population have undergone FGM, including 66,000 women and girls living in the UK.[25] The procedure inflicts severe pain, and carries with it the risk of haemorrhage and shock. Girls and women who have undergone FGM can later experience infection, pain during sexual intercourse, bladder problems, difficulties in childbirth, and other severe psychological consequences. A study of 30,000 African women by the World Health Organisation found that excised women were 31 per cent more likely to have a Caesarean birth and 55 per cent more likely to have a child who died before or very shortly after birth.[26]

Many forms of violence against women, like FGM, have a common driver: the desire to control women's sexuality. And they are frequently defended as important to ethnic or national identity. I spoke to Dr Faith Mwangi-Powell, previously director of the British charity Forward which campaigns against FGM and currently director of the African Palliative Care Association in Uganda, about how the practice has become embedded in some communities. She said, 'It's been going on for such a long time that even when you ask the people who are practising it they won't tell you the reason we do it is because of a-b-c. They will say things like "My mother did it and my sister and my grandmother did it." It's seen as an initiation right – where girls become women. They are prepared for marriage. That's why it is so difficult to deal with because people feel like you are taking away a very important piece of their culture.'

In March 2009 I attended a public meeting organised by the Iranian and Kurdish Women's Rights Organisation (IKWRO) in London to discuss the failures by police to protect twenty-year-old Banaz Mahmod. Banaz was tortured and murdered on 24 January 2006 by men hired by her family after she had fallen in love with someone they disapproved of. She was amongst the estimated 5,000 women worldwide who are murdered each year in what are referred to as 'honour killings'[27] – another harmful cultural practice recognised by the UN. I asked IKWRO founder and director Diana Nammi what motivates these killings: 'Honour killing take place when a woman is killed for bringing shame on the family by having a kind of attitude or something not acceptable to the family, wearing make-up, having a boyfriend, having a sexual relationship out of marriage, losing virginity or become pregnant outside of marriage, being a victim of rape. Honour killing is happening in more than fifty-four countries . . . Honour killing is organised crime. If a culture is criminal, it must be changed.' Indeed, culture is not a static, ahistorical, inflexible entity. Quite the contrary. It is a series of social practices that not everyone has an equal hand in forming, which can privilege certain groups, and which are constantly being contested.

However, there is a problem in recognising these forms of violence against women as uniquely cultural. As I'll argue later in this chapter, culture plays a crucial role in *all* forms of violence against women – including Western mainstream culture. Feminist author and activist Rahila Gupta suggests that 'culture is the prism through which we view only the actions of minorities. In 1994, Roy Greech, a white man, stabbed his wife twenty-three times and left the knife in her throat because she was having an affair. Crime of passion? Jealousy? Honour? Different labels, but they are all about the control of a woman's body and mind.'[28] Yet there is often a tendency to notice the role of culture only if it is outside the mainstream/ majority or if it is occurring abroad.

Something else that becomes apparent when browsing

typical lists of harmful cultural practices is the absence of any that are customary in Western culture. As I explored in 'Mirror, Mirror on the Wall', millions of women in Western societies undergo practices that are harmful to their health and status as equal citizens – but which are widely endorsed by society and rarely questioned. Millions have their flesh sucked, foreign bodies inserted under their skin and, increasingly, parts of their labia minora cut off for non-medical purposes. We don't name this as a harmful cultural practice stemming from gender inequality; we call it plastic surgery. As feminist author Sheila Jeffreys points out, 'Harmful practices in the west will most usually be justified as emanating from consumer "choice", from "science" and "medicine" or "fashion"; that is, the law of the market.'[29] Western practices are veiled by the language of choice, but it is crucial to understand the coercive pressure that culture can exert – both in the UK and worldwide. Sometimes when discrimination is etched out on women's bodies they don't need to be physically held down because, intangible as it is, culture can do the job just as effectively. Dr Mwangi-Powell points out that in the case of FGM it is practised 'by women on women, so it's seen as a way of empowering women'. And the World Health Organisation report that some girls may actively desire it due to social pressure and fear of rejection by others if they don't have it done.[30] Violence against women takes place throughout the world – sometimes justified according to culture, often compounded by other forms of discrimination, but always stemming principally from the enduring inequalities between women and men.

Fight like a man

If at first you don't succeed, buy her another beer

This slogan appeared on a T-shirt sold in the UK by Asda. The supermarket withdrew the garment from their 'comedy range' in 2007 after complaints were received, but maintained they were 'just a bit of fun'.[31]

A terrifying proportion of men and boys decide to inflict violence against women. Why? Who are these men? What is it driving their decisions? Attempts to uncover answers to these questions are hampered by the fact that two common portrayals of the phenomenon are contradictory, or 'double-faced'. On one side, when talking about victims, its features appear 'natural'. Rape, for example, is presented as just one of those things that 'happens' to women and so it is crucial they remain vigilant; much like not standing in a field during a storm lest you attract lightning. Yet the other face of violence against women, the perpetrator, is unnatural, otherworldly, or monstrous. When the serial rapist John Worboys was convicted in 2009 of assaulting female passengers in the back of his taxi, he was typically described in the media as 'evil' and a 'demon'. The truth is that both faces – natural and unnatural – are masks, part of the equality illusion.

In discussing convicted sex offender Francisco Montes, who sexually assaulted and murdered thirteen-year-old British schoolgirl Caroline Dickinson in 1996, Fiona Phillips wrote in her *Daily Mirror* column that he was 'driven by an uncontrollable sexual urge', adding, 'there's no doubt the man is sick'.[32] However, most violence against women is perpetrated by 'normal', average men and boys, and represents an attempt to assert and gain control, not a loss of it. Despite much early psychoanalytic literature postulating that rape was, as Phillips suggests, an uncontrollable sexual urge, a classic series of interviews with over 500 men convicted of rape conducted by A. Nicholas Groth in 1979 showed that the men tended not to be sexually aroused either before or during the rape. They frequently had to obtain erections by masturbating or forcing their victims to sexually stimulate them.[33] He classified 55 per cent of the men as 'power rapists', meaning, for them, rape was a conquest – a demonstration of their masculinity. A second category that emerged was 'anger rapists', and 40 per cent of the men fell into this. The aim of their rapes was to humiliate and hurt the victim as revenge because they perceived they had been harmed by women. The remaining 5 per cent of men Groth interviewed were classified as 'sadistic rapists'. These men were sexually aroused by domination and violence, and they took narcissistic pleasure in their victims' pain. In committing rape, the men were gaining control, not losing it.

The true face of violence against women is gender inequality – embedded firmly in mainstream culture. Sociologist Jamie Mullaney asked convicted perpetrators of IPV to explain their behaviour to researchers and to their partner separately. When talking to researchers the men overwhelmingly justified their behaviour by claiming that they had entitlements by virtue of being the head of the household, financial provider, or 'protector' of their partner. They claimed they had rights as men to control their partner. When it came to providing an account to their partner, however, they overwhelmingly blamed it on her behaviour or refused even to bother offering her an account at all.[34] The justifications offered were – researchers believed

– an attempt by the perpetrators to save face 'as men', having had their so-called entitlements challenged by the criminal justice system and other agencies. And researcher Dalit Yassour Borochowitz found perpetrators' accounts of their violence revealed they had disciplined their partners when they felt they had lost control over their partners' behaviour. The violence represented attempts to 'tame the shrew'.[35] Violence against women was a way for these men to express and uphold their masculinity – their power over femininity.

In today's culture, being a 'real man' (often referred to by academics as 'hypermasculinity') involves being violent and embracing the notion that men are naturally dominant over women and that male/female relationships are naturally antagonistic. Masculinity has to be proved, and one way of doing this is through the 'sexual conquest' of a woman or girl. This is an adversarial venture that he can either win or lose. And of course, as the Asda T-shirt illustrates, advertisers have been quick to capitalise on it. Unilever have managed to make Lynx deodorant (or Axe as it is known in most of the sixty-plus countries where it is marketed) the bestselling 'male grooming product' in the world. They have achieved this largely on the back of advertising campaigns that portray the deodorant as having a drug-like effect on (thin, white, large-chested, conventionally beautiful) women and making it easier for 'ordinary' men to have sex with them. Lynx's 2009 offering, New Lynx Bullet, is a case in point. It is described to consumers as 'Pocket Pulling Power', with billboards loudly calling on men to 'NEVER MISS AN OPPORTUNITY'. In the Lynx Bullet, Unilever are offering men ammunition in their hunt for a sexual conquest. It is sexually callous, and it will undoubtedly sell by the bucket-load. It really doesn't require a great stretch of the imagination to see how a culture of hypermasculinity lays fertile ground for violence against women. Indeed, studies of sexually aggressive men and per-petrators of IPV show heightened adherence to hypermas-culine ideologies,[36] and incidences of sexual assault are higher in cultures where women are treated as sex objects and where aggression and violence are glorified as male traits.[37]

Dr Michael Flood, a Research Fellow at La Trobe University in Australia, suggests that rape can be a way for men to bond and prove their masculinity to each other. He points out that, to a large extent, men's lives are organised by relationships between men, and individual men's rela-tionships with other men are often prioritised over those with women (else they risk being branded 'pussy-whipped'). I asked Flood how this could translate into violence against women: 'Boys and men often try to "prove themselves" as men in front of other men, through displays of power, dom-inance, or physical or sexual prowess. Male peer groups often police and reward or punish males' performances of gender, giving status to males who prove their manhood and attacking others as "fags", "girls", and "sissies". Sex with women – with lots of women, or particularly attrac-tive women . . . is a key path to status amongst male peers.' An identity based on both rejecting femininity and achiev-ing sexual conquests is a toxic mix. 'Rape may be both a means to and an expression of male bonding, especially when it's perpetrated by groups of males. More generally, men who have male peers who tolerate or condone vio-lence against women are more likely to use it themselves.' With alarming regularity there are reports in the media of women being raped by groups of male sports stars. In 2008 two England rugby players were alleged to have raped an eighteen-year-old woman while two other players watched. The players denied the allegation, insisting it was consensual 'three-in-a-bed' sex. However, Flood highlights disturbing research evidence that shows cultures of male bonding amongst male athletes, fraternities, and friendship circles foster sexual assault of women.

The collective rape of women is also a literal game for some. In 2009 Amazon.com was forced to remove a computer game which was being sold on its website called Rapelay – a Japanese 'rape simulation' game which allows players to rape any female character in the game and get other male characters to join the attack. And while rape represents the most serious manifestation of male bonding through coercive sexual practices, it is on a spectrum with something everyone will be familiar with – the sexual harassment of women in public by groups of men. A man who decides to wolf-whistle, holler or beep his car horn at a woman walking past is not realistically going to get a date with her – and he knows that. She is likely to feel intimidated from the very public proclamation that she is a sex object, and he will have proved his masculinity to his friends or co-workers looking on. Within a society of unequal gender relations and cultures of hypermasculinity, violence against women makes a disturbing amount of sense.

Asking for it

Another reason sexist violence manages to evade scrutiny is society's tendency to blame the victims. Women are frequently held to be responsible for acts of violence committed

against them by men, so the perpetrator and the wider cultural context remain hidden from view. A 2009 government survey of people living in England and Wales found
that 20 per cent thought it was acceptable, or at least acceptable in some circumstances, for a man to hit or slap his
wife or girlfriend for dressing in sexy or revealing clothing
in public.[38] Sixteen per cent considered nagging or constant
moaning justified similar retribution and 13 per cent
thought that flirting with other men was deserving of such
punishment. And women who don't remain passive but
defend themselves or fight back are seen as less warm, and
so more blameworthy.[39] After US pop singer Rihanna was
violently attacked in 2009 by her then partner, fellow pop
singer Chris Brown, a survey by the Boston Public Health
Commission in the US found that 46 per cent of teenagers
thought Rihanna was responsible for the violence.[40]

Women are also blamed for staying in violent relationships. When in August 2008 Sheryl Gascoigne reportedly got
back together with her ex-husband – footballer Paul Gascoigne
– Daily Mail columnist Carol Sarler wrote an article titled
'I'd like to slap Sheryl Gascoigne . . . at least it would save
Paul the bother'. Paul Gascoigne is reported to have been
violent towards his wife during their marriage. However,
Sarler's central argument was that, because Paul was evidently a 'recidivist thug' and 'palpably disturbed', it was
entirely Sheryl's responsibility if she was subject to any violence from him in the future: 'It would be an understatement
to say that she seems to be a sucker for punishment.' Sheryl
is described in the article as a 'self-selected victim' who has
'some insatiable mania for sadomasochism'. Yet there are
countless reasons women return to or don't leave violent
relationships. She may still care for her partner and hope he

has changed. Elaine, whose story appears earlier in this chapter, attempted to leave her husband on several occasions prior to her final departure following fourteen years of abuse. But each time he bullied her into staying and convinced her that it would be better for the children if she did so. Caroline, another woman previously subject to abuse who contacted me, found it difficult to leave because her partner made her believe the abuse was all her fault. 'He put all of his behaviour on to me because he said I had mental health problems and needed help with my violent personality. I know now that this was just his way of projecting his own violence on me.'

Even when a woman does manage to escape from a relationship, the intimidation can continue. Sarah endured both sexual and physical assault by her boyfriend before eventually leaving him. 'I told him I was never going to change my mind. It was over.' But it wasn't as far as he was concerned. 'It started with notes appearing around the place. He would leave all sorts of notes. Suicide threats. Love notes. He wrote me one letter in blood. His car would be places he knew I would be but I would never see him.'

We see a similar pattern of blame when it comes to rape. The 2009 British government survey mentioned above found that 43 per cent of people think a woman should be held responsible or partly responsible for being sexually assaulted or raped if she was flirting heavily with the man beforehand; 42 per cent think the same applies if she was using drugs at the time, 36 per cent if she was drunk, and 26 per cent if she was wearing sexy or revealing clothes. Actress Dame Helen Mirren gave voice to these attitudes when she was interviewed for men's magazine *GQ*. Mirren said that if a woman is naked in bed with a man, engages in sexual activity with him, and then says 'no' to sexual intercourse at the last second, she doesn't think the woman 'could have that man in court . . . I guess it is one of the many subtle parts of the men/women relationship that has to be negotiated and worked out between them'.[41]

These attitudes also influence the treatment of rape victims. In 2008 it emerged that the Criminal Injuries Compensation Authority (CICA) had, over the previous year, reduced the compensation offered to fourteen victims of rape on the basis that they had been drinking before the attack. Journalist Michael White defended the policy in the *Guardian*: 'But surely compensation is not about blame, that's a matter for the criminal law. It's about weighing up the injury, what long-term distress, financial outlay or even unemployment, it may cause, and – one factor amongst several – whether the actions of the claimant may have contributed to his/her misfortune. In sum, it's about personal responsibility.'[42] He then goes on to use this comparison. 'You put yourself at risk, just as you do by speeding when the idiot coming the other way loses control of the car: his fault, but you were going too fast or (another common one) tail-gating.'

I would like to offer a slightly more apposite comparison for this situation. A woman decides to go for a drive. She doesn't speed during her journey and her car is fully insured. Part-way through her journey the driver of a car slowly approaching on the other side of the road from the opposite direction notices her. At this point, he abruptly swerves his car onto the woman's side of the road, puts his foot down on the accelerator and intentionally collides with her car head-on. The woman survives the crash and later goes on to make a compensation claim for the injuries he inflicted on her. The CICA respond and say they will give her some money as compensation for the attempted murder, but not the full amount because she was driving a car when the man tried to kill her and by getting into a car she knew she was taking on a statistical risk of injury. In fact, even that's not a fully accurate comparison, because the driver would have to have been in an armoured tank and come away from the crash injury-free for it to be an accurate comparison with a man who chooses to rape a woman who has consumed some alcohol. Our daily lives are filled with mundane activities that expose us to some form of risk – getting into a car, riding a bike, or crossing the road. But we would never suggest that an individual deliberately harmed by another person while doing any of these activities would be partially responsible. So why do we contend that women should be blamed for being raped because they've had a drink?

Rape isn't a 'natural hazard' like a cliff edge that women must be careful to avoid when drunk – it is a wilful act of violence perpetrated by another human being and the responsibility lies with the perpetrator, not the victim. Drinking alcohol is not illegal or wrong. Perpetrators are in control of their actions. A woman is never responsible for a man raping her. But society's morals and logic currently display a yogic ability to bend over backwards to accommodate, accept and normalise the reality of violence against women. Studies show that people who display high levels of sexism are more likely to accept the idea that women can be to blame when a man rapes them.[43] This propensity to blame victims and often to absolve the perpetrators allows the cultures that breed sexist violence to go unchallenged. Victim-blaming must also end for the real cause of sexist violence – gender inequality – to come into full view.

Awaiting justice

'That means no one believes me.'

Those were Tanya's words on hearing that, after half an hour's deliberation, a jury had found the man who had raped her 'not guilty'.

State institutions are also implicated in society's denial of the reality of violence against women. Nowhere is this better illustrated than in cases of rape: in the UK, only 6.5 per cent of cases reported to the police end in a conviction. In 2008 this equated to just 2,021 convictions for rape.[44] Or, put another way, rape – on the whole – is easy to get away with. This appallingly low conviction rate has attracted significant debate amongst policy makers and the public at large, but its stubborn endurance means it continues to demand discussion. As the Fawcett Commission on Women and the Criminal Justice System reported in 2009, violence against women fails to be treated with the same 'professionalism and vigour devoted to other crimes'.[45] The failure by states to prosecute the vast majority of perpetrators means individual women are denied justice and all women remain at risk of sexist violence. Most women choose not to report their experiences of rape to the police. It is estimated that between 75 and 95 per cent of rapes are never reported to the police, and the British Crime Census in 2001 revealed that 40 per cent of rape victims had told no one at all about their experience.[46] Sharon Smee, Fawcett's policy officer for violence against women, believes this is in no small part due to the myths and stereotypes surrounding rape: 'Survivors of rape may fear that they will be blamed for the attack or disbelieved, particularly if alcohol was involved or if the rape was committed by someone known to the victim. The low conviction rate for rape, the media representations of how a "proper victim" should behave and the lack of priority which has been given to the investigation of rape cases will also affect a woman's confidence in reporting rape.'

Selena, who earlier spoke about being raped by a friend, did report her rape to the police, but almost wishes she hadn't. 'I wouldn't advise anyone to go through this again. I would advise them to invest in a good counsellor and get on with their life because I wasted six months of mine. I do think that the whole system really needs to be revised in all sorts of ways.' Her experience of the criminal justice system was negative from the start, including the crucial bodily forensic examination. 'My examination was a bit brutal. It wasn't even a proper examination room, which is why it was terrible. The bed was horrible. It wasn't meant for sexual assault work, it didn't have stirrups or anything.' Similarly she felt the subsequent police investigation was inadequate. 'The police weren't supportive. It is quite difficult when you are a victim and [the police] don't call you back and you are just waiting and waiting and waiting.' The Crown Prosecution Service (CPS) is the public body responsible for deciding whether or not a case proceeds to court, based on whether they think there is enough evidence – as gathered by the police – for a realistic prospect of convicting the defendant. In Selena's case the CPS decided there wasn't. But she is adamant the CPS were 'proactively sceptical' about her case. 'I think the way my case has been handled, anyone can get away with it.'

Indeed, failures by police to take allegations of rape seriously, and thus build the necessary body of evidence, have been repeatedly exposed. In 2009 the Independent Police Complaints Commission found that a Metropolitan Police Service 'Sapphire team' (an elite unit set up to spearhead best practice in rape investigation) had consistently mishandled rape cases and failed to search for evidence. A PC working within the unit condemned management failures to allocate the team necessary resources: 'The picture painted was that greater importance was given to motor vehicle crime than victims of serious sexual assault.'[47] And it's not just a failure to investigate rape properly that police have been found guilty of. In many cases they don't even record that a rape case has been reported. Nearly 25 per cent of rapes reported to the police are 'no crimed'. This means that the police decide no crime has taken place, so they don't investigate it or include it in official crime figures. Yet government research has found that over 30 per cent of reported rapes ignored by police should have been investigated according to the police's own rules.[48] The police have also been found to overestimate the scale of false accusations of rape, yet in reality only 3 per cent of reported rapes are found to be 'probably or possibly false' – no more than any other crime.[49] The net result of all this is that between half and two-thirds of rape cases reported to the police don't advance beyond the investigation stage, and most victims never even get close to justice.

Those women whose cases do proceed to court find the odds similarly stacked against them there. Tanya, whose rapist was found not guilty, was twenty years old when she was assaulted. Tanya has physical and learning disabilities and is cared for by her parents. I spoke to Tanya's mother, who described the traumatising effect the court case had on her. In court the defence barrister challenged Tanya's disabled status, and derogatory remarks were made about her disabilities by both the judge and the prosecuting barrister, who remarked to the jury that 'she isn't the sharpest knife in the drawer'. The defence also used a previous incident of sexual assault upon her (which had resulted in a conviction) to imply that Tanya had either encouraged or fabricated the assault currently in question – the implication being that rape was very unlikely to have happened to the same person twice. Tanya told her mother, 'It made me feel so angry. I wished I hadn't told anybody [about it].' A diversity or vulnerability issue is identified in over 40 per cent of reported rape cases, mental health or learning disabilities being the most frequent. Yet the conviction rates for these cases are even lower than the overall rape conviction rate. Since the court case Tanya has attempted suicide, and is still self-harming and experiencing flashbacks to the assault. The impact of failing to see justice done has been profound for her. As her mother explains, 'She thinks if he does it again, it'll be her fault. We try and tell her if he does it again, it'll be the court's fault.'

A common myth is that rape convictions are so low partly because the evidence usually comes down to 'her word against his'. This is rarely the case. In nearly 90 per cent of prosecuted rape cases there is supporting evidence such as forensics, previous convictions or witnesses. So how is it that so few perpetrators are found guilty? It is in large part because rape myths count in the courtroom. Rape myths are false beliefs about rape that have the effect of denying or minimising the crime ('Lots of women make up rape accusations when they later come to regret sex that had been consensual'), or shifting responsibility for it from the perpetrator to the victim ('It was her own fault for being drunk'). The notion that women are responsible if they are raped is just one of many 'rape myths' which are prevalent throughout society and influence jury members' perceptions, making them less likely to find a perpetrator guilty. Studies of jurors' perceptions reveal that they often believe it is 'reasonable' for a man to assume silence equals consent, even if this was due to the fact that the woman was completely intoxicated at the time.

How is it that rape myths could become so widespread that they sway verdicts in court cases? Because they are broadcast to literally millions through newspapers, TV and the internet. When researchers in the US looked at how the media reported an allegation of rape against Kobe Bryant, an NBA basketball player, they found over 65 per cent of news articles about the case contained at least one popular rape myth. The most frequent were 'she's lying' and 'she wanted it'.[50] Similarly, 10 per cent of media headlines about it were found to contain rape myths.[51] While most pre-trial publicity is typically found to bias jurors against defendants, the opposite happens in rape cases. Popular stereotypes and myths are sometimes seized upon by the defence. One woman who contacted the Fawcett Society to share her experience in the courtroom said, 'The defence barrister was a female QC paid for by the rapist's wealthy parents. She raised her voice to me and used vulgar expressions to describe a fictional sex scene. She laughed at my responses. She made inferences about my decision to get drunk and socialise without my boyfriend's supervision. She told the jury I was crying because my boyfriend was in the public gallery and hearing the "truth" from her about what happened. She was very aggressive and the prosecution never objected, but the judge did.'

It isn't only justice that states fail to provide to victims of sexist violence. Even the most basic of support services are scant on the ground. In 2009 the Equality and Human Rights Commission threatened over 100 councils with legal action because they were failing to provide domestic violence support services or rape crisis centres.[52] Despite government estimates of 100,000 women being raped each year, there are just thirty-eight rape crisis centres in England and Wales, something I explore further in 'A New Day', below. Some women also face additional barriers to accessing what scant support services do exist. A couple of years ago I worked at the Northern Refugee Centre in Sheffield developing a number of 'Women's Conversation Clubs' at which women refugees and asylum seekers could practise their English and meet other people. One morning I received a call at the office from Saran, who had been in the UK for just three months since coming from Côte d'Ivoire with her two young children to join her husband who had sought asylum here. In very broken English she managed to communicate that her husband had hurt her since she had arrived, and that she wanted to leave now while he was at work. A colleague and I immediately drove to her house to collect her and her children, and I contacted a local domestic violence refuge to see if she could stay there. The first question they asked me was what Saran's immigration status was. They explained that if she didn't have a particular status then they could not afford to accept her. Anyone living in the UK on temporary admission does not have recourse to public funds – meaning they cannot claim any benefits, including benefits that would fund a place in a domestic violence refuge.[53] Saran did not have any options. She didn't have any family or other friends living in the UK, she didn't have any money, and she couldn't speak English. After hours of phone conversations we were able to establish that her husband's immigration status meant she was in fact entitled to benefits so she was able to move into the refuge. However, it is estimated that up to 1,000 women fleeing gender-based violence are subject to the 'no recourse' rule each year in the UK.[54] And this means that some of the most vulnerable women in society are being trapped in abusive relationships.

Violence against women embodies many of feminism's central concerns, demonstrating the continuity between the private and the public, the personal and the political, and between abstract beliefs and actual physical harm. While every single act of violence against women is a unique and very personal tragedy, together they form a pattern. For too many men in society today, perpetrating violence against a woman is a logical way to affirm their masculine identity. And for too many women, the threat of sexist violence looms large in their daily lives. Acts of violence are gender inequality in chilling action. No amount of rape alarms and self-defence classes are going to protect women from sexist violence as they go about their day-to-day lives, not least because that violence is likely to come from someone they know, trust, or even love. We need to put an end to the illusions that surround violence against women and recognise it for what it is: the inevitable consequence of a society riddled with sexism. Only then will we be able to start putting an end to one of the greatest human-rights scandals of our time.

20:30 | The Booty Myth

A Night Out in the Sex Industry

Lucy glances up at the clock as she takes another sip of wine. She's fine for time, and will easily be able to get her make-up done before leaving the flat. It's a daily routine she has perfected but increasingly loathes: shave legs, armpits and pubic hair. Then apply fake tan, fake nails, straighten hair, put make-up on, and pack shoes and outfits in a bag. It's all a far cry from the glamorous job Lucy thought she was getting when she auditioned to work at a lap-dancing club five months earlier. 'I was fired from my office job and needed money fast because I had just moved into a new flat. I felt worthless and as if I couldn't do anything, wasn't qualified for anything. I was also bored of working nine to five and thought it would be an easy, exciting way of making good money. I had a friend who'd done the job before and I realised you didn't have to look like Jordan.' But working in a lap-dancing club hasn't turned out the way Lucy imagined it would.

As she waits for the hair straighteners to heat up, Lucy rummages through her bag for her purse to make sure she's got enough money to get a taxi home at the end of the night. A few weeks ago she hadn't made enough at the club to pay her cab fare back and had to walk home in the early hours of the morning. 'Some nights it is possible to actually lose money. You pay to go to work, a flat fee of a minimum of twenty pounds, usually more. From the first night, I was in debt to the club. You have to buy your outfits from the club. You pay for any drinks you have when you're there, and believe me, you feel like you need to drink. The only money you earn is from customers who come in and want you to dance. If you start work at half past eight, it can be eleven o'clock or midnight before you get a dance. Sometimes later. Sometimes never.' Then there are the club's fines. 'Usually twenty quid. And it seems like you can get fined for anything: being late, having the wrong shoes or a dress the manager doesn't like. The one they're really strict about is the pole – you have to do your pole dance when your name is called or that's a twenty-quid fine straight away.' The management also fills the club with dancers so there's always heavy competition for custom.

Once she's ready, Lucy pours herself one last glass of wine and quickly downs it. She tries not to go to work sober. She then takes a small folded paper envelope out of her bag and chops up a quick line of coke. It's too expensive to use much before work starts, but she needs a little something to wake her up.

'Lap dancing is one of the hardest things I've ever done. I've found it tough, soul-destroying. You are constantly lying about who you are, because you don't want to tell these men about your real self. You don't know them, and yet you are exposing yourself sexually and physically. Worst of all, for me, you are forced to behave in a way which is consistently demeaning and submissive. I always thought I was quite good at talking to people, but you quickly find out that the chatting is not really about getting on with the customers as their equals. The last thing they want is a clever lap dancer. You have to play dumb, that's the way to make the most money. Be agreeable, submissive, charming, seductive, alluring, feign interest in anything from their tie to their job to their newborn baby, and perhaps most importantly pretend to find them attractive when you do not find them attractive. The whole transaction is entirely false.'

Lucy also learned early on that in order to make money she would have to let her boundaries slip. 'You never think you will, but you end up letting men touch you. And touching them. The rules say no touching, no exposure of your genitals, no letting customers touch you. But when everyone else is breaking the rules, you have to join in. Why would a man pay twenty quid for a lap dancer who stays three feet away, when the next one he chooses lets him touch her? The rules are broken all the time.' Despite Lucy's growing contempt for what goes on inside the club, with every shift she works it seems harder and harder to leave. She describes her drinking as 'out of control', and is worried about her chances of landing another job. How would she explain the period she has been lap dancing on her CV? But the biggest obstacle to leaving is her self-esteem, which is now at an all-time low.

Lucy grabs her bags and hurries out the front door. Once on the train she glances around at the other passengers. She wonders, of the couples there, how many of the men have been to a lap-dancing club and whether their partners know or even care. Lucy is pretty confident that most people who have never been to a lap-dancing club have no idea what they are really like, and that many women don't take issue with their partners going because they don't want to seem prudish or illiberal. 'It's seen as uncool to take issue with stripping or porn. And I think lots of girlfriends or wives have this idea in their head of Moulin Rouge, or those American clubs you see in films. As though men go to the clubs to watch dancing. That isn't what happens! If you realised your man was actually kissing another woman's breasts, or putting his fingers in her vagina, or being masturbated by another woman, then would you still not mind? Would you mind if he did those things to a woman he met in the pub? The amount of physical contact involved in going to a lap-dance club, in any other context, would be called infidelity.' Once she reaches her stop Lucy makes her way up the escalators and walks the short distance to the club. She's got ten minutes left to get her dress and shoes on before she has to be on the floor ready for her turn on the pole.

I met Lucy through my work at the Fawcett Society, where we have been campaigning alongside the women's rights organisation OBJECT for the licensing of lap-dancing clubs to be tightened. Lucy's story is typical of many of the women who came forward during the course of the campaign to share their experiences of what it is really like working in a lap-dancing club. At the start of the campaign lap-dancing clubs were licensed in the same way as cafes and restaurants – which is part of the reason the number of lap-dancing clubs in the UK doubled between 2004 and 2008 to at least 300. Lucy is currently receiving therapy to help her deal with events from her past, and it has led her to reflect on her reasons for starting work in a lap-dancing club, aside from needing money quickly.

'I was raped in my late teens and was increasingly abusing drugs and alcohol into my twenties. For me, getting a job as a lap dancer seemed in some way to be an expression of who I believed myself to be: a sexual object.' Lucy wants to use her experiences of lap dancing to dispel the myths that surround the industry. 'I went into this job mistakenly believing that it was in some way going to be – for me as a sexual being – empowering. You're a dancer, of independent means, you're glamorous, exciting. You honestly believe you're going to make really good money. Whereas in reality you are totally skint, this promised money just never comes. Added to which you're potty, exhausted, hung over. You have a rash from constantly shaving your pubes. And with every night that goes by you begin to feel less and less like a human being. I truly believe that the reason men pay for lap dances is not because they are titillated visually by the sight of a naked woman, or even because the sexual contact is particularly stimulating. They do it because they get a power rush from the act of paying a woman to take her clothes off. She is vulnerable, and he is powerful, and that's the real allure – that's the real reason the clubs are getting so popular. Lap-dancing clubs are places in which you can all pretend that feminism never happened.'

Lucy is one of the many millions of women whose lives are directly caught up in the global sex industry. The scale on which stripping, pornography, and prostitution now take place is unparalleled in human history. Free-market ideology, the proclaimed 'sexual revolution' of the 1960s and 70s, and developments in technology all aligned to make the 1990s the decade during which sex became managed, manufactured, marketed, and consumed. Yet the gender-neutral term 'sex industry' betrays the very specific nature of the transaction involved: in the sex industry, it is overwhelmingly men who are the consumers, and women who are the product. Statistics published by the internet technology reviewer TopTenREVIEWS.com reveal that, in 2006, 96 per cent of internet searches including the word 'porn' were made by males. Oiling the wheels of this industry has been a PR campaign by its representatives and promoters that has successfully overhauled its previous image of seedy exploitation. Instead, we are told that today's sex industry represents a natural and harmless pursuit, engaged in by 'gentlemen' and catered for by liberated, empowered women choosing to express their sexual identity. Hugh Hefner, founder of *Playboy*, insists, 'Twenty years ago, *Playboy* was perceived as a chauvinist publication. Today the rabbit symbol has been embraced by women as a form of their own sexual empowerment.'[1]

Similarly Douglas Fox, founder and business partner of Christony Companions – one of the UK's largest escort agencies – claims prostitution is 'the consensual labour of a worker' and frames himself as a supporter of 'a woman's right to express her sexuality as she [chooses]'. He describes himself as a 'sex worker and human rights activist'.[2] Fox is an active member of the International Union of Sex Workers – who campaign for prostitution to be recognised as a conventional occupation and whose membership is open to anyone who works in the sex industry, including pimps, pornographers, and brothel owners. As a result of these 'liberating' credentials the sex industry has been freely waved into our leisure activities, workplaces, high streets, and homes. You would now have a hard time locating a teenage boy who had never masturbated to pornography, or a newsagent or supermarket that didn't sell pornographic newspapers or lads' mags. But what if the industry's credentials were fake – and its apparent embodiment of liberation just a carefully crafted illusion? What if 68 per cent of the women in prostitution have post-traumatic stress disorder (PTSD) as a direct result of the 'work' they do – a rate comparable to that of rape victims and survivors of state-sponsored torture?[3] What if 88 per cent of the pornographic scenes men were masturbating to contained physically aggressive acts – nearly all directed at women – such as slapping, gagging, and choking, and if it had reliably been shown that consuming such images led to an increase in sexually aggressive attitudes and behaviours? What if the sex industry didn't represent sexual liberation at all but, instead, one of the most profound challenges to women's status as equal citizens in the world today? Then, we would have a problem.

The truth is, nearly all of us are implicated in some way in the ubiquity of the sex industry: either as those who have used pornography, attended a pole-dancing lesson, visited a lap-dancing club, or simply remained quiet as the sex industry became louder and ever more dominant. But we have to face up to the fact that the problem is real and we have a responsibility to confront it – however uncomfortable that may be for us personally. For all the multitude of ways that the product is packaged, delivered, and consumed, the sex industry boils down to a very simple product concept: a person (usually a man) can access a sexual interaction with someone (usually a woman) who doesn't want to have it with him. She may consent to her body being used to sexually gratify him for a range of reasons: because she needs money, because she needs a drugs fix, because she wants to please her pimp, or because she thinks that's all she's good for. But a genuine desire to have an intimate sexual interaction – to gain emotional or sexual satisfaction – are not amongst her reasons for sexually stimulating him. And the purchaser knows full well this is the case – otherwise he wouldn't have to pay her for it. There are (at least) two disturbing elements to this scenario. One – the physical and psychological consequences for women who engage in unwanted sexual interactions can be devastating. Two – there is a culture in society causing millions of men and boys to feel at ease with, or even desiring of, a sexual interaction with a woman who doesn't want to have it with him.

At its heart, the sex industry requires its consumers to detach mentally from the living, breathing human being stimulating their sexual arousal, as if she were simply a collection of body parts. The stripper, the prostituted woman, the porn actress: her history, desires, needs, boundaries and vulnerabilities are all knowingly denied. She is made a sexual object. For too long, the sex industry has managed to deflect attempts to interrogate it by co-opting the language of feminism; the language of 'choice', 'power', and 'liberation'. It is a strategy that has proved all too successful, with even some people active in feminism embracing the notion that the sex industry can be congruous with women's equality. In a 2007 interview for US magazine *The Nation* Jessica Valenti, founder of feministing.com and author of three books on feminism, said, 'I'm not anti-porn. It's there, I watch it sometimes, it's fine.'[4] Marcelle Karp and Debbie Stoller, founders of *BUST* – a magazine that proclaims it has been 'BUSTing stereotypes about women since 1993' – also wrote in their 1999 book *The Bust Guide to the New Girl Order*: 'We don't have a problem with pornography unless, of course, it doesn't turn us on.'[5] When journalist Ariel Levy published *Female Chauvinist Pigs* in 2005, a critique on the rise of 'raunch culture' and the notion that the mainstreaming of pornography is empowering, the book was described as 'dangerous' by Jennifer Baumgardner – former editor of *Ms.* magazine.[6] She alleged that 'Levy contributes to that mean finger, pointed only at girls, which apparently tells them, "You're a slut and people are making fun of you."' Yet by asking some tough questions of women's and girls' behaviour Levy issued a crucial warning against a mainstream culture which relentlessly sexualises women. In this chapter I trace everyday instances of 'raunch' back to their source: the global sex industry – an industry whose alibi is wearing thin. Arguments that prostitution, pornography, and stripping are harmless – or even empowering – simply because a woman engaging in these acts usually does so without a gun being held to her head spectacularly fail to take into account the context within which that 'choice' was made, the motivations driving it, the consequences of it, and the role of others involved. It is high time to reveal that the sex industry is not only based on gender inequality, it makes sexism sexy.

Dear John

'She's an independent, witty young woman . . . At work she is in total control and a complete professional – the ultimate seductive call girl.'[7]

This is the description of 'Belle', the high-class title character of ITV2's drama series *Secret Diary of a Call Girl* from the TV show's website. The show averaged over 1.2 million viewers per episode during its first series.

Rebecca Saffer, who worked as a 'high-class call-girl' in America for seven years, has a rather different description:

'Prostitution is absolutely frightening. Every night I risked my life. I risked my health of a condom breaking and ending up infected. I risked my safety by being raped and beaten because some men feel they deserve it and look at me as nothing more than a whore. I risked everything for money. People will never understand how it feels to be strangled until your feet collapse because that's just what turns him on.'

Calculatingly marketed as the 'world's oldest profession', prostitution is the sex industry's quintessential product. The *Pretty Woman* branding retains strong currency in today's society, and programmes such as *Secret Diary of a Call Girl* continue to propagate the notion that prostitution is a financially lucrative lifestyle choice. Or, if not quite the ultimate money-spinner, it is at least framed as 'work like any other'. Douglas Fox, escort agency owner and member of the International Union of Sex Workers, says he provides a 'much-needed service' and that 'the National Health should contribute to the cost because it's a really human need for companionship'.[8] The International Union of Sex Workers is affiliated to the GMB, Britain's third largest trade union, which proclaims that 'the sexual behaviour of consenting adults requires no regulation by the state' and that their role is 'to support workers in any industry'.[9] Even Jobcentre Plus (JCP), the British government's employment agency, advertises jobs to work as 'masseuses' and 'escorts' despite full knowledge of the fact that women applying for these jobs through JCP have gone on to find they were expected to sell sex acts.

The idea that selling sex acts is like serving a cappuccino or stacking shelves carries little truck with Rebecca Saffer. 'Whoever says that prostitution is just ordinary work has never walked even a minute in my shoes, or any other [call] girl's that I know. Prostitution is far from ordinary. It's demeaning and degrading and by no means a way to an end. It's actually a trap. A trap that most women believe for far too long.' I got in touch with Rebecca after she spoke at a meeting recently in London about the realities of prostitution. Now twenty-eight and living in the US, Rebecca was able to escape prostitution just over a year ago, 'by calling my mom and having her book a plane ticket for a day that I knew my pimp was leaving town to visit his sick mother'. She has chosen to speak out about her experiences because of the false image people are fed about prostitution. 'I think the way society has glorified prostitution is very sad. I believe young women all over the world are going to become more curious [about going into prostitution] due to the positive light that is shown on this horrid profession.'

The last two decades have witnessed a startling growth in the global prostitution industry. During the 1990s the number of men paying for sex acts in the UK doubled and there are now an estimated 80,000 people involved in prostitution in the UK.[10] In London alone there are at least 921 brothels spread across every borough, mostly in residential settings.[11] Sheila Jeffreys, a professor in the School of Social and Political Sciences at the University of Melbourne, reports the industry is most advanced and embedded in countries where militaries set up large-scale prostitution systems, for example the US in the 1930s and 40s, in countries like Korea, the Philippines, and Thailand.[12] Today, prostitution is big business: it is estimated to account for 8 per cent of the Chinese economy alone. And wherever large-scale, male-dominated events go – so does prostitution. The

German government reported that there was a significant increase in demand for prostitution as a result of the 2006 football World Cup. As with the sex industry as a whole, prostitution itself is 'packaged' in a variety of ways. Customers can choose amongst street prostitution, women who sell sex acts from home, brothels, massage parlours, escort services, and prostitution tourism, or even mail-order brides. The essential product, though, is the same.

So who are the women whose bodies are the raw materials of this industry? Does their involvement represent a free, liberated choice – as so often touted by the industry? A single glance at the statistics suggests not. Between 50 and 75 per cent of women in prostitution in the UK began selling sex acts before they were eighteen years old,[13] and they are found to have been sexually abused as children at much higher rates than women not involved in prostitution. Interviews with over 100 women prostituting in Vancouver found that 82 per cent had been sexually abused in childhood.[14] This finding makes sense in that common consequences of childhood sexual abuse include sexualised behaviour, difficulties in asserting boundaries, and an increased risk of future sexual victimisation. But for Emma, it wasn't childhood sexual abuse that led to her involvement in prostitution. It was instead an abusive relationship she found herself in shortly after graduating from university: 'First it was controlling behaviour, then an occasional physical incident. For the last two years, the violence was a constant threat. Things were also fucked-up in my family and I was left to cope on my own as well as in a relationship that was careering out of control. I turned to substances – alcohol and sleeping tablets being the main ones.' Her partner also had a worsening drug addiction, and used all their money to feed his habit. 'His dealer said he'd provide him with drugs in return for the use of me, for himself and his friends. I was trapped with no money, terrified, in the grips of raging alcoholism and totally isolated. If I refused or fought I was beaten.' Emma did eventually manage to escape this abuse, but it had devastated her, and she couldn't hold down a job. 'I was basically too fucked-up for work, and I knew it. So when I saw an ad in the paper for escorts, there seemed little choice. I figured I was really fucked-up about men, and had been truly fucked over by them, and didn't trust them an inch, so I might as well make some money from it. This was not a free "choice". It was the opposite. I needed money, but was a mess. Where else do they greet you with such open arms in such a state as the sex industry?'

Poverty, racism and marginalisation are other hallmarks of an entry into prostitution. Of the 100 women interviewed by researchers in Vancouver about their experiences in prostitution, 52 per cent were from Canada's First Nations, despite the fact that this group comprised less than 7 per cent of the city's general population. Black women are also found to be over-represented in prostitution in the US, and African-American women are additionally arrested at a higher rate than women from other ethnic groups who are charged for solicitation.[15] Rebecca Saffer, who is half Choctaw and half Caucasian, grew up in the US in poverty. 'The main reason for me entering prostitution was definitely economic hardship. I remember being hungry and being teased at school about my clothes. When I had my daughter at eighteen years old, I swore she would never go through what I went through, regardless of the cost.' Shortly after having her baby, Rebecca started working in a lap-dancing club, 'to make ends meet while I went to university during the day'. A year later, she entered prostitution. Experiences like these, and findings reported by the British government – such as the fact that 70 per cent of women in prostitution have previously spent time in care – suggest that the sex industry's credential of being populated by 'liberated staff' is fraudulent. Abuse, homelessness, poverty, marginalisation, family breakdown: these are the lights illuminating the path to prostitution.

But what of the 'work' itself? Putting aside the vulnerabilities that lead women into prostitution, what effect does selling their bodies for sex acts actually have on the individuals involved? 'I saw up to eight or nine clients in a day,' Emma recalled. 'Such frequent sex was painful and I numbed myself out with drink and drugs from the humiliation and degradation of it. I gave longer blowjobs where possible to shorten the time they had intercourse with me. My mouth tasted of rubber condoms all day long. I only had chance between clients to go to the bathroom, wipe up, and reapply lipstick sometimes and then it was back upstairs with the next one.' Emma was required by the escort agency she started out at to use a fake name (she chose 'Angel'), and to always officially deny she sold sex acts; rather she had to say that she sold 'time'. 'When I had sex I think I numbed out, or tried to, tried not to think. I tried to pretend this was happening to Angel, not Emma, that they couldn't hurt me, that I was in control.' Two years on, Emma is still struggling with the consequences. 'I suffer nightmares, flashbacks and am triggered by numerous things – scents, sounds, groups of people . . . I still struggle massively around sex. I still dissociate, and feel like I split off from myself.' Emma has been diagnosed with PTSD

– a common 'side-effect' of prostitution. (As mentioned earlier, a research project conducted across nine countries found the rate of PTSD amongst women in prostitution was 68 per cent – a rate comparable to survivors of rape and state-sponsored torture.)[16] The dissociation that Emma describes occurs when people are under extreme stress; it is a means of enduring severe abuse.

In addition to the psychological trauma, women in prostitution are also subjected to extremely high levels of violence, regardless of whether they are involved in street prostitution or 'high-class' escorting. This violence is often on two fronts: both from the pimps and from the men paying them for sex acts. Rebecca had two pimps during her time in prostitution. 'I entered with a pimp who courted me for a year before, making me believe he was my boyfriend and actually cared about me. My second pimp, who I was with for three and a half years, was extremely violent. He hit us on a regular basis. We were all scared of him, and that's what kept us there so long.' Rebecca describes receiving all forms of abuse while in prostitution. 'I have been raped, strangled, beaten, yelled at, cussed at, spit on, told I was nothing but a whore, a hooker, no one would ever want me as a wife. Things that really hurt my heart.' Emma was similarly subjected to extreme violence. 'Some of them [the men paying for sex] hated women and were sadistic. I learned not to respond if a john was deliberately rough, because it spurred them on. Some would suck my nipples so hard they hurt, or bite them, or push my head down when I was giving oral, or fuck me extra hard and penetrate me without warning. I went in on myself.' What Rebecca and Emma experienced was no aberration. A mortality survey of over

1,600 women in prostitution in the US found that murder accounted for 50 per cent of the deaths.[17] Nine out
of ten of the women interviewed in Vancouver had also
been physically assaulted and 78 per cent had been
raped.[18] As a result of such high levels of trauma and violence, it is perhaps no surprise that many women in prostitution take to using drink and drugs as a coping
mechanism. Researchers in Canada analysing the economic costs of being in prostitution found that over two-
thirds of the women they interviewed hadn't used drugs
or alcohol before they entered prostitution, and only 12.9
per cent entered prostitution solely because of an addiction problem. Yet once in prostitution, all but three of the
sixty-two women interviewed for the study proceeded to
develop a serious addiction. The amount they went on to
spend on drugs and alcohol averaged C\$12,617 for each
year they were in the sex industry.[19]

For all the factors that make women vulnerable to prostitution, it is crucial to remember that they aren't the
'cause' of the industry. Prostitution exists because there
is demand for it – huge demand. (It would be a mistake,
however, to confuse existing demand with inevitability
of demand. As I'll show in 'A New Day', countries that
have effectively tackled prostitution, such as Sweden, have
been able to dramatically reduce demand.) So who exactly
are the people currently using women in prostitution?
The British government reports that the profile of an average 'user' is a man aged around thirty, in full-time employment, married, and with no criminal convictions. To
establish a fuller profile, Jan Macleod and colleagues at
the Women's Support Project in Glasgow interviewed 110
men who bought women in prostitution in Scotland and

found nearly a third of them had attitudes tolerant of rape.[20] Twenty-two per cent said that, once a customer has paid, he is entitled to do whatever he wants to the woman and 12 per cent said it wasn't possible to rape a woman in prostitution. The men came out with various justifications for their use of women in the sex industry, such as women in prostitution being qualitatively 'different' from other women, a need to satisfy their sexual desires, and prostitution providing an opportunity to dominate women. Perhaps most crucially of all, however, was that the researchers found the men who were most accepting of prostitution were those who were most hostile towards women and whose identity was most based on valuing sexual and psychological dominance. Crudely speaking, the more sexist they were, the more acceptable they thought it was to use women like Rebecca and Emma. Findings like these illuminate why such high levels of violence are perpetrated against women in prostitution.

I asked Emma what she thinks about the media's portrayal of prostitution: 'I still define myself by these experiences [prostitution] and it tears me apart when programmes like *Diary of a Call Girl* are on TV. It devalues my whole experience. It makes me feel hopeless and utterly and wretchedly alone, drowned out by the vast noise of the sex industry and its all-powerful lobbying. At times I have felt suicidal with it. When I was working, I had to join in the lie and say I liked it and I chose it, and I think that that is what upsets me the most now. Only now that I am out of it am I free to tell the truth. It's hard to have a voice when you have a cock thrust down your throat.'

Uncomfortable viewing

Taking more than just inspiration from the product of prostitution, pornography can be seen as a form of filmed prostitution and is the sex industry's most prolific output. As a result, our world has been 'pornified'. Pornography – sexually explicit material produced solely for the purposes of sexually stimulating the viewer – is inescapable, with a reach that extends to even the most mundane aspects of everyday life. Simply buying milk from the local corner shop usually involves unwittingly viewing a display of pornographic 'lads' mags'. Never has pornography been so easy to access, deemed so acceptable, or been so embedded in mainstream culture as today. According to TopTenREVIEWS.com, the average age of first exposure to internet pornography is just eleven years old, and every day there are 68 million search engine requests for porn. The rather obvious conclusion we can draw from all this? There are few people who have never seen pornography, and perhaps even fewer young men who have never masturbated to it.

Individuals who have dared to question whether this is an entirely positive thing have been frequently dismissed as 'illiberal' or 'prudish'. When Labour MP Clare Short criticised the *Sun*'s Page 3 as being degrading to women, the paper launched an attack on her, superimposing her face on a topless model and labelling her a 'killjoy' who was 'fat and jealous'. Feminist concepts have also been adopted into the language of pornography industry representatives, as when Christie Hefner – daughter of Hugh and CEO of Playboy Enterprises – told Ariel Levy in *Female Chauvinist Pigs* that the company's rabbit logo symbolises a female attitude of, 'I'm taking control of how I look and the statement I'm making' and that women appearing in *Playboy* are making a 'statement'. 'It's a moment that lets them be creative.'[21] It is inevitable that any discussion about what role pornography plays in a society riddled with sexism is going to be uncomfortable. We may have used pornography ourselves, our partners might use it, the seemingly 'feminist' language used by the industry can be confusing, and the prospect of someone labelling you a 'prude' isn't exactly the nicest thing in the world to contemplate. But it is a conversation that cannot be avoided. The ubiquity of pornography means no one is left untouched by its effects. It is time to start asking questions: Exactly what are men masturbating to? Who are the women in the images? What effects does pornography have on viewers? And does pornography represent an attack on gender equality?

It all started with a bunny. While the existence of pornographic imagery can be traced significantly further back, Rebecca Whisnant, Associate Professor of Philosophy at the University of Dayton, and Gail Dines, Professor of Sociology at Wheelock College, pinpoint 1953 as the year pornography became an 'industry'. This was the year the first issue of *Playboy* magazine was published.[22] But the production of pornography is now unrecognisable from its inception. The scale and speed of its growth has been phenomenal. Political and economic policies of the 1980s and 90s, coupled with advances in technology, enabled pornography to become a global, multi-billion-dollar industry and transform the Western cultural landscape. Consider the following findings from 2007 TopTenREVIEWS.com:

- 12 per cent of all websites are pornography sites
- 25 per cent of all daily search engine requests are for pornography
- At any given moment 28,258 people are viewing pornography online
- Every month there are 1.5 billion peer-to-peer downloads of pornography
- Every thirty-nine minutes a new pornography video is created in the US

The profits, of course, are astronomical. Over $3,000 per second is spent on pornography and the industry is estimated to be worth $97 billion worldwide – more than the combined revenue of Microsoft, Google, Amazon, Yahoo!, eBay, Apple, Netflix and Earthlink. And where money goes, so too does respectability. In 2002 the then British prime minister, Tony Blair, invited Express Newspapers owner Richard Desmond to a meeting at Downing Street. Desmond also happens to be a pornographer and publisher of magazines such as *Asian Babes* and *Mega Boobs*. That same year the Labour Party accepted a £100,000 donation from him.[23] The sheer scale of the industry testifies to the size of its market. So who are the people putting the 'demand' into the transaction? In 2006, 96 per cent of the people who searched the internet using the word 'porn' were male, 97 per cent who searched using the term 'free porn' were male, and 86 per cent of those who searched for 'Playboy' were also male. While it is apparent that some women do use it, pornography is very much a gendered phenomenon.

The first question to ask is what exactly are men masturbating to? What does twenty-first-century pornography, which is overwhelmingly heterosexual, look like? To find

out, I decided to do what millions of others do every day:
I Googled 'porn'. Over 200 million pages came up, but I
restricted my review to the first ten. Bear in mind, this was
the most easily accessible material, and all of it was free.
The first website proudly proclaimed to serve 'over 9 MIL-
LION "satisfied" people a day'. The first four videos it
showed had the following titles, 'Dp for a French slut',
('Dp' is short for 'double penetration' – when a woman is
penetrated vaginally and anally by two men at the same
time), 'Adorable teen Jassie is one tight Asian slut', 'Hot
blondie powerfuck and squirting!' and 'Barbie gets double
treatment'. Other videos you could watch on the home page
included 'Victoria takes some deep dicking' and 'German
fisted and fucked'. Site visitors could also choose from a
range of 'categories' including 'interracial', 'anal', 'ass', 'big
tits', 'bondage', 'bukkake' (where multiple men ejaculate
on one woman's body), 'cum shot', 'fisting' (where someone inserts their fist in a woman's vagina), and 'teen'. The
video titles on the other top nine websites I looked at were
all pretty similar to this; they were relentlessly degrading
and aggressive: 'Teen screams as she takes a dick in the
ass', 'Suck my toes bitch' and 'Teen gets spanked, slapped
and choked' were representative titles. Website number
three on the Google search had a video on its home page
called, 'Passed out brunette teen girl gets fucked silly', which
linked to the external website, 'Sleep Surprise'. The site's
description of the video read, 'Because the hotel is booked
full he is allowed to sleep with her, provided he is not going
to touch her. Of course girl! But as soon as the girl is asleep
he grabs the opportunity and slides his fingers into her
panties. That feels like a really soft pussy! So he gives her
a good fucking and a wad of night cream too!'

I hadn't watched any of the videos by this point, but then on website number eight in the Google search I clicked on a video link on the homepage to reveal the full title and introductory text. It read, 'Nasty Latina is Abused and Humiliated: Fuck, this chick risked her life to get to the US from Cuba just to end up in this humiliating porn . . . Ah, tears of freedom, welcome to America.' The video started playing. A woman is shown sitting fully clothed on a chair. A man off-camera asks her how she's enjoying America. She doesn't understand and it becomes immediately obvious that the woman speaks very little English. The film then abruptly cuts to a scene of a man repeatedly thrusting his penis down her throat so far that she throws up. He then continues to repeat this until she throws up a second time. The film cuts again, this time to show a man having sex with her. Her face is on full view to the camera, and she is crying. The sounds she makes while crying suggests she is also in physical pain. All the while there is a man off-camera 'encouraging' her with words like, 'yeh, good whore' and 'that's a good girl'. The video had received 445,373 hits and an average rating by viewers of 7.84. I didn't feel able to watch any more pornography after that.

A content analysis of contemporary pornography presented at the International Communication Association's 2007 annual meeting reveals that the deeply disturbing results of my quick web survey were by no means anomalous. The study analysed the most popular rented VHS and DVD pornography titles as compiled from the monthly sales records of online and retail shops across the US.[24] It found that contemporary pornography is incessantly aggressive: 89.1 per cent of scenes contained aggressive acts, with the average scene containing 11.52 acts of verbal or physical aggression (physical being the most common, featuring in 88.2 per cent of all scenes). Of all aggression in the films, 94.4 per cent was directed towards women. The study also found that in pornography women apparently don't mind being abused and many of them apparently like it: 95.2 per cent of the victims of aggression responded with either neutral or pleasurable expressions. And it also found that there is a high demand from viewers for pornography which includes watching women participate in sex acts that they don't generally like in the 'real world'. Surveys of sexual preferences show the vast majority of women don't find the act of anal sex appealing. But 55.9 per cent of pornography scenes feature anal sex, with 41 per cent of these scenes also involving 'ass-to-mouth' (ATM). ATM entails a man penetrating a woman's anus, then removing his penis and placing it immediately into the woman's mouth. As Gail Dines points out, this act delivers no apparent increase to the man's sexual pleasure outside the woman's degradation and humiliation.[25] While degradation and aggression against women is an overwhelmingly dominant theme, Dines and Whisnant also point to another disturbing trend in pornography: racist sexual ideology. Films such as *Bangkok Suckee Fuckee* and *Me Luv U Long Time* portray Asian women as exotic 'others' who are obedient and slavishly willing to please. Websites like 'Hoodhunters' and 'Pimp My Black Teen' depict African-American women as hypersexual and even more worthy of abuse. The text for one of the latter site's films reads, 'This girl was just too ghetto, baggy jeans, flannel and nappy hair. After we done her up, she was bad ass and ready to get on camera with a big black cock inside of her.' Today's pornography is almost unrecognisable from the pornography ushered in by *Playboy* in 1953 – which now seems positively tame. This is the reality of pornography in the twenty-first century. This is what a disturbing number of men are masturbating to.

Second question: who are the women in the images? There is little research that focuses specifically on women involved in pornography, but what we do know is that pornography is a form of prostitution. It is a variant on the 'traditional' theme, of course, because the 'customer' doesn't get to physically interact with the woman being paid to sexually stimulate him. But she is being paid to undertake sex acts (i.e. to prostitute), recorded on film, explicitly for that purpose. So, we already have the extensive evidence from women not routinely filmed while prostituting to indicate what makes women vulnerable to the industry and what impact being prostituted has on them. In fact, when Emma was working in a massage parlour, some of the men would make pornography of her. 'I found myself and one of the "girls" having a foursome – two men paid for us. We both gave both of them oral, they had sex with both of us (without changing condoms) and we had to perform a lesbian show for them, giving one another oral sex and pushing dildos up each other. They filmed us on their mobiles.' The types of sex acts men requested at the massage parlour also mirrored those in pornography. 'Anal, being the most painful, was in great demand – only one other woman did it, and that was only because you could charge ninety pounds. Towards the end of my time there, I contemplated it on many occasions for the cash, but my experiences of anal with my ex-partner had been incredibly painful to the point of vomiting and luckily I exited [the sex industry] before I had to do that.'

Biographies of porn stars also give an indication of what

life is like in pornography. Sheila Jeffreys, in her book *The Industrial Vagina*, translates an account by European ex-porn star Raffaela Anderson, who describes it this way: 'Take an inexperienced girl, who does not speak the language, far from home, sleeping in a hotel or on the set. Made to undergo a double penetration, a fist in her vagina plus a fist in her anus, sometimes at the same time, a hand up her arse, sometimes two. You get a girl in tears, who pisses blood because of lesions, and she craps herself too because no one explained to her that she needed to have an enema . . . After the scene which the girls have no right to interrupt they have two hours' rest.'[26]

A common theme in such biographies is that before entering pornography women were often desperate for money and had little self-esteem or support. Jenna Jameson, one of pornography's biggest stars, describes in her autobiography *How to Make Love Like a Porn Star: A Cautionary Tale* how she was raped as a teenager and pimped by men she knew.[27] Once in the industry, we also know that women face extremely high health risks from sex acts that are standard in pornography. The US-based Adult Industry Medical Health Care Foundation lists these as including HIV, rectal chlamydia, gonorrhoea of the throat and damage to the vagina and anus. And another fundamental fact we know is that every single woman featured in pornography, on sites like analsuffering.com and gagonmycock.com, is a human being with a past, with pain receptors, and with authentic desires and emotions, despite the industry's best efforts to persuade viewers otherwise.

Now the big question: how and why is there such huge demand for images that show women being sexually degraded and aggressed against? Yet again, we see that far

from this demand being inevitable or natural, it has everything to do with masculinity and gender inequality. Robert
Jensen, an associate professor in the School of Journalism
at the University of Texas, describes pornography as a mirror, reflecting the way men who buy into conventional or
'hyper-' masculinity see women. I asked Jensen how he
could explain the predilection to watch a woman have a
penis thrust so far down her throat she gags, or watch a
man penetrate a woman anally and then place his penis
immediately into her mouth. 'All these practices are quite
clearly about male domination and female submission. Men
know most heterosexual women don't like anal. It's a way
to act out their aggression.'[28] Pornography, then, and men's
use of it, is intrinsically linked to inequalities between
women and men; it eroticises the dominance of masculinity over femininity, of men over women.

In our culture, to have sex and be a 'real man' at the
same time requires that he controls and dominates his
female sexual partner. He has to 'give it' to her or 'take it'
from her; a fuck is a conquest. The very fact that the pornography exists, that the woman is there on screen having sex
to stimulate him, represents a conquest for the viewer in
itself. That conquest could be tied to the fact that she had
to be paid to be there, that she is participating for his pleasure and not her own sexual or emotional satisfaction, or
that her privacy has been invaded. And with the simple
on/off button the viewer can also control when and where
the woman sexually stimulates him; he sets the terms. When
the dominant form of masculinity infuses sex with power
and control, the additional violence found in pornography
is practically inevitable. As Jensen says, 'Films that exist to
provide sexual stimulation for men in this culture wouldn't

work if the sex were presented in the context of loving and affectionate relationships.'[29] Pornography also allows men to bond with each other through the shared conquest of women's bodies. Men's pornography use is often a communal act. As Michael Flood from La Trobe University in Australia points out, men often get together to watch pornography, and share and exchange pornographic films and publications.[30] This 'homosocial bonding' is also represented in the content of pornography itself. A dominant theme in contemporary pornography is multiple men having sex with one woman.

This leads then to the final question: what effects does watching pornography have on the viewer? When I started researching this, I assumed from the public controversy over this question that I would find little conclusive evidence. After all, pornography doesn't exist in a social vacuum and demonstrating cause and effect in any social scientific research is notoriously problematic. But on surveying the literature I found that the scientific evidence demonstrating harmful effects from watching pornography, both experimental and non-experimental, is compelling. In a 2007 report commissioned by the British Ministry of Justice, researchers Catherine Itzen, Ann Taket and Liz Kelly detail a range of meta-analyses providing strong and stable evidence of the effects of viewing pornography. (Meta-analyses enable researchers to scrutinise, compare, and average the results of multiple studies, thereby providing more robust and reliable conclusions.) One such meta-analysis of over thirty studies found that consuming pornography increased aggressive behaviour in the viewer.[31] A separate meta-analysis of forty-six studies found that exposure to pornography reliably had the effect of making viewers more likely to commit sexual offences, experience difficulties in intimate relationships, and accept 'rape myths' as true. Finally, a meta-analysis of nine studies revealed a statistically significant relationship between attitudes supporting violence against women and pornography consumption. As Itzen and her colleagues conclude, 'Taken together they constitute a substantial body of mutually corroborative evidence of the harm effects of extreme – and other – pornographic material.' Considering what pornography represents, and what it contains, it would frankly be bizarre if it wasn't having these effects. Men masturbating to pornography are experiencing one of the most physiologically powerful and rewarding sensations there is to images of women engaging in unwanted and abusive sex acts.

Stripping the illusion[*]

Prince Harry, Simon Cowell, Christian Slater; all three have reportedly been customers at lap-dancing clubs – now familiar features of UK high streets. The term 'lap dancing' has come to encompass a variety of routines, including table dancing, erotic dancing, stripping and striptease. Another term sometimes aptly used to describe it is 'live pornography'. Lap-dancing clubs originated in the US, and the UK's first lap-dancing club opened in London in 1995. Since that time, it has proved itself to be a hugely profitable industry, spawning at least 300 clubs across the UK. There are now at least 3,000 in the US, and the lap-dancing industry is estimated to be worth a whopping $75 billion worldwide.[32] Key to its success has been the effectiveness of a market-

[*] 'Stripping the Illusion' was the campaign name for OBJECT's work challenging the normalisation of lap-dancing clubs. The name comes from research on lap dancing by Julie Bindel (2004).

ing campaign which replaced the image of seedy, neon-lit strip joints with one of high-class, respectable 'gentlemen's clubs' where women command fortunes with their sexual power.

Tatyana, who I met through my Fawcett and OBJECT campaign work, is incredulous about this claim by the industry. 'We are the main attraction yet we're treated worse than anyone in the business. In this hierarchy, female dancers are at the bottom of the food chain. We have no rights to speak of. We can be fired for no reason. There is no sick pay or pension.' Tatyana is originally from eastern Europe and started working in a lap-dancing club shortly after arriving in the UK. 'I wanted to be "Westernised" and sexy like the way the media portrays women should be in the West, and I was bullied and racially abused in other jobs.' There are a variety of reasons women start working in lap-dancing clubs. For one, it is frequently portrayed as glamorous, lucrative, and a way for women to express their sexuality. Anna is upfront about why she started working in a topless bar. 'I was a student and heard from a friend that the topless bar in town had jobs going. I think I had a sense of topless dancing being a daring, edgy thing to do. That it was bold – not something people who knew me would expect. So it was more an egotistical choice than anything else.' Another disturbingly familiar theme in women's entry into the industry is abuse. For Lucy, who had been raped in her teens, lap dancing seemed to offer her a way of recapturing what she described as her 'sexual power'. A study of exotic dancers by Jennifer Wesley at the University of Central Florida found nearly half of them had been molested or raped as children or teenagers.[33]

When Sandrine Leveque, campaigns manager at women's

rights organisation OBJECT, and I gate-crashed a meeting of the Lap Dancing Association (LDA) in 2008 we got a very literal illustration of who exactly does hold the power in the lap-dancing industry. The LDA was set up in response to Fawcett and OBJECT's campaign to re-license lap-dancing clubs, and this meeting had been organised to come up with a strategy to combat our campaign. Obviously curious as to what their strategy would be, we went along. It was held in the offices of the LDA's lawyers, and we entered the meeting to find a long board table filling the room, with owners and managers of various UK lap-dancing clubs sitting round it – all except one of whom were male. Because the truth is that the owner/worker divide is a wholly gendered one. And despite being 'independent contractors' instead of employees of the clubs, women performers have very little control over their work. As Anna recalls, 'We were working for ourselves and not the owner – or that's how he wanted us to see it, at any rate. We each had to pay a fee for the privilege of working – twenty pounds on quieter nights, thirty on Fridays and Saturdays.' In fact, many of the women we spoke to had to pay much higher fees than Anna did, commonly up to £80 or £100 a night. It is the clubs that set the schedule, the hours, the fees, the prices of dances, the uniform stipulations, and it is the club that often mandates the performers to tip bouncers and DJs. It's no surprise, then, that there weren't any performers present at the LDA strategy meeting that day. After we had taken our seats at the board table Sandrine and I were required to introduce ourselves to all the assembled club owners, who seemed somewhat bemused to see us there. And although the chair of the meeting eventually asked us to leave, this wasn't before they had spent an hour – half the allotted meeting time – trying to persuade us that Fawcett and OBJECT's campaign was unnecessary (and thus happily halving the amount of time the LDA had to strategise against us).

Lap-dancing clubs also frequently exploit vulnerabilities and inequalities experienced by women performers. Migrant women in particular can face heightened exploitation because of their status. As writer Sayyadina Thomas recalls from her time spent working in a US strip club, 'Two Asian girls I worked with were illegal and everybody knew the boss liked illegal immigrants. Since an illegal immigrant is a security risk the club owner may demand she pay three times the normal house fee.'[34] Thomas also found racial stereotypes were marketed by the club. 'A strip club is almost always a demeaning environment to women, and it is racist because every girl has to label herself. Blacks and mulattos are exotic beauties. Whites are American beauties.' Jennifer Danns encountered a similar environment in the UK lap-dancing club she worked in. '[The manager] intentionally chose the girls working to ensure a range of choice for the men, so there were blondes, brunettes, older girls, younger girls, slim girls, bigger girls etc. My place was assured as I was one of the few black girls and at one time the only black girl. At the time this process seemed normal but with hindsight it is dehumanising and basically a form of cattle market. Men would come in and ask the manager did she have any black girls and I would be wheeled over like a prize cow.'[35]

Women working in lap-dancing clubs also face extremely high levels of harassment and violence. Tatyana recalls what it was like in the clubs where she worked. 'I was constantly looking over my shoulder and the stress I was under, constantly, without a respite would become unbearable. That's why I drank, I believe. We were all propositioned for sex on daily basis.' Research conducted by the Child and Woman Abuse Studies Unit for Glasgow City Council found that prostitution does indeed take place in some lap-dancing clubs.[36] Similarly, research in Scotland into men who bought women in prostitution found that 31 per cent of the interviewees have bought sex acts in a lap-dancing club.[37] Anna also recalls the pressure to offer 'sexual services' after a new group of performers arrived at her club from one of the more established lap-dancing clubs. 'I vividly remember one woman putting her finger into her vagina, drawing it out again and waving it under the customer's nose so he could smell it; this happened often, and a number of the women did it. They charged more for that. They also had an impossible-looking move that involved doing a headstand right in front of the customer and spreading their legs wide open. The effect of this was that there was an expectation from the customers that the rest of us would do the same things.' Lap-dancing clubs don't just foster prostitution within the clubs themselves, but also implicitly normalise and legitimise the practice more widely. Research into men who pay for sex acts has found that the mainstreaming of lap-dancing clubs and the sexualisation of culture more widely plays a key role in their motivation to pay for sex acts. This led researchers at the Child and Women Abuse Studies Unit to conclude that 'where there are clubs in which women perform sexualised dance in order to titillate men, nearby premises offering sexual services will benefit'.[38]

Kelly Holsopple, who herself worked in stripping for thirteen years, conducted research into women's experiences of violence in strip clubs.[39] She found 100 per cent of the women she surveyed had experienced physical abuse while working in a lap-dancing club, which variously included being bitten, slapped, pinched, or punched. All of the women had also been sexually abused in a club. This ranged from having their breasts grabbed to men attempting and succeeding to penetrate them vaginally with fingers and bottles. Every woman had been verbally harassed, frequently being called names such as cunt, whore, bitch, and slut, and every single one had been propositioned for sex. The women surveyed also reported that almost all of the perpetrators suffered no consequences for these behaviours. Tatyana sums up her experience of lap dancing: 'It's not glamorous and exciting at all, it's a horrible world that is cruel and abusive to vulnerable women. On one hand, you're this glamorous creature that everyone apparently desires and wants to be like (regular women told us many times they were jealous of us and wished they'd looked like us or could dance/do pole work like us). But on the other, we were openly disrespected, exploited, abused and treated with hostility and contempt.'

Given what goes on in lap-dancing clubs, how can we explain their popularity with so many men? Anna believes that, contrary to the popular notion that lap dancing is empowering for women, in reality 'it is empowering for men. And it's not just sexual; these men like being in an environment where women give them lavish attention, laugh at their jokes, flirt with them, and ultimately get their tits out for them. Women in the "normal" world are not usually so biddable.' A study of men who regularly visit lap-dancing clubs backs up this analysis of 'empowerment'. Cultural anthropologist Katherine Frank found that over half the men she surveyed who frequented lap-dancing clubs said they felt relaxed in the clubs because to them it was an escape from the everyday rules of conduct they had to follow when interacting with women in other settings.[40] The men described relations between women and men as being 'tense' and 'confused', particularly in the workplace, where they felt their interactions with women were constrained by the threat of being accused of sexual harassment. Some of the interviewees explicitly said they visited clubs in order to interact with women who weren't 'feminist' and would interact with them in more 'traditional' ways. As with other elements of the sex industry, it is clear that much of the appeal of lap dancing is intimately tied up with a desire by customers to bolster their masculinity. It is a dedicated space in which to be a 'real man'. Tatyana concurs with this. 'With us they didn't feel the need to pretend that we were "equal". We were there to be used and they carried on like to them it was obvious that women are inferior to men, discussion closed. And that we were "all the same", easily interchangeable, one substituted for another in a blink of an eye and also a nuisance when we talked.'

As part of my work at Fawcett I have participated in multiple radio debates with lap-dancing club owners who have argued that 'if you don't like lap-dancing clubs you don't have to go in them'. But this is to wilfully deny the profound impact lap-dancing clubs have on wider society as well as on the performers and customers. The streets surrounding lap-dancing clubs can become 'no go areas' for women, who fear and experience harassment while walking by. This issue is flagged up by the UK Royal Town Planning Institute in guidance on spatial planning[41] and was also revealed in a review of lap-dancing club licensing conducted by the London Borough of Tower Hamlets.[42] Sarah contacted the Fawcett Society about how she had been affected by a lap-dancing club opening in her town. 'There is a bus stop near the railway station that I have used very often since I have lived here. Until a strip club opened outside this bus stop, I had never experienced a single instance of harassment, intimidation or any antisocial behaviour while waiting there at up to eleven at night. Since it opened I have been subjected to numerous counts of verbal abuse best described as sexual harassment. It's most often on Friday and Saturday evenings. On separate occasions, I have had men say to me "How much for a dance love? I'll give you £20 to get yours out," "Show us your titties, darling," "Give us a dance sweetheart, just a treat for the lads like, give us flash of your titties."' It got so bad that Sarah made a complaint to the police. 'They were very kind, very sympathetic and listened to what I had to say. They then advised me to stay away from the bus stop for my own welfare and to find another way of getting home.'

Lap-dancing clubs are also having a negative impact on UK workplaces – contributing to the sexist workplace culture that I explored earlier in 'Sexism and the City'. At the Fawcett Society we received numerous reports from individual women that, in their jobs, out-of-office socialising and entertaining was taking place in lap-dancing clubs. My colleague Hannah Stapley and I conducted some research to ascertain the prevalence of corporate use of lap-dancing clubs. We surveyed the websites of UK lap-dancing clubs and found 41 per cent specifically tailored their marketing to businesses. Venus Table Dance Club in London advertises a special corporate membership rate of £1,000 per annum, while Peter Stringfellow proudly proclaims on his website, 'Stringfellows

Covent Garden and Peter Stringfellow's Angels Soho are both perfect for your discreet corporate entertaining but still keep their very sexy and exciting edge. OK so you've just done the big deal, or you're about to do the deal but they need that extra little push. So tell me, where are you going to take them to clinch the deal??? Exactly, there's only one choice – either one of my clubs . . .' We were also receiving reports that some lap-dancing clubs provided 'discreet receipts' that customers could then claim back on company expenses without it being apparent where the money had been spent. We contacted London-based lap-dancing clubs to inquire about this facility and found that 86 per cent offered it.

To ascertain the impact of corporate entertaining in lap-dancing clubs on female employees researchers at the University of Michigan conducted a study of the sales industry – a sector in which it had previously been revealed that almost half of all salesmen have reportedly entertained clients in topless bars.[43] They found that women in sales were mostly not invited to the clubs, deceived into not going, or simply told not to come and as a result were denied access to professional information exchange and industry contacts. The researchers found that some women were actually disregarded by employers for certain jobs precisely because it would involve entertaining in lap-dancing clubs. Those women who did accompany colleagues to lap-dancing clubs reported feeling embarrassed and out of place. The increasingly common practice of entertaining staff and clients in this manner puts female employees in an impossible situation. If they don't go they risk jeopardising their career development. If they do, they have to watch their male colleagues and clients treating other women like sexual objects. What this points to, then, is the rather obvious fact that lap-dancing clubs don't exist in a social vacuum. What goes on in the clubs, what they represent, affects society as a whole and cannot be avoided or ignored.

Pimp my mainstream

'Unleash the sex kitten inside . . . simply extend the Peekaboo pole inside the tube, slip on the sexy tunes and away you go!'

The foregoing description is from a pole-dancing kit sold on Tesco's website for £49.97. Following complaints, the store was forced to remove it from the 'toys' section of the site, but the product remained on sale as a 'fitness accessory'.[44]

The sex industry has reached such heights of quantity and profitability that it is spilling over into mainstream culture, influencing both the images we see and the things we do on a day-to-day basis. Media, fitness routines, beauty practices, and even children's toys: all are increasingly taking their inspiration from prostitution, pornography, and stripping. And while these things obviously represent a dilution of the original, this seep into the mainstream helps dissolve boundaries of acceptability and drowns out critique of the sex industry. Lads' mags are prime examples of this. These publications, categorised as 'men's lifestyle magazines', sit neatly alongside home furnishing magazines and children's comics in over 50,000 shops in the UK alone. Magazines such as *FHM* and *Loaded* emerged in the 1990s, and the burgeoning market was joined a decade later by titles including *Nuts* and *Zoo*. It is a lucrative market: even during the current recession 272,545 copies of *FHM* are sold every month in the UK, while 234,034 copies of *Nuts* are sold each week.[45] As part of some research we were conducting at Fawcett I contacted all the major UK supermarkets to inquire what their policies were on the display and sale of lads' mags. All of them assured me they didn't sell 'adult', pornographic titles but, yes, they did sell lads' mags. And there lies the success behind the lads' mags market: they have managed to evade the top shelf by declaring themselves not to be porn magazines. But just a quick glance at the cover of a lads' mag unmasks that as a wholly incredible claim. My colleagues and I did a content analysis of six popular lads' mags and found they all had pornographic imagery in them – images designed primarily to sexually arouse the reader. While women's genitalia are covered by hands, clothes, or other women's bodies, their breasts are routinely exposed in lads' mags and the poses, pouts, props, and positioning all derive from pornography.

Attempts to pass lads' mags off as 'general interest' or 'lifestyle' aren't just restricted to their positions on the supermarket shelves and the publishers' descriptions on the back. Annabelle Mooney, a senior lecturer at Roehampton University, has pointed out that the pornographic content is subtly normalised and made part of the everyday within the magazine itself. For example, a staple of lads' mags is pornographic spreads and features where the models are presented as 'real women' – i.e. not professional models but authentic, accessible women who have contacted the magazine. *FHM* run an annual 'High Street Honeys' competition while *Nuts* has a weekly feature called 'Real Girls UK' – and both make the pornographic content normal by using 'normal' women. Lads' mags also borrow features from women's and more general lifestyle magazines, like letters pages, film and book reviews and TV listings.

Features such as these, and direct references to other mainstream magazines, put a veil over the pornographic content of lads' mags and ensure they can sit quietly on supermarket shelves next to *Woman's Own* and *Grazia*. It is a strategy that has proved remarkably successful. In 2007 Ofsted, the UK schools inspectorate, commended the sexually explicit content in lads' mags such as *Nuts*, claiming that they offer a 'very positive source of advice and reassurance for many young people' despite 'at times reinforcing sexist attitudes'.[46]

The portrayal of women as sex objects on billboards and in shop windows is now a staple tool in the advertisers' repertoire. In 2008 researchers at Wesleyan University analysed 1988 advertisements from fifty-eight popular magazines in the US and found that 50 per cent of ads featuring women portrayed them as sex objects.[47] Women were most likely to be portrayed as sex objects in men's magazines, followed by women's fashion and adolescent girls' magazines. Similarly researchers at Old Dominion University in the US found that female-only characters were significantly more likely than male-only characters to feature in magazine ads where sex was used to sell the product (51 per cent versus 13 per cent) and that, where a single character was featured, 33 per cent of females were objectified while only 2 per cent of males were similarly dehumanised.[48] The aviation industry in particular seems to exemplify the predilection of advertisers to portray women as sex objects. Ryanair ran an advert showing an adult model dressed up as a 'sexy schoolgirl' to highlight its 'HOTTEST BACK TO SCHOOL FARES', and a clip from a media conference held by the firm received the accolade of being the 'most viewed' on YouTube after a Ryanair spokesperson informed assembled journalists that the working title for their new business-class service was 'Beds and Blowjobs'.[49] Also keeping to the theme is the American company Southwest Airlines, which in 2009 covered the length of one of their Boeing 737s in a magnified image of supermodel Bar Refaeli lying in a bikini. The stunt was part of a promotional deal with *Sports Illustrated*'s 'swimsuit issue'.[50] Sexualised images and direct references to the sex industry are also common fodder in music videos. Britney Spears pole dances in the video for her song 'Gimme More', as does Kate Moss in a White Stripes video. Destiny's Child gave lap dances live on stage to three famous audience members at an awards ceremony they were performing at, while singer Ciara did the same for Justin Timberlake in the video for her song, 'Love, Sex and Magic'.

But what of it? 'Sex sells' – surely everyone knows that? Well, 'sexism sells' would be a more accurate description of this trend, because a wealth of evidence shows that the portrayal of women as sex objects in the media causes acute harm. Princeton University psychologist Susan Fiske took brain scans of heterosexual men while they looked at sexualised images of women wearing bikinis.[51] She found that the part of their brains that became activated was pre-motor – areas that usually light up when people anticipate using tools. The men were reacting to the images as if the women were objects they were going to act on. Particularly shocking was the discovery that the participants who scored highest on tests of hostile sexism were those most likely to deactivate the part of the brain that considers other people's intentions (the medial prefrontal cortex) while looking at the pictures. These men were responding to images of the women as if they were non-human. The American

Psychological Association also report a range of studies showing that viewing media which portrays women as sex objects leads people to become significantly more accepting of gender stereotyping, sexual harassment, interpersonal violence, and rape myths.[52] Men's behaviour towards women has also been shown to become more sexualised after exposure to this media, so they actually treat women in the way they are portrayed – like sex objects.

Not only is the sex industry increasingly within our line of gaze, but it is also starting to guide our choice of leisure activities, clothes, and beauty practices. More and more leisure centres offer pole-dancing classes as a way for women to get fit. In 2009 a college in south Devon hosted two demonstrations of pole dancing for its fourteen- to nineteen-year-old students as part of its 'Be Healthy Week'.[53] Burlesque has also been experiencing a revival since the 1990s. But according to Laurie Penny, who became the headline act in a burlesque troupe when she was eighteen years old, it 'differs from lap dancing less and less these days'. Laurie originally started performing in burlesque in a bid to improve her body image: 'I was so desperate for self-esteem anywhere I could grab it that sexual performance seemed to fill the hole, just a little bit.' Yet despite proclamations of contemporary burlesque being 'subversive' and 'artistic', Laurie, now twenty-two and no longer performing in burlesque, believes it only really differs from stripping on one main measure: class. She says, 'Burlesque has become a sanctioned way for middle-class women to get involved in self-objectification.' There would also seem to be the assumption at play that because the clothes the women are stripping off are from previous decades this somehow makes the performance 'ironic' and defuses it of sexism. Retro it may be, but it is still 'retro sexism'.

As 'Mirror, Mirror on the Wall' explored, women's beauty practices are guided by ideals – and increasingly these are reflecting the standards and norms portrayed by women in pornography. In most contemporary porn women don't have pubic hair. In fact, so dominant is the pre-pubescent-like image of women with hairless vaginas that pornography consumers sometimes have to select an 'unshaven' category to see it, alongside categories for 'big tits' and 'anal'. And it's no coincidence that the Brazilian bikini wax, which involves removing the hair from the entire pubic region aside from a small patch just above the vaginal area, has become a staple on the menu of the average beauty salon. Women's fashion is borrowing from pornography too, and it is a trend that I can personally recall influencing my fashion choices as a teenager. I remember thinking nothing of it while shopping in Topshop for clothes to take to uni when my friend bought a hoodie that had the words 'pornstar' emblazoned across the front. I also remember sometimes wearing a see-through top without a bra when I went clubbing. The magazines I read and videos I watched were full of women dressing like this, so the thought of wearing a dress with a zip down to my belly button (and no bra) really didn't seem to me to be a big deal. I wasn't dressing this way to show how 'up for it' I was, to make myself feel 'powerful', or to 'creatively express my sexuality'. I just wanted to look OK, hopefully even 'nice'. And making yourself look like a sex object was just how I understood you were supposed to achieve this.

In fact, young girls are one of the targets as the sex industry marches into the mainstream. Abercrombie and Fitch developed a line of thongs for ten-year-olds with the words 'wink, wink' emblazoned on them, and the UK firm Bhs brought out a 'Little Miss Naughty' clothing range, which included push-up bras for pre-teens.[54] Thousands of young girls also now own bright pink pencils, pencil cases, duvet covers, and bedside lamps which bear the emblem of a cute little bunny on them. That bunny is the logo of a pornography empire, yet Playboy's children's products are now commonly stocked by high street stationers, department stores, and toyshops. Sadly, it is of little surprise, then, that when mobile entertainment providers The Lab surveyed 1,000 UK young women aged fifteen to nineteen in 2005 about their ambitions, 63 per cent said they would rather be a glamour model than a nurse, a doctor or a teacher. And while just 3 per cent aspired to a teaching role, a quarter thought lap dancing was an appealing profession.[55]

The mainstreaming of the sex industry provides pornography, prostitution and lap dancing with an alibi, creating the illusion of benign normality. Because surely if pornography really was so deeply misogynist then five-year-olds wouldn't be sleeping under Playboy duvets. And lap-dancing clubs can't be that oppressive to women if Britney Spears is singing about how good stripping feels and the Pussycat Dolls are pole dancing while singing about how empowered they are. The disturbing reality behind all of this is that young girls are being what can only be described as groomed by mainstream culture to be sexualised. They are learning that sexuality is a performance they must act out for others, not a genuine desire of their own. Young boys are taught that women are sexual objects that you do things to, not human beings to be treated with respect and dignity like themselves. And all the while, the industry of sexual exploitation continues to grow.

22:57 | Bedroom Politics:

Reproductive Rights and Wrongs

Latisha very gently pulls Sean's door shut. It's the second time this evening she's had to take him back to bed, and she knows when Andy gets home that's bound to wake him up again. When she found out two years ago she was pregnant Andy had promised he would do his fair share of the caring when the baby came. But tonight is the third night in a row he's gone to the pub with his mates, while Latisha hasn't been out once in the last six weeks. 'He can have his own life; I'm stuck with that child for the rest of my life. I know that sounds really horrible, but I'm stuck with that child. He'll say I'm going to such and such, see you later. But I'm like, "What about me? What if I want to go out? They're your kids n'all."' Even when he does stay in he doesn't help much. 'He's at work ten till seven and is like, "he's done his chores". He's been at work for the day and life stops there.' Latisha is getting increasingly frustrated by how old-fashioned it feels. 'He comes home from work and is like, "I go to work and I expect my dinner on the table." Then he just lays on the sofa and is ready for bed.'

   I was introduced to Latisha by the young women's organisation YWCA, which provides support to socio-economically disadvantaged young mothers. Latisha and Andy struggle with money, though Latisha has got budgeting

down to a fine art. On a good week, once they've accounted
for bills, food shopping, and necessities for Sean, they usually have about £5 left over. Despite their best efforts, however, the debt is mounting up. 'When you start to think
about how much you're actually in debt you're like, woah.
I get worried. I don't sleep, I don't eat.' Latisha wants to
go through the pile of bills on her living-room table, and
Andy said he'd be back early to go through them with her
but it's now quarter to eleven. She reaches for the remote
and starts aimlessly flicking through the channels. This isn't
how she imagined she would be spending her evenings as
a twenty-year-old. All her friends would probably be at the
pub now as well, but they've stopped bothering to ask
Latisha along as she always has to say no.

Latisha was still in college when she found out she was
pregnant, and to say it was a shock is an understatement.
Sex-education lessons at school had done little to prepare
her. 'They were absolutely rubbish. When I left school I
knew nothing about sex.' Despite not losing her virginity
until college, she had a 'reputation' at school. 'I was known
as one of the biggest sluts in my year and I hadn't even
done nothing with any boy.' She hadn't even particularly
wanted to lose her virginity when she did, but her boyfriend
at the time had been pressuring her for weeks. Her friends
weren't much help either. 'I could've waited but everyone
was sort of saying, "Go on, we've all done it." I had my
own mind, but I was so young.'

Latisha adores Sean and wouldn't change him for the
world. But she does wish she could have had him a few
years later. But her mum and boyfriend were against the
idea of Latisha having an abortion. Latisha, on the other
hand, believes 'at the end of the day it's everyone's deci-

sion'. But she didn't want them to think badly of her, and had herself recently come across an anti-abortion group campaigning in her town centre: 'Those people in the high street . . . They bring [a] foetus that looks like a baby. They stand there and they grab you over. It looked like a real baby.' That image had stuck in her mind, and in the circumstances she decided she ought to go ahead with the pregnancy.

As usual, there's nothing decent on telly, so she grabs one of the childcare course brochures from the coffee table, sits down at the small round dining table they have squeezed into the corner of the living room, and half-heartedly leafs through it. She's been thinking for a while now about training to be a nursery worker. Ideally she would like to do veterinary nursing, but there's just no way she could fit in the training and work around caring for Sean. Nursery work is a lot more flexible, but the pay makes it seem hardly worth doing. The average pay for workers in full day care is £6.90 per hour.[1] Any kind of a career feels a long way off right now though. It's nearly eleven o'clock, Andy's not home, the bills aren't sorted out, tomorrow she's got a list of chores as long as her arm to get through, and right now she's absolutely knackered. So at 22:57 Latisha walks over to the living-room door, switches out the light and goes to get changed for bed, ready to start another day much the same as today.

Women's reproductive capacity – and the need for individual women to have full control over their own – is fundamental to feminism. Unless a woman can control her sexual, reproductive, and maternal life (if, when, and who she has sex with; if, when, and how many children she has, and being able to care for her children without suffering societal penalties), her ability to access other fundamental human rights is severely jeopardised. Without this control, women are unable to participate in society as citizens equal to men. The long list of positive outcomes that stem from women having control over their own bodies and reproductive capacity includes the reduction of poverty, improved health, environmental sustainability, enhanced education, and – of course – gender equality. For example, frequent and multiple births limit women's ability to do paid work and make them more physically vulnerable to complications during childbirth – putting them at higher risk of maternal death.[2] The World Health Organisation state that 'the reproduction revolution – the shift from six births, of whom several might die, to around two births, nearly all of whom survive – represents the most important step towards achievement of gender equality by boosting women's opportunities for non-domestic activities'.[3] And, especially in developing countries, reproductive and sexual rights are crucial to accessing even the most basic of rights: that of the right to life. In 2003, 504 million women living in developing countries used modern contraceptive methods, thereby preventing 187 million unintentional pregnancies, 215,000 deaths from pregnancy-related causes, and 79,000 deaths from unsafe abortions. In fact, Sarah Blaffer Hrdy, Professor Emerita of Anthropology at the University of California Davis, suggests in her book *Mother Nature* that women's control over their own reproduction has been crucial to human evolution: 'the single most important source of variation in female reproductive success is not how many young are born; what matters is how many survive and grow up to reproduce themselves. For such creatures, survival of at least some young requires reproductive discretion. This is why being pro-life means being pro-choice.'[4]

Latisha was born in the UK thirty years after the much-vaunted 'sexual revolution' began. The social changes during the 1960s were lauded as a key to unlocking women's reproductive rights – and even women's rights as a whole. In the UK, abortion was decriminalised and contraception made more readily available. The approach to sex education became more liberal, sexual relationships outside marriage began to be more accepted, and sex started to be talked about more openly and freely. So far, so good. But in her book *Anticlimax*, Professor Sheila Jeffreys from the University of Melbourne argues that the sexual revolution wasn't all it was cracked up to be.[5] For one, it was largely heterosexual. While these social developments provided a fertile landscape for the development of the gay rights movement, the scant coverage given over to homosexuality in the 'manuals' of the revolution such as *The Joy of Sex* belies the apparent inclusive, tolerant nature of this social transformation. And, crucially, she proposes the greatest benefactor of the revolution wasn't women, but the international sex industry, which was greeted as sexual liberation.[6]

It can sometimes seem like the sexual revolution was a success because today 'sex' is all around us – freely discussed and portrayed on billboards, in newspapers and magazines, and on computer and TV screens. We couldn't be 'freer'. But, as I argued in the previous chapter, closer inspection reveals that what is often referred to as 'sex' or 'sexualisation' in society is in fact the sexual objectification of women; women made (or unmade) into dehumanised sex objects. Today we live in a society saturated by pornography; a society where women are still subject to a sexual 'double standard'; where a staggering proportion of women and girls have complied with unwanted sex; where women still don't have full control over contraception and abortion; and where women and men are straitjacketed by outdated stereotypes about whose role it is to do the caring once children are born. While the sexual revolution brought sex on to our TV screens, it failed to unpick unequal sexual power relations. Sex – and its potential consequence, reproduction – do not take place within a social vacuum. Unequal power relations between women and men remain an influential feature of every societal sphere – including the bedroom. So, for example, easy access to contraception can mean little for a girl if her boyfriend says he'll dump her if she doesn't agree to sex without a condom. In Latisha's case she found herself pressured into sex, discouraged from having an abortion, expected to do most of the childcare, and paying a 'poverty penalty' for having a child. It might be easy to dismiss Latisha's current situation simply as the result of some unwise choices. But we have to recognise that Latisha's experiences are not unique, rather they are part of a much greater pattern of women being denied their full reproductive rights – a pattern driven by gender inequality and hidden by the equality illusion.

Not tonight

Despite the much vaunted sexual revolution, a high proportion of women and girls continue to acquiesce to sex they don't actually want to have. I'm not writing here about rape as defined in law, but a subtler form of coercion that stems from sexual stereotypes and unequal power relations. Jennifer Katz and Vanessa Tirone at SUNY College at Geneseo found in 2008 that over one-third of sexually active women in heterosexual relationships had agreed to unwanted sex,[7] something the psychologists described as a form of 'self-sacrifice' or 'voluntary sexual submission'. Each night a disturbing number of women go to bed to find themselves coerced into sex they don't want to be having. And it is very much a gendered phenomenon, with significantly more women than men complying with sexual activity that they don't want. Researchers at the University of Buffalo asked women who had had unwanted sex what their motivation for complying was and found that many spoke of feeling obliged to satisfy their partner's sexual wishes.[8] Other reasons included believing their partner is beyond 'the point of no return' or being pressured by their partner. Charlotte found herself regularly complying with her ex-boyfriend's sexual requests: 'I had a lot of problems with my body in terms of pain and often couldn't have sex without it hurting, but it got to the point where I would let him "finish" because I knew that if I didn't he would guilt me into doing something alternative for/to him despite being in pain and not getting any sexual pleasure myself. I hated this so much and I would be really distressed but he really didn't seem to care.' Charlotte isn't alone in feeling the negative effects of 'complying'. Research has shown that 65 per cent of women who comply with unwanted sexual activity experience physical and emotional discomfort, relationship tension or other harmful consequences.[9] When the traditional gender roles of feminine passivity and masculine agency play out in the bedroom they can do serious damage.

In 2006 researchers at Rutgers University and the University of California found that, at a subconscious level, women tend not to associate sex with active and equal participation in sexual or emotional pleasure, but instead associate it with submission to their sexual partner (revealed by testing through a word-association experiment).[10] And the consequences of this aren't 'all in the head'. Women who experience less autonomy and agency in sexual relationships report greater sexual dissatisfaction – feeling less aroused and finding it more difficult to reach orgasm. This link between sex and submission also exists amongst women at a conscious level. In 2002 researchers in the US found that 78 per cent of adolescent and young adult women agreed that they should always be able 'to make their own decisions about sexual activity, regardless of their partner's wishes'. However, further questioning revealed that nearly half of these same women and girls didn't think such autonomy extended to the right 'to stop foreplay at any time, including at the point of intercourse', 'to tell a partner he is being too rough', or 'to tell a partner "I want to make love differently"'.[11]

Sadly, it makes sense that so many girls and women feel disempowered when it comes to sex. They are correctly reading the dominant meaning of sex in modern culture. As I've already shown in relation to violence against women and pornography, for those aspiring to be 'real men', sex is a conquest. He 'does it to her', 'takes her', 'has her', or 'scores'; i.e. he is the one in control. Lads' mags are littered with evidence of this (despite proclamations that the women they feature are sexually liberated, empowered individuals). To introduce a ten-page topless spread in *ZOO* titled 'Britain's Boobiest Babes', the writers make clear just who are the ones in control: 'You can smile again, gentlemen, because just as the country's been stripped of cash, we've stripped Ms Brady of her clothes.' The subtitle of another topless feature in the same edition reads, 'ZOO persuades another campus cutie to undress!'[12] In addition there is, of course, still a huge sexual double standard between women and men, which is intimately connected to this idea of men acting and women being acted upon when it comes to sex. I asked some young women at a YWCA group about the double standard. Their response was unanimous: 'It's always been like that.' They said girls thought they risked being labelled a slut if they slept with a boy, but the opposite wasn't true: 'Boys can sleep with ten girls in a night and no one would give a fuck. It doesn't matter to them.' The asymmetry of this sexual status is crucial. The more a man has sex, or the 'further he gets' with a woman, the more he has conquered and therefore the more manly he is. The more a woman has sex, the more often she has been conquered. She is thus a cheaper, easier target, a victim – therefore a loser in the situation.

The pressures on women in the bedroom each night are only intensified by pornography. Expectations about sexual behaviour have been influenced by pornography in the same way that expectations about beauty and bodies have been. 'I felt a lot of pressure to look like those women, and act like those women as well, and as a result our sexual relationship didn't have any intimacy at all because I spent the whole time trying to please him and trying to appear as if I was this porn queen who could come at the slightest touch and who wasn't really there for my own gratification but solely for his.' Jo had felt like there must be something wrong with her for feeling distressed about pornography being used in her sexual relationship. 'He would say that I was a prude for being uncomfortable with [pornographic magazines], or that if I had sex with him more often he wouldn't need to look at them. It got to a point where I was buying the mags for him, just so that I could prove that I was "OK" with it and that I was modern and hip and not old and prudish. I just didn't have the ability to truly verbalise the things I felt about pornography, and how it affected my self-esteem or how I felt it reflected on women.'

A survey of 15,246 adults in the US by researchers at the University of Southern California found that men who used pornography reported being significantly more critical of their partner's body as a result.[13] This is something another interviewee – Stacey – experienced with a previous boyfriend. 'He convinced me that it would be a good idea to shave off my pubic hair. We went to Asda especially to get a razor with protective bars across the blades, so I wouldn't cut myself, and some shaving foam. Given that I already had problems with pain in that area and had had several infections during our relationship it wasn't the greatest idea! I gained nothing from doing this. And it felt weird because I had always had hair and since then always have.' Women I interviewed also reported feeling pressured to perform sexual acts their boyfriends had seen in pornography. Holly recalled from a past relationship, 'He became obsessed for a while that he should cum in my face, which is for me an utterly unattractive enterprise. I kept refusing (as you can imagine) and that became something of a contention; if you can believe it, he acted like I was denying him his rights!' Kacie similarly felt pressured by a boyfriend: 'He would use porn to distance himself from me and would expect me to behave like a porn star. If I didn't then I would get rejected and he'd use porn instead. By the end of the relationship he was using porn daily and we'd stopped having sex.' The pressure that many women feel to acquiesce to sex, and the entitlement that some men feel to have sex (and in particular ways), are deeply personal experiences. But they are also deeply political. This common scenario hasn't randomly appeared from nowhere. It has emerged from a cultural backdrop in which men are encouraged to sexually conquer women. It is the entrenched notions of masculine/active, feminine/passive being played out in the bedroom, with damaging effect.

Faithful

'I just think that abstinence is the only way you can effectively, 100 per cent foolproof way you can prevent pregnancy' (Bristol Palin)[14]

Bristol Palin is the daughter of former Alaskan governor and vice-presidential candidate Sarah Palin. Her pregnancy at the age of seventeen caused controversy during the 2008 US presidential elections not only as a piece of political gossip but also because Sarah Palin is a vocal campaigner for abstinence before marriage. Bristol went on to become an advocate for teenage abstinence herself, assuming a prominent role in what feminist author and blogger Jessica Valenti terms 'the virginity movement', which advocates against sex before marriage and proscribes teaching children about any form of birth control other than abstinence. Bristol's situation highlights the absurdity and ineffectiveness of this approach to birth control, but it is still hugely influential in the American education system and also in parts of the UK school system. Driven by conservatives and evangelical Christians, the virginity movement has transformed the sex-education landscape in the US and seriously undermined women's and girls' control over their own reproductive health. In addition, behind the virginity movement lie many damaging assumptions about sexuality, gender and control. In light of this, it is perhaps no surprise that over half of all women in the US aged between fifteen and forty-four have had at least one unintended pregnancy.[15] Among economically disadvantaged women the rate is four times higher than among the rest of the female population. Access to contraception and comprehensive, accurate information about sex are crucial to the ability of girls and women to control their reproductive lives, yet this access is today being challenged on multiple fronts in both the US and the UK.

By 2000 only 55 per cent of teachers in US high schools and just 21 per cent of those in junior high schools taught pupils how to use a condom.[16] However, 96 per cent of high schools and 92 per cent of middle and junior high schools were teaching abstinence as the best way to avoid sexually transmitted diseases (STDs), HIV and pregnancy. (Theoretically, of course, this is correct. But as I argue later, it is a wholly inadequate prevention strategy in reality.) In financial year 2005/6 the US government allocated $168 million in federal funding to abstinence-only education programmes. A common funding condition of these programmes is that no information on contraceptive services or sexual orientation is to be provided. The federal regulations themselves are steeped in culturally specific morality. An abstinence-only programme must teach that 'a mutually faithful monogamous relationship in context of marriage is the expected standard of human sexual activity'.[17] Same-sex marriage is excluded from this definition, and it is taught that harmful psychological effects are a likely consequence of sex outside marriage. In fact, a review of US abstinence-only policies and programmes found they largely ignore the issue of homosexuality except when discussing how HIV/AIDS is transmitted. Gender stereotypes also abound in the teachings, with men framed as being ruled by their sexual urges, thereby requiring women to act as sexual 'gatekeepers'.[18] Here again, we can see the gender ideology of male/active, female/passive being played out. He is the doer, she is the receiver – and yet she is the one held to account for birth control.

Accompanying the abstinence-only education in the classroom are a growing number of social initiatives aimed at amplifying the message. An estimated 4,000 purity events were held in the US in 2007,[19] including father–daughter purity balls, which commonly involve daughters pledging their abstinence until marriage before their own and the other assembled fathers, while fathers also commonly make declarations 'before God to cover my daughter as her authority and protection in the area of purity'.[20] Of course, you would be hard-pressed to find a father–son or mother–son purity ball – and this underlines how the cultural notions of both girls/women as sexual gatekeepers and male ownership of female sexuality lurk behind the ceremonies. Purity rings are another way young women and men can demonstrate their commitment to abstinence until marriage, as worn by *Hannah Montana* star Miley Cyrus. The Silver Ring Thing, a US programme begun in 1995, has alone bestowed rings on 110,000 students.

The problem is, abstinence-only education doesn't actually work. There is no evidence it has any success in delaying the initiation of intercourse. In fact, Add Health data show that people who took virginity pledges were less likely to use contraception when they did go on to have sex – so their sexual health was endangered.[21] A review of commonly used abstinence-only education programmes conducted by minority staff of the Committee on Government Reform of the US House of Representatives found that there was information on reproductive health in eleven out of thirteen curricula which was false, misleading or distorted. The full impact of the abstinence movement on young women's sexual and reproductive autonomy will probably never be fully quantifiable. Happily, however, there have been recent moves in the US to roll back the tide of ineffective abstinence-only programmes. In May 2009 President Barack Obama announced in the 2010 budget that most US federal funding for abstinence-only education is to be eliminated.[22]

Unlike in the US, a strong abstinence movement hasn't yet taken hold in the UK and in 2009 the government announced sex education (or personal, social and health education – PSHE) is to be compulsory for school pupils from the age of five. However, the government's proposals include a clause that will allow faith schools to teach against homosexuality, sex outside of marriage and using contraception.[23] The plans enable this by including a clause that allows religious schools to teach the lessons in line with their religion's 'context, values and ethos'.[24] The British Humanist Association report that approximately one-third of all state-funded schools in Britain are 'faith' schools or schools 'with a religious character'.[25] Approximately 1.75 million children will be affected by this provision.[26] The government's plans also continue to allow parents to withdraw their children from sex-education lessons on religious grounds.

Regardless of the complicating role of religion, however,

gender inequality – and the constructs of masculinity and femininity – act as a barrier to contraception everywhere. As I've explored in previous chapters, boys' relations with other boys play a central role in their lives, and the main source of boys' information about sex is their male peers. Researchers at Nottingham Trent University have found that they are far less likely than girls to turn to teachers for information on sexual matters, and are more likely to actively try and disrupt sex education lessons at school.[27] This is likely to compromise the quality of sex education they receive. In addition to their peers, many boys also get information about sex from pornography. A Channel 4 survey of over four hundred pupils aged between fourteen and seventeen found that three in ten said they learned about sex from porn.[28] Quite aside from the very damaging effect pornography usage has been found to have on attitudes and behaviour, it is worth noting that condoms are very rarely used in pornography.

Even when women are fully informed about and can access contraception, some still don't use it. Researchers have shown that women are more willing to risk their sexual health than they are to risk the disapproval or embarrassment involved in either purchasing a condom or asking a partner to use one.[29] Just as gender inequality creates pressures on women to please or submit to their sexual partner, it can also disempower them when it comes to using contraception. A study by sociologist Jennifer Pearson at the University of Texas revealed that adolescents who don't feel a sense of control over their sex lives are less likely to use condoms if they have sex,[30] and multi-country studies have shown that the single greatest predictor of whether women will use contraception is whether their partner approves.[31] Furthermore, where women are subject to intimate partner violence, their reproductive rights are frequently denied. Women who have an unintended pregnancy are approximately two and a half times more likely to have experienced physical violence around the time they became pregnant.[32] Just as reproductive rights are crucial to gender equality, so gender equality is crucial to women realising their reproductive rights.

She decides

Worldwide, approximately 25 per cent of all pregnancies end in abortion and a third of all women will have one during their lifetime.[33] There is a wide range of reasons that women decide to have an abortion. Olivia, for example, was eighteen when she became pregnant. She had just finished her A-levels and was looking forward to starting university later that year. 'When I found out I was pregnant I was suicidal. I imagined how I would try and abort the baby myself if the doctor couldn't help me, otherwise I planned on taking an overdose. I do not want children. I would not have been able to support the child.' For Olivia, the abortion offered a means of keeping 'the life I had planned and wanted'. After the procedure, 'I was so happy and relieved, the best word to describe how I was feeling is elation – all of my problems had gone and I knew I could keep on living . . . I still think that this was the best decision I had ever made and I have not regretted it for a day.' Mel was in an abusive relationship when she became pregnant: 'He was very controlling and I was scared of him really. [I] was terrified of being tied to him for ever and ending up struggling at the same time.' Mel already had five children at the time and was experiencing health problems. 'Medication that could help [the illness] would harm the fetus and also I was advised that my pregnancy and childbirth would be difficult. It was also suspected that the fetus was "abnormal" . . . I was not willing to risk my health [and] the well-being of my existing family to bring a human into the world who had less than full quality of life. I consider my decision the act of being a good mother.'

For Kerri, her pregnancy had been the result of a one-night stand when she was eighteen: 'I'd acquiesced in having sex rather than actively wanting it. I didn't want to have further contact with the man and certainly not to have a life-long link to him through a child . . . I didn't want a child and didn't think I could cope raising one alone and living a very different sort of life than the one I had planned.' Then there was Mani, who was living with her partner 'in a rather grotty one-bed rented flat' at the time she became pregnant. They knew that they wanted children together one day, but not then. For Mani, it was a straightforward decision. She felt 'it would not be fair to raise a child in those circumstances and that we would make a very bad job of it'. Six years later, Mani and her partner now have two children. 'We have a good life and have devoted ourselves to our kids . . . both taking equal responsibility for childcare and domestic life. We feel very lucky that life has panned out so well.'

The decision to have an abortion is, of course, a serious one, as it has huge implications for a woman's life, and none of the dozens of women who shared their experience of abortion with me suggested that she had taken it lightly. A key theme to emerge amongst my interviewees was their deep feeling of responsibility to avoid bringing an unwanted child into the world, or one for whom they felt unable to provide an adequate quality of life. When I asked how they had felt after having an abortion, a commonly expressed emotion was relief: 'I felt the most immense relief I think I've ever felt. I felt like I could enjoy my life again'; 'Immediately after, I was hit with a massive sense of relief, almost epiphany like. I was fourteen again and could be fourteen again instead of being as stressed as I was'; 'Both times afterwards I felt a massive sense of relief that it was all over and cried only because I was relieved that what I had had to keep secret for weeks had now come to an end.'

Sadly, another theme to emerge was the stigma that is still associated with abortion. Many of the women had told only their closest friends and family about it and were nervous about telling other people. In fact, when Olivia's mum found out she'd had an abortion, 'she called me names, told me I was a slut and that I was wrong. She has a Catholic background and very strong convictions.' The reluctance of some women to reveal that they have had an abortion is not surprising, given that only 29 per cent of seventeen-year-olds in the UK say they are strongly pro-choice. The majority are either ambivalent or negative about a woman's right to an abortion.[34] Nicky was seventeen years old when she first fell pregnant and chose to have an abortion. Now thirty-four and with one child, she is more convinced than ever of the need for women to be able to access abortion: 'I feel sick at the prospect of losing such hard-won rights . . . I think women of my generation have become too complacent about these issues and the rights which previous generations fought for are being eroded so subtly we won't know it's happened until we need to invoke them.'

Being able to obtain an abortion is a crucial aspect of

reproductive rights – and therefore gender equality – but it is also an aspect of the universal right to control over one's own body, whether male or female. Access to a safe abortion is enshrined in international human rights law because it is necessary for reproductive self-determination – implicitly guaranteed in the human rights to physical integrity, liberty, privacy and family life. Reproductive self-determination is also explicitly guaranteed in the Convention on the Elimination of all forms of Discrimination Against Women (CEDAW) – the international bill of rights for women. In discussing abortion rights and how they relate to wider human rights issues, bioethicist Donna Dickenson points out that 'no competent adult other than a pregnant woman can be forced to submit to pain and suffering on behalf of another person'[35] – and the fetus isn't even a person, only a potential one which goes on to become an independent human being solely because of a woman's willingness to labour arduously for it – both physically and emotionally – during pregnancy and childbirth. And as *Guardian* journalist Zoe Williams puts it, 'if you do not consider the fetus human, then [abortion] becomes no more of an issue than getting a tumour removed . . . I do not consider a fetus which a woman has a one in three chance of involuntarily rejecting anyway to be a viable life unless she deems it so.'[36] But even putting this medical context aside, being able to have an unwanted fetus removed is crucial to a woman's human rights regarding her own body. The labour required in pregnancy and childbirth entails real costs and serious risks to health and well-being. If a woman is forced to do this against her will, it is no exaggeration to say that she is fundamentally enslaved.

Yet despite these international proclamations, now more

than ever we need to defend the right of women to seek a legal, safe, free abortion and ensure that every woman and girl knows that it is her decision whether or not she has one, and hers alone. A lack of access to reproductive health services means that nearly half of all abortions are performed in unsafe conditions, almost all in developing countries. The World Bank estimates that 5.1 million women are permanently disabled or left infertile and 68,000 women die each year as a result of unsafe abortions.[37] This problem was exacerbated by the US's 'global gag rule', reimposed by George W. Bush in 2001 and eventually rescinded by Barack Obama in 2009. The ruling prevented US funding going to international family planning and population assistance organisations that provided information about abortion to its service users and was described by Marie Stopes International as 'an unmitigated disaster for the world's poorest women'.[38]

Furthermore, 26 per cent of the world's population live in countries where routine abortion is illegal.[39] Indeed, where Catholicism has traditionally been dominant, strict abortion laws are still the norm.[40] In 2009 the family and doctors of a nine-year-old girl living in Brazil were excommunicated after the girl had an abortion. She had become pregnant after being raped by her stepfather.[41] Yet a 2007 study by the World Health Organisation and the Guttmacher Institute revealed women are just as likely to get an abortion whether it is legal or not.[42] The most severely restrictive abortion laws can be found in Latin America – along with the highest rate of clandestine abortions.[43]

Even in countries where previous campaigns for legal abortion have been successful, that right is increasingly coming under fire. Between 2004 and 2007, thirty-eight abortion bans were introduced in the US in seventeen separate states. These bans cannot take effect because of the federal legal ruling of *Roe* vs *Wade* (which legalised abortion in the US), but they have been introduced as 'bans in waiting' or as attempts to trigger a Supreme Court challenge. If *Roe* were overturned it is predicted that thirty US states would be likely to restrict or outlaw abortion.[44] Another major challenge in the US came in 2007 when the Supreme Court upheld the Partial Birth Abortion Ban Act, originally adopted in 2003, as constitutional. The US charity Center for Reproductive Rights point out that 'Partial-birth abortion' does not refer to any specific medical procedure, it is not a medical term, and it allows no exemptions to protect a woman's health. Depending on interpretation, the legislation has the potential to limit a range of abortion procedures, including those performed early in the second trimester of pregnancy.[45] Medical professionals who carry out abortions in America are also often the targets of violence. In May 2009 George Tiller, one of the few doctors in the US who provided 'late-term' therapeutic abortions (performed to preserve the health of the woman), was murdered while he attended church. (The alleged killer was an anti-abortion activist.) But this wasn't the first attempt on Tiller's life: in 1993 he survived an assassination attempt,[46] his clinic had been bombed in 1985, and he and fellow staff wore bulletproof vests to work each day. In the context of increasingly inflammatory and violent words and action by mainstream anti-abortion groups his murder was shocking, but not surprising. Even in those countries where abortion is legal, it is a right that is under constant attack.

Abortion is generally thought of as less contentious in

the UK, yet it is increasingly being challenged there. In Northern Ireland it remains illegal to have an abortion except under exceptional circumstances. The 1967 Abortion Act – which applies to England, Wales and Scotland – has never been extended there. Since that Act was passed over 50,000 women have been forced to travel from the province to England or other European countries and pay for an abortion. This, of course, has huge class implications. An abortion can cost between £600 and £2,000. Add that to travel and accommodation expenses and a woman's economic status can dictate whether or not she is forced to continue with an unwanted pregnancy. Even in England, Wales and Scotland, the right to abortion is under threat. In 2008 all but one of the Conservative Party front bench voted (unsuccessfully on that occasion) to reduce the upper time limit of twenty-four weeks for abortions in the UK.[47] The focus on so-called 'late-term' abortions has been a particularly effective tactic of anti-abortion campaigners, despite the fact that only 1.4 per cent of abortions take place after nineteen weeks. The reasons that women have abortions after nineteen weeks include delays in suspecting and confirming they were pregnant. Nearly 90 per cent of abortions are conducted in the first twelve weeks.[48]

These legal challenges have been supported by a wide-ranging propaganda campaign by anti-abortion advocates. For Latisha, whose story opened this chapter, seeing anti-abortion campaigners in her town centre had a considerable impact – and it appears she is not alone. In May 2009 it was revealed that for the first time since 1995 (when Gallup Polls began assessing relative support for abortion) the majority of adults in the US identify themselves as pro-life. In the UK, anti-abortion organisations have been targeting young people in particular with their message. In 2008 the Society for the Protection of the Unborn Child offered its educational PowerPoint presentation to every secondary school in the country.[49] During 2007–8 the UK charity Life gave 810 talks in UK schools and colleges, claiming to have reached 38,000 young people.[50] They have even begun to deliver 'Life Before Birth' presentations to children in Year 6. According to Life's website, these talks are 'designed to give them information about the beginning of human life and the development of the unborn child'.[51] The presentation preview on their website features graphic 4D images of the fetus and ends with the assertion, 'When the baby is born it has been alive for 9 months. What changes at birth is its environment and location, not his status as a human being.' What the children presumably won't be told in their presentation is that while part of the woman's body, the collection of cells that make up the fetus at no point achieve consciousness, or that, as Stuart Derbyshire concludes in the *British Medical Journal*, 'it is not possible for a fetus to experience pain'.[52] Life allege a causal link between abortion and sterility and also provide a 'post abortion counselling service' for the 'many women' they say experience psychological harm after an abortion, commonly termed 'post-abortion syndrome'.[53] There is no scientific evidence for either of these claims. It is more risky to carry a pregnancy to term and deliver the fetus than to have an abortion,[54] and 'post-abortion syndrome' is not a recognised or proven medical condition.[55] The editors of the scientific journal *Contraception* state that 'the best literature to date concludes that there is no evidence of psychological harm from abortion and that the most reliable predictor of a woman's mental health after an abortion is pre-pregnancy mental health'.[56] For nearly all the women I interviewed, having an abortion was a relief and the consequence of a positive and carefully considered decision. What continues to make these decisions harder, however, is the societal stigma of abortion – meaning that many women are reluctant to acknowledge to others what was a positive choice and a responsible act.

Each day a staggering number of women acquiesce to unwanted sex, experience difficulties in accessing an abortion or feel compelled to keep hidden the fact that they've had one, are being denied crucial information about contraception, and – like Latisha – are shouldering most of the caring responsibilities if they do have children. (And in an economy that penalises workers with caring responsibilities – they are paying a high price for this.) Full access to reproductive rights and sexual equality are a prerequisite for women to be able to participate in daily life as citizens equal to men. Yet every night, millions of women go to bed having had these rights challenged, restricted, or denied.

Part 2

TOMORROW

00:00 | A New Day

Sexism casts a long shadow over our daily lives. It has been present for so long and spread so far that it can seem part of the natural landscape. It isn't. None of the problems you have read about in this book is inevitable. Body hatred, poverty, violence, sexual exploitation: none of these things has to exist. That is why the many women and girls featured in this book have chosen to speak out about their experiences – so that we can learn from them and work towards a world where no woman or girl has to experience the same. Amy, who spoke in 'Tough Love' about the abuse she suffered at the hands of her partner, wrote this to me: 'I've got to decide I'm not ashamed about what happened, and the only way I can do that is by letting this experience count for something. I need it to help someone else, which is why I wanted to tell you what happened.' I hope that the experiences of the women and girls featured in this book will shatter the illusion once and for all that women and men at the beginning of the twenty-first century are equal. And I hope that this chapter will inspire you to take action and help make gender equality a reality.

Every so often a book is published or an article is written calling for a new kind of feminism. But the feminism we need today is the feminism we've always required: one driven by truth, bent on justice, and founded on the fundamental belief in the equality and rights of all people. That's not to say, however, that we need it to be static and inflexible. On the contrary, it must constantly respond to changing circumstances and be acutely attuned to the complexity of people's lives. Sexism doesn't operate in a vacuum, but instead interacts with the multitude of other forces shaping our lives, such as race, class, age, disability, and sexuality. Gender equality can only be achieved if these are taken into account. Additionally, as I have argued throughout this book, it is crucial that we don't fall into the conceptual trap of confusing a process (choice) with feminism's aim (ending the subordination of women). This produces a dead-end situation whereby almost anything can be justified as feminist simply by identifying that individual 'choice' and 'agency' were involved. When discussing whether being pro-pornography can be a feminist position, Jessica Valenti, author and founder of feministing.com says, 'What I love about the third wave[*] is that we've learned how to find feminism in everything – and make it our own.'[1] I would seriously challenge the usefulness of this approach. Much of the feminism 'found' in pornography, stripping and so on hinges on the fact that the women participating aren't explicitly forced – and are thus exhibiting a form of agency. But the question must always be: what impact does the practice have on gender relations as a whole? Does it help end the subordination of women – or does it further perpetuate it? That is the litmus test.

There is no blueprint for how to build a 'feminist utopia', nor do we know precisely what this new society will look like – because nobody alive today has ever witnessed a world

---

[*] 'Third wave' is commonly used to denote a period of activity by young feminists that emerged in the early 1990s.

without sexism. But what we do know is there has to be something better than what we see today, and we can look to feminist successes of the past as inspiration for future actions. And what is abundantly clear is that ending discrimination against women will require no less than a total transformation of society at every level: international, national, local, and individual. This will involve campaigning not only for new legislation and better policies, but also challenging cultures, practices and, perhaps most difficult of all, ourselves. That means unlearning old habits, questioning long-held assumptions, and rethinking our actions.

Happily, recent years have seen a resurgence in feminist activism, particularly in the UK. Feminist conferences, magazines, blogs, websites, and groups have been proliferating throughout the country. The task facing us now is to build on and expand this activity. We need to move it firmly into the mainstream and ensure that feminism becomes widely recognised as one of the most important movements for social justice of our time. My great hope is that this book will play some part in that. For this chapter I have interviewed a small selection of people currently taking action against gender inequality, particularly those involved in grassroots activism, campaigning organisations and, vitally, men who are active in feminism today. What these individuals and groups demonstrate is that, by using or creating opportunities in our daily lives to challenge the equality illusion and further the ideal of a world without sexism, change is possible, and everyone has a crucial role to play.

DIY revolution

You don't have to be the leader of a feminist organisation or a member of parliament to effect change – it can come from the grassroots members of organisations, communities, and society. And because gender inequality is intimately tied up with our everyday lives, that is a good place to start. The possibilities for action are endless. A first step is to look inwards and assess your own behaviour and beliefs – something that can be extremely difficult. We have all been raised in a society arbitrarily segregated along sex lines, and no one is immune to the messages bombarding us daily that a woman's worth lies in her appearance, that pornography is harmless, that boys and men have to 'be a man' by rejecting femininity. In addition it is also crucial that we look outwards, and actively start to unpick the sexism that surrounds us, whether it be in the home, in the street, in the office, or on our TV screens. Grassroots feminist activism doesn't have to be arduous and time consuming (though it can if you want it to be!). All you have to do is ask yourself a few questions: what are the issues you're most passionate about? What time and resources do you have available to you? How could you most effectively make a difference? You might challenge a boyfriend who is planning to visit a lap-dancing club as part of a stag party, write to your MP during your lunch break, set up a feminist society at your university, or arrange for your football team to hold a charity match in aid of a local women's refuge. It's up to you. While such actions might seem minor, they can alter the everyday fabric of relations between women and men. And collectively they can create a tidal wave of change.

Sam Lyle decided to set up the Warwick Anti-Sexism Society – a feminist activist group for men and women at the student union – while completing her Masters in Social Research at Warwick University. It was a mixture of the subject she was studying and her daily experiences during lectures that spurred her into action. 'I was shocked by the number of young women who were on the same courses as me with titles such as "Birth of Feminisms" who, when asked in class, would not or did not consider using the term feminist to describe themselves despite seemingly holding "feminist" views and studying gender.' Sam was also frustrated by people's failure to realise how urgent these issues were and had a 'slow-burning belief that I could and should do something about it'. Grassroots activism involves making use of whatever resources are available. For those at university, a flexible timetable and the student union – which is often ready and able to support campaign work – provide unique opportunities for effecting change. They can help you influence other members of the student community – who are each at a pivotal time in their lives, on the cusp of entering the workforce, and likely to carry the formative experiences they have at university with them for the rest of their lives.

Sam never imagined WASS would be as popular as it turned out to be. 'I used a flyer at the Fresher's Fair to convince people to join. I got fifty members the first year, a hundred the next, and currently membership is above a hundred and fifty! We had stalls with information, we had awareness weeks, wrote articles for the student newspaper, spoke on the radio, had a website, went on national demos, held meetings. We did a collection of gifts that children could give to their mums every Christmas for our local women's refuge. WASS was also closely linked to Union Council, we got ourselves elected and successfully put through policies which got anti-sexism on the agenda.' Sam is now doing a PhD, but is still closely connected with the group. I asked her, looking back, what impact setting up a feminist group had on her personally: 'Putting WASS together was a very important and exciting time in my life, it was a time when I got to put into practice a lot of the things that I had been learning and thinking about for a long time.' There are dozens of grassroots feminist groups active across the UK, each one coordinated by dedicated volunteers in their spare time – yet their collective action is able to bring about change on both a local and national level.

'Doing something about it' doesn't have to mean being a member of a feminist group, diligently turning up to regular meetings. It can also be a one-off response to a specific incident or issue. Kirsty Bowen was propelled into action after reading on an online forum that the American restaurant chain Hooters was planning to open a branch in her home town of Sheffield. A website called The Smoking Gun got hold of a copy of the Hooters Employee Handbook, which revealed the chain required its 'Hooters Girls' to sign the following: 'I hereby acknowledge and affirm that (1) my job duties require I wear the designated Hooters Girl uniform; (2) my job duties require that I interact with and entertain the customers; and (3) the Hooters concept is based on female sex appeal and the work environment is one in which joking innuendo based on female sex appeal is commonplace. I also expressly acknowledge and affirm I do not find my job duties, uniform requirements, or work environment to be offensive, intimidating, hostile or unwelcome.'[2] Kirsty was horrified at the prospect Hooters would be opening up near her. 'I can't believe in this day and age it seemed acceptable to go to a restaurant that recruits women to wear hot pants and tight vests when serving burgers to its customers, forcing the women to accept any harassment they experience in the process.'

Kirsty had never been involved in feminist activism before, and didn't anticipate her frustration turning into a fully fledged campaign. 'I just wanted to let people know what was planned and [demonstrate] the support of people I knew would be against it.' To kick things off she set up a 'No to Hooters in Sheffield' Facebook group and after just four days was approached by a local radio station about the campaign. Sensing there would be significant interest, she contacted a local feminist group, Sheffield Fems, to get extra campaign support and together they designed leaflets and a petition. 'We soon had articles in the *Star*, *Sheffield Telegraph*, *Yorkshire Post* as well as national media such as the *Independent* and the *Guardian*. We were interviewed live on BBC's *Look North* and Radio Five.' Supported by local councillors and MPs, after just two months of campaigning Kirsty was contacted by city developers to say that they had ceased negotiations with Hooters; it would no longer be opening in Sheffield. 'They were frightened that negative attention would ruin the reputation of Leopold Square [a new city development].' Kirsty remembers the experience as being 'incredibly enjoyable and empowering', and the campaign also opened doors for her professionally. 'Soon after, I had an interview for a marketing and media-related role and they heard about the campaign and were impressed with the amount of press I created and the initiative I had to make the campaign a success.'

While the development of the internet has brought with it huge challenges to feminism (enabling the unfettered dissemination of pornography on an unprecedented scale for one thing) it does, of course, present opportunities for organising. In 2001 the then twenty-one-year-old Catherine Redfern was eager to get in touch with other feminists. Searching online for ways to contact people, Catherine discovered lots of US-based feminist websites and discussion groups – but nothing in the UK. So to plug that gap she set up The F-Word – an online magazine and blog dedicated to contemporary UK feminism – which now receives around 80–100,000 hits a month. She says that 'it was just done for the pure excitement of discovering different feminist opinions'. I asked Catherine what role she thinks websites and blogs like The F-Word play in activism: 'It's about sharing our opinions and voices and making it more visible. A lot of people have emailed the site and said, "I didn't think I was a feminist, then I read this".' Also, 'a lot of people have found feminist activity through the website and gone on to join other groups and form other groups'. Catherine is currently writing a book with academic Kristen Aune called *Reclaiming The F-Word: The New Feminist Movement*, due to be published by Zed Books in summer 2010. The book will feature the results of a survey of over 1,300 self-identified feminists, including questions on what first got them interested in feminism. 'If we know what sparked all these other feminists – why they're feminists – maybe we can learn something from that.'

Grassroots feminist activism can also connect up with and support national feminist organisations and campaigns. For example, grassroots activism is at the heart of OBJECT's campaign work against sex-object culture in the media. The organisation itself grew out of a newsletter started by Sasha Rakoff (now director of OBJECT) in her spare time to raise awareness of and promote activism on the issue as she was frustrated by the lack of discussion about the increasing normalisation of the sex industry in mainstream media. Sandrine Leveque, campaigns manager at OBJECT, explains: 'No one was really holding the media to account. [We wanted to] provide a voice to people who were fed up with it.' The organisation is continually short of funds and without an office to work from, so the efforts of its three paid staff hinge on the commitment and support of its volunteer activists. The results of their combined efforts have been impressive and include policies against sexist advertising in London transport systems.

Thanks also to their efforts, there is now a media-industry code of practice on the sale of lads' mags, although OBJECT believes this requires improvement and continues to coordinate grassroots activism around the issue. Because the code has had little real impact on how lads' mags are displayed, OBJECT have recently started organising 'Feminist Fridays' – direct action against lads' mags carried out by activists in shops across the UK. Anna van Heeswijk, grassroots coordinator at OBJECT, described to me how this works: 'We write anti-sexist slogans on brown paper bags . . . phrases such as "women not sex objects", "FHM – For Horrible Misogynists", for *Maxim* we write "MAXIMum sexism". We put all the lads' mags in these bags so the whole display is covered in our messages.' This form of activism has proved very effective in raising awareness and collecting signatures for their petition for greater regulation of lads' mags and pornographic newspapers. It has attracted local and national media coverage and recently led to the Equality and Human Rights Commission inviting OBJECT to discuss the issue with them.

Grassroots activism was also at the heart of the Fawcett Society and OBJECT's successful campaign to re-license lap-dancing clubs in England and Wales. The message to government that lap-dancing clubs shouldn't be licensed like cafes because they are part of the sex industry needed to come from more than just two organisations. It was the thousands of supporters' signatures on petitions, the hundreds of letters written to MPs, the countless articles in local and national newspapers, and the individuals that packed out our campaign rally in Parliament that together formed the most convincing argument. Numerous local campaigns against proposed lap-dancing clubs were run by activists in towns and cities from Durham to Newquay.[3] This meant that when Sandrine and I had meetings with ministers and spoke to the press we were able to point to the huge public support there was amongst the British public for licensing reform. As a result of this, Home Secretary Jacqui Smith announced on 21 September 2008 at the Labour Party Conference, 'We'll give communities a stronger say in stopping lap-dancing clubs opening in their areas.' As I write, the bill to reform lap-dancing club licensing is still making its way through Parliament, but should become law before the end of the year. Writing a letter to a local newspaper, signing a petition – these are quick, easy actions you can take in your own time, but the impact they can have is huge.

Taking part in collective grassroots activism is also about more than just achieving campaign goals. It can have a much more personal impact. I spoke to Katie McGrainer about why she decided to set up Birmingham Fems – a community-based feminist group. Katie was sexually assaulted in a previous relationship and had witnessed domestic violence in her own family, and she was becoming increasingly frustrated by people's reactions to issues like these and the blatant sexism she saw in her day-to-day life. 'I felt really alone. I didn't feel I could talk to anyone who would understand. People would just say "that's the way it is".' After searching online she found the wealth of feminist blogs that now populate the internet and was able to speak to people who felt the same. 'I thought, oh, I'm not a weirdo. I'm a feminist.' Katie set up her own blog, then decided to start a local group where she could talk face to face with other people about feminist issues. She set up an email group, advertised for members, and Birmingham Fems started meeting at the beginning of 2008. 'It's made such a difference. It's really improved my confidence.' The meetings, held fortnightly in a local coffee shop, allow the group to plan various actions as well as providing everyone with a space to offload 'feminist frustrations'. So far Birmingham Fems' activities have included picketing outside the Conservative Party Conference in 2008 to protest against the inclusion of discount vouchers for a Birmingham lap-dancing club in delegate packs. (The vouchers, provided by the Conservative-run local council, entitled delegates to £10 off the entry fee to the Rocket Club – which describes itself as an 'exclusive gentlemen's entertainment venue' featuring 'up to 50 of the most beautiful girls from around the world'.)[4] They have also attended national anti-violence demonstrations such as Million Women Rise and Reclaim the Night and held a fundraising event at a local cafe called 'Veg Out Against Violence'. What's clear is that anyone can bring about change, whether it's from a home computer or from outside the Houses of Parliament.

To harness people's desire for change my colleagues Sandrine Leveque, Anna van Hoeswijk and I have set up a new organisation – UK Feminista – to support grassroots feminist activism and build a broad-based movement of women and men committed to ending sexism. Anyone can become involved, and more information on how to do so is provided in the resources section at the end of this book.

Organising resistance

Feminist campaign organisations are key to the promotion of women's rights throughout the world. These funded groups can run sustained, strategic, and resourced campaigns and coordinate grassroots activism on the ground. Right now, feminist organisations throughout the world are raising awareness, influencing cultures and lobbying governments. They too demonstrate that, despite all the odds, change is possible.

Established two decades ago, Southall Black Sisters has proved to be one of the most influential feminist campaign organisations in the UK. When I went to interview the campaigner Pragna Patel at their offices I thought I had the wrong address: it looked just like any other house on the quiet suburban street in west London. But when I stepped inside I found a feminist powerhouse: huge photos lined the walls recounting the victories the organisation had enjoyed over the years, including the jubilant image of Kiranjit Ahluwalia and Southall Black Sisters campaigners, hands held high in the air, outside the High Court. Ahluwalia, an Asian woman who arrived in the UK following an arranged marriage, was convicted of murdering her husband and jailed for life in 1989. Yet the conviction took no account of the fact that she had been subject to severe domestic violence by her husband for a period of ten years and was suffering from severe depression at the time of his death. Believing that a miscarriage of justice had occurred,

Southall Black Sisters launched a campaign to appeal her sentence, arguing that the ongoing domestic abuse amounted to provocation. The campaign mobilised huge public support, with Ahluwalia becoming a household name. She eventually won her appeal on the grounds of diminished responsibility and the conviction was reclassified as manslaughter. Ahluwalia was freed three years and three months after she had first been imprisoned – setting legal precedent for 'cumulative provocation' that would go on to help many other abused women. Ahluwalia remains a member of Southall Black Sisters to this day.

Southall Black Sisters grew out of the intense anti-racist activism of the 1970s. The founders wanted to look at how race and gender intersected to affect black women's lives. Patel explains, 'They felt, along with many other black women, that they fell between two stools. A lot of the race agenda was dominated by men and a lot of the gender equality work was dominated by white women . . . Black women's voices were rarely heard.' Today the organisation continues to provide support to ethnic minority women suffering violence alongside their campaign and advocacy work. Other campaign successes include obtaining concessions from the government over immigration rules and domestic violence. Previously, women who had come to join their spouse in the UK and then proceeded to experience domestic violence within the first year of their arrival had the choice of either remaining in that abusive relationship or leaving it but facing deportation. Thanks to campaigning by Southall Black Sisters, such women are now safe from deportation. However, as I found at the Northern Refugee Centre in Sheffield when trying to find a refuge place for Saran who was being abused at the hands of her husband (discussed in 'Tough Love') – the no recourse to public funds rule means that women with insecure immigration status cannot access benefits within two years of their arrival. This means that, while women can now leave their abusive partners without the threat of deportation, they still can't access funds to cover a stay in a refuge – something Southall Black Sisters continue to campaign intensively on. 'That's a very urgent issue, a pressing issue. It's making it very difficult for us to protect certain women who have immigration uncertainty. We try to do what we can to find them some accommodation but it's not always easy.'

Patel and her colleagues are also currently campaigning against legislation seeking to enshrine religion as an aspect of people's identity requiring legal protection from discrimination on a par with people's race, sex, age, disability or sexuality. They believe this will 'only reinforce the discrimination that women face'. Southall Black Sisters are deeply concerned that such legislation will lead to local authorities funding religious organisations in order to meet their legal equality objectives and that these organisations will in turn 'subvert the kind of work that we have done over the years and encourage women to return to abusive situations because religiously their duty is to conform to traditional roles . . . [Statutory] resources are allocated according to whether you are within a particular religious identity. But who decides what that religion is, what those values are, are often very powerful, authoritarian, patriarchal, religious leaders. They're the ones the government is listening to.' Patel is deeply worried about this trend. 'In our daily experience we see the way religion and culture – and the two are indistinguishable – often is used to justify violence and abuse against women.' I asked Patel how individuals can support the work of Southall Black Sisters, and she was resolute in her response: 'Funding. Funding is the number one priority. We live hand to mouth year in, year out . . . If there are individuals who have any little bit of spare cash – funding would be great, [or] organising fundraising events for us.' Southall Black Sisters face huge challenges in their work, not least in resourcing their activities, but the courage and commitment so evident within the organisation gives great cause for hope.

Another pioneering campaign organisation based in the UK is WOMANKIND Worldwide (WKWW). Established twenty years ago, the organisation currently runs a programme for secondary school students and teachers designed to tackle the endemic levels of sexual bullying in UK schools – which I explored in 'Hands Up for a Gendered Education'. Working alongside schools to raise awareness of the problem, WKWW provides preventative strategies and educational resources like CD-ROMs and lesson plans. The organisation is clear about why schools should be addressing this issue: 'We believe that if schools do not challenge sexual bullying, they are acting as a training ground for violence against women later in life.'[5] WKWW's UK schools programme is just one aspect of their work – the majority of which is focused on projects overseas. They work with around thirty-seven partner community groups in fifteen developing countries to fund and support projects focused on empowering women. I asked Kanwal Ahluwalia, senior programmes and policy manager at WKWW, how their relationship with partner organisations works. She described their role as 'that of a conduit . . . We seek funding from the UK or the EU' and 'bring that money from these donors and collaboratively work with partners'. They can also provide support for specific projects and organisational development. For example, WKWW supported the Gender Centre in Ghana to conduct a strategic review of the organisation by visiting them and holding workshops to share best practice from other organisations, as well as enabling the Gender Centre to bring in a consultant to assist on strategic planning.

Feminism has a long history of transnational organising. Jan Jindy Pettman, formerly Director of Women's Studies at the Australian National University, reports this was a particular feature of campaigns for women's suffrage.[6] International networks have burgeoned particularly since the UN sponsored a series of world conferences on women held between 1975 and 1995. This transnational approach is something WKWW is very keen to foster. 'We try and facilitate learning and exchanges between our partners. If something works in Peru we can certainly share it with Ghana, for example, and see whether they can learn from it and adapt it to their own context.' The organisation also uses what policy forums they can access to make the voices of their partners heard, such as the UK Department for International Development, and forums connected to the EU and UN. Since the fall of the Taliban in Afghanistan, for example, WKWW have produced four research reports with partners in Afghanistan to assess the progress of women's rights in the country. WKWW have then used these findings to lobby British MPs and government departments such as the Foreign and Commonwealth Office to do more to support women's rights organisations in Afghanistan.

While feminist organisations throughout the world work on similar themes – such as violence against women and women's political representation – the political, social, and economic environments they operate in are, of course, unique to each country. And the challenges facing activists are perhaps no greater than in Afghanistan – described by WKWW as one of the most dangerous places in the world to be a woman.[7] Afghanistan has one of the highest maternal mortality rates in the world with one in nine women dying in childbirth, and also, at 88 per cent, the highest female illiteracy rate in the world. In addition, 60 per cent of marriages in the country are forced, and domestic violence is endemic. I asked Maryam Rahmani, who works at one of WKWW's partner organisations – the Afghan Women Resource Centre (AWRC) – about the current status of women in her country: 'Since September 2001, Afghan women have begun to increase their activities. Numerous events were organised during the last few years by Afghan women's organisations inside and outside Afghanistan, such as panel discussions, conferences and international meetings, in order to ensure needs of Afghan women would receive the required attention.' AWRC was established by a group of Afghan refugee women in 1989, and has been operating in Afghanistan since 2002. The organisation provides a range of training and education programmes as well as advocacy and lobbying for the rights of Afghan women. Prior to the fall of the Taliban in 2001, the organisation was unable to operate from within Afghanistan because women and girls were forbidden from working or going to school and banned from leaving their home unless accompanied by a close male relative. They were not allowed to speak in public or to men who were not relatives, and could be beaten or killed for violating these rules.

Despite recent advances, progress for women in

Afghanistan since then has been painfully slow. As Rahmani points out, 'Gender equality is an important element for the overall reconstruction and development of a country.' Yet international development funding has been slow to reach women's rights organisations, and the worsening security situation further limits women's participation in development. Since 2007, 640 schools in Afghanistan have been burned, bombed or closed by the Taliban and its allies – 80 per cent of which have been girls' schools.[8] Women's rights defenders have also come under specific attack. On 25 September 2006 Safia Ama Jan, Director of Women's Affairs in the Kandahar province, was shot and killed outside her home by suspected Taliban gunmen.[9] Ama Jan was a former teacher who had run an underground school for girls during the Taliban's reign, and her role at the time of her murder included championing efforts to get all girls back to school.[10] Just before I wrote this section it was announced that Afghanistan has passed a new law, backed by President Hamid Karzai, that permits Shia men to deny their wives sustenance and food if they don't obey their husband's sexual demands. Women are now also legally required to obtain permission from their husbands to work, and guardianship of children is now the exclusive right of fathers and grandfathers.[11]

Defenders of women's rights across the world are faced with colossal challenges in their work, with many experiencing daily threats to their lives; yet still they keep campaigning. I am acutely aware from my own experience at the Fawcett Society of how crucial the active support of members of the public is to the day-to-day work of feminist organisations, and there are countless ways that this can be offered. Whether it be through donating or fundraising, signing petitions, attending campaign events, or volunteering, public support is invaluable. Again, further details of international feminist organisations may be found in the resources section or on the UK Feminista website.

Safe spaces

Fundamental to the movement for gender equality is providing support for those suffering most acutely under sexism, like those women fleeing abusive partners and women being sexually exploited. Social change takes time, but there are women and girls who need support now. And until women and men are truly equal, there will be a need for women-only spaces – particularly in the case of support services like refuges. For Emma, who spoke in 'The Booty Myth' about her experiences of prostitution, support services have played a key role in helping her to rebuild her life. 'It has been just over two years since I exited [prostitution] and I am still in therapy and anticipate that I will continue to need help for some years to come. I think specialist services for prostituted women are vital . . . I don't think many people understand the complex trauma that selling yourself or being sold causes.' Sadly, fewer than one in ten local authority areas in the UK currently provide these specialist services.[12] And of the service providers that do target women in prostitution, many take a basic 'harm reduction' approach, such as visiting women on the streets and giving out condoms. Eaves Housing for Women report that often these approaches frame women's involvement in prostitution as relatively harmless as long as they don't contract a sexually transmitted infection or are attacked and, as a result, de-prioritise helping women exit prostitution.[13] Roger Matthews, a professor of criminology at South Bank

University who has studied street prostitution for over twenty years, suggests these kinds of services can actually end up keeping women in prostitution rather than helping them out of it.[14]

Thankfully there are some pioneering projects in the UK making a huge difference to the lives of women in prostitution, one of those being the GAP project at Tyneside Cyrenians which offers support to women in the Newcastle area. GAP stands for 'Girls Are Proud', and was originally coined by women using the project. Starting out as a weekly drop-in for women in prostitution, GAP now offers a range of services, including outreach visits to women's homes, accompanying women to appointments, and organising various group activities. I asked Laura Seebohm, who manages GAP, how women have responded to the service: 'A lot of them say it's their family. They always use quite dramatic language with it, like "GAP saved my life".' The project provides a holistic service, which means addressing all and any needs the women have. 'We do whatever is needed, basically. It's very much about looking at the women's priorities and not making assumptions.' And the range and severity of needs is staggering. 'The women's lives are fraught with different abuses going on. Life can be very violent for the women we work with.' Many have experienced childhood abuse and 'all of the women we work with are either in domestic abuse relationships or have been'. Laura also refers to the local drug treatment centre as 'our second office'. In 2007 GAP trained some of the women using their service to conduct research with others involved in prostitution in order to find out what issues they were facing. The researchers found that the vast majority said they would no longer prostitute if they could stop taking drugs, with the average daily spend on drugs being £137.

While you might expect that basic needs like accommodation or drug treatment would top the list of what women ask GAP to provide, Laura has actually found that frequently these issues can't be dealt with until women simply start enjoying being at GAP, through taking part in activities like horse riding or drama workshops. 'One thing we prioritise is making sure they've had some fun. They'll say very clearly to us, "We want to be off our face, that's why we take drugs" or "that's why we drink". So in some ways, unless there's something going on where they don't want to be off their face then they don't always have the need to address these problems.' GAP has only been running since 2006, but already many of the women who have used the service have exited prostitution, and two have won awards for voluntary work. Laura points out, however, that what constitutes success very much depends on the individual. 'For one woman, turning up at something once a week is a massive success, or for another woman getting through drugs treatment is a massive success.'

Kelle Holliday was previously involved in prostitution in the Newcastle area and volunteered to help set up GAP. She is now a paid worker at the organisation, and her personal experience of the sex industry helps her to connect with the women she works with: 'I've had similar experiences to what some of these women have had so I understand where they're coming from.' I asked Kelle how helping to set up and run GAP has affected her life: 'Now I've got my own house, a full-time job, I've got a little girl. I didn't have any of that before. It's made a massive impact on my life.'

Laura suggests that one of the most important things people can do to support women who use the GAP project is simply to understand. Often, she says, the women's behaviour towards other services or to the public can be quite challenging. But she stresses the need to 'understand why that might be and just scratch the surface, and underneath their needs and aspirations are the same as anyone else's'. The project is also always pleased to receive donations, with one-off gifts usually being spent on a one-off activity for the women, such as a trip to the theatre. 'Stuff like that they talk about for months and things like that can be a really good catalyst [for starting to tackle other issues].' Kelle also adds that 'donations of clothes always come in really handy because a lot of the women have been homeless or move about a lot so they lose their belongings'. Services like GAP provide a lifeline to women currently involved in prostitution and provide a model for what should be made available to every woman whose life is currently caught up in the sex industry.

The backbone of the movement in the 1970s to get domestic violence recognised as a crime and not just a 'private matter' was a network of refuges which offered accommodation to women fleeing abuse. In 1974 the National Women's Aid Federation was established, and this brought the individual refuges together formally into one network. In turn, the experiences of the individual women arriving at these refuges informed the political lobbying by Women's Aid. Their first lobbying success came in 1976 when Parliament passed the Domestic Violence and Matrimonial Proceedings Act, the first piece of specific legislation in the UK offering protection to women from domestic violence. Today, Women's Aid supports over 500 domestic and sexual violence services in the UK, helping up to 250,000 women and children a year. The size of the refuge movement is a testament to the efforts of feminist campaigners over the last forty years, but it is also a damning indictment of how big a problem violence against women is. Yet despite this, a recurring theme amongst organisations supporting victims of sexist violence is that they themselves are struggling to survive. In 2006, Devon Donkey Sanctuary received £20 million in donations from the general public – more than Women's Aid, fellow national domestic-violence charity Refuge, and Eaves Housing for Women received combined.[15]

Another crucial form of support is provided by a network of rape crisis centres. Nicole Westmarland, a criminology lecturer and researcher at Durham University, currently sits on the management committee of Tyneside Rape Crisis. Set up in 1978, it was one of the UK's first rape crisis centres. Westmarland described to me how, similar to refuges, the rape crisis movement emerged out of grassroots feminist work in the 1970s. The number of centres soon grew, reaching a peak in the mid-1980s, and they were supported by a national federation that provided links between the centres. The range of services provided by rape crisis centres can include a helpline, group work, face-to-face counselling, and training. But today rape crisis centres are themselves in a state of crisis. In 1984 there were sixty-eight rape crisis centres in the England and Wales network, but by 2008 that number had almost halved.[16] In the past three years eleven centres have had to close or reduce their services, five have no paid staff at all, and two-thirds describe their funding as 'unsustainable'. This is not because there has been any decrease in demand. Between 2001 and 2006 the number of rapes reported to the police in the UK increased by 41 per cent,[17] and now approximately 100,000 rapes are committed every year. As a result, the majority of women now don't have access to a centre.

However, there are signs that the funding situation is changing. Following a high-profile campaign by Rape Crisis and its partners the government made a significant funding injection in 2008, making it the first year there were no centre closures. The priority now is to stabilise funding and start opening new centres in major cities. 'The long-term aim is to have none,' Westmarland points out. 'We want to close them because there's no demand for them.' As such they hope to do more prevention work in the future, and much of this will depend on members of the public stepping forward to support the centres. 'The Rape Crisis movement is crying out for people to volunteer their skills. For example, book keeping, or if you had a marketing degree you could come up with catchy campaign banners'.

Services like Rape Crisis, Women's Aid and GAP play a vital role in supporting individual women to deal with the very real and very brutal consequences of sexism: rape, violence and other abuse. Those services, in turn, urgently need everybody's support.

FHM (Feminism Helps Men)

In 1871 John Stuart Mill, philosopher and radical MP, wrote: 'The most vitally important political & social question of the future [is] that of the equality between men and women.'[18]

Men have a long history of being actively involved in feminism. John Stuart Mill introduced the first parliamentary amendment requiring MPs to vote on women's suffrage in 1867 and two years later wrote the political tract, *The Subjection of Women*. He spent a significant portion of his working life engaged in feminist campaigning: gathering petitions, giving countless speeches on the subject and, according to Mill's biographer Richard Reeves, dedicating half of all the letters he wrote in the last four years of his life to issues facing women. Millicent Garrett Fawcett, the suffrage campaigner and begetter of the Fawcett Society, described Mill as the 'principal originator' of that campaign.[19] More recently, Anthony Lester played a key role in the introduction of the Sex Discrimination Act 1975 as Special Adviser to Roy Jenkins. A leading human rights lawyer, Lord Lester QC has subsequently argued many of the leading discrimination cases in Britain and the European Courts. I asked Lord Lester what originally inspired him to get involved in campaigns for gender equality, and his answer was short and simple: 'My belief in equality and justice.' The involvement of men in feminism has been crucial in the past, and it remains paramount today.

Jeremy Coutinho started becoming aware of the acute need for feminist campaigns in the 1990s when 'gentlemen's clubs' started opening up with regular frequency in UK cities and magazine racks started being populated by pornography. He is now chair of OBJECT, the leading UK organisation campaigning against sex-object culture, and is adamant that sexism isn't just a 'women's issue': 'It is an issue for society. These issues affect our mums, sisters, daughters, friends. We would have to be extremely selfish not to realise that in this way they also affect us men.' As bell hooks, acclaimed activist and author who writes on the intersection of race, gender and class, insists, 'feminism is for everybody'. To bring about gender equality, one major change we need to make is to redefine what it means to be 'a man'. Because at the moment, being a man is not just biological, it is political. As I've explained, it requires individuals to prove their masculinity and, in doing so, disprove their femininity. Men are boxed in by restrictive stereotypes and pressured to demonstrate how 'manly' they are. As long as this culture of sexism continues, some men will prove their masculinity through violence, sexually 'conquering' women, and treating them as dehumanised sex objects. That is why feminism must target men for change.

Damian Carnell, project manager at Nottinghamshire Domestic Violence Forum, describes his involvement in feminist work specifically targeting men and boys as 'the most valuable fifteen years of my life'. In his current work Carnell develops best-practice models for work with domestic violence perpetrators, conducts education projects for children on healthy relationships and gender respect, and spearheads various anti-domestic violence campaigns. Carnell is adamant about the need to target men: 'We have to find ways of engaging men and boys to understand, take seriously, and actively support feminism and reject the messages being fed to them that devalue, exploit and stereotype women and girls.' However, he is well aware of the battle feminism has on its hands. 'Thankfully, not all men and boys take on sexist beliefs or behaviour, but the opportunity is there for them, perpetually drip fed through the media, religions, sport, family cultures and traditions, pornography and prostitution, music, TV and other mediums, education, employment, law, and politics. We make choices based on our awareness or lack of, and here rests the case for education in gender equality and about the oppression and discrimination women and girls experience.'

Such fundamental changes to people's lives cannot simply be imposed from outside; boys and men need to be actively engaged in the process. To bring about change, established male groups and cultures – such as football – will need to be tapped. The White Ribbon Campaign is a good example of this. It was started in Canada in 1991 by a group of men on the second anniversary of the murder of fourteen women by one man, and is now a campaign run in over fifty countries to end violence against women.[20] The aim is to educate men and boys and get them to actively speak out against violence against women and to wear the campaign's white ribbon as a public statement. As a way of connecting with established male cultures, the UK branch has been working alongside football clubs in its 'Blow the Whistle' initiative, which involves football players and managers pledging their support and publicly speaking out against violence against women. Initiatives like these, where boys and men are actively engaged in campaigning, encourage them to take more responsibility for doing something about the sexism they witness or even perpetrate in their daily lives.

It is also important to remember that, if we can broadly say that gender inequality currently affords men as a social group certain power or 'privileges', not all men share in that equally. Some actually suffer harmful consequences as a direct result. UK-based gay rights organisation Stonewall conducted a survey in 2007 amongst lesbian, gay, and bisexual school pupils and found that nearly two-thirds had experienced homophobic bullying.[21] In addition, 95 per cent of secondary school teachers reported hearing pupils use the phrases 'you're so gay' or 'that's so gay' in their school, and 90 per cent observed that children were subject to homophobic bullying, name-calling or harassment regardless of their sexuality.[22] Researchers at Nottingham Trent University who have investigated teenage sexual identities suggest this kind of homophobia has links with sexism, asserting that 'the construction of masculinity and femininity takes place within a heterosexual matrix'.[23] In more general terms: being a 'real man' not only involves being tough and dominant, it also means being heterosexual. Saying to a boy 'you're so gay' calls into question his masculinity and implies he is the worst thing of all – feminine. I asked Ruth Hunt, head of policy at Stonewall, if this rang true in their organisation's experience: 'Sexism and homophobia are intrinsically linked. In our work with schools, [we] find that homophobia is often the product of sexism. For example, young boys and girls who do not conform to strict ideas about how they should behave are often called "gay". We hear from teachers who tell us that a simple act of choosing a pink pencil if you are a boy is enough to prompt scorn and homophobic abuse.' The same cultures that encourage the disturbing levels of sexual harassment spoken about by girls in 'Hands Up for a Gendered Education' also lead to boys who fail to conform to set rules on masculinity being punished.

US filmmaker and anti-sexism activist Byron Hurt works to call attention to how race and gender specifically intersect to effect black men's experiences of 'male privilege'. In documentaries like *I Am a Man* and *Barack and Curtis* Hurt explores the issue of black masculinity in America. I asked Hurt how he thinks racism has shaped black masculinity in the US: 'I think black people have been socialised and conditioned that we are less than, that we're not as valuable, that our lives do not mean as much as white lives.' As a result, Hurt feels that 'African-American men have been placed in this really difficult position of trying to attain a certain level of manhood or masculinity in this very patriarchal culture but have not been given all of the means and access to become what is considered to be a standard level of manhood or masculinity.' A self-described 'hip-hop head', Hurt also produced the award-winning documentary *Hip-Hop: Beyond Beats and Rhymes* to interrogate the hyper-masculinity, misogyny, and homophobia he saw in mainstream hip-hop music. Hurt has previously written that he was motivated to make the film 'for boys and men who felt uncomfortable with an image of manhood in Hip-Hop that was too narrow but had a hard time breaking out of the "man box" because they didn't want to risk being called "soft", "weak", or a "punk"', as well as being moti-vated by the 'girls and women who felt dissed, betrayed, and unsupported by the people who run the Hip-Hop indus-try, and because the racist, sexist representations of women of colour in Hip-Hop were raging out of control.'[24] I asked Hurt what he thinks is the biggest challenge to efforts to end sexism, and he was resolute in his answer: 'Denial. I think that men are in denial about the level of violence against women. That's what makes it so difficult. We as men don't really want to take a look at ourselves, at our behaviour and our attitudes . . . We have to get over it and beyond if we're going to have really serious conversations about what we can do as men to end violence against women.' More about Hurt's work may be found in the resources section of this book.

Feminism helps men. Gender inequality forces them into a mould of dominance, aggression and control. John Anderson, who works at youth-work organisation London Youth, first got involved in feminist campaigning while studying and working at Sheffield Hallam University. His subsequent professional work with young people has

demonstrated the very tangible ways men would personally gain from the eradication of sexism. 'I see a lot of young
men frustrated by the gender stereotype they are confined
to follow. I think feminism offers men the opportunity to
fulfil their potential and interests, not those imposed on
them. In the starkest terms, I think feminism is the solution to countering the machismo culture which is so prevalent in young people in London and is, I think, one the
main factors behind the terrifying levels of knife crime which
kills mostly young men.' He is categorical about why men
should be active in feminism: 'Because it's right and we
need to register our opposition to those who are wrong.'
It is crucial that men get active in feminist campaigns and
that gender equality initiatives specifically target men. The
very future of feminism depends on it.

Demand an end

There is no silver bullet for sexism. But a campaign in which
grassroots activists, organisations, support services and legislation all come together to tackle a problem is about as
close as we're ever going to get. And Sweden's approach
to tackling prostitution – which hinges on stamping out
demand for commercial sexual exploitation – is a demonstration of what can happen when it does.

Recent debates around prostitution have focused on
whether or not it should be wholly decriminalised and
classed as ordinary work and whether this would benefit
the women involved. At the end of 2007 the Hampshire
section of the Women's Institute launched a high-profile
campaign to legalise prostitution in the UK, and conducted
an international search for the 'perfect brothel' that could
act as a model for ones in Britain. It was justified by mem-

bers on the basis that 'there will always be prostitution'.[25] But Emma, who spoke earlier about her experiences of prostitution, vehemently disagrees with this approach: 'I strongly believe that prostitution should not be legalised because what the law permits it approves and to permit prostitution is to permit the abuse of women. The argument that it can be "made safer" is a fallacy put forward by pimps and the sex industry lobby . . . it fails to take into account that the experience of being prostituted in itself . . . The public need to know the truth, and to be reminded that it doesn't have to be like this.'

Sweden's campaign against sexual exploitation suggests Emma is correct in her insistence that prostitution is not inevitable. It is now illegal in Sweden to pay for sex acts, but still legal to sell sex acts. This approach recognises prostitution as a gender equality issue: a form of violence against women that involves a victim and a perpetrator. I spoke to Gunilla Ekberg, former special adviser to the Swedish government on prostitution and trafficking, about the policy. She explained that 'if you criminalise women you are in a situation where victims are penalised. It is in violation of international law.' The Swedish Law that Prohibits the Purchase of Sexual Services came into force on 1 January 1999 and is designed to tackle the root cause of prostitution: demand. Men who are found guilty of paying a woman for sex acts are either fined or imprisoned for a maximum of six months. To Emma, criminalising the buying of sex is a 'no brainer . . . it makes sense to lay the blame where it belongs – firmly with the pimps and johns who have the money and power. If you cut off the demand for the "services" of prostitutes, and combine this with increased exiting services for the women involved, you begin to tackle the problem.' Integral to the change in Swedish law have been government-funded education and awareness-raising programmes targeting public authorities, the media, NGOs, and the general public about the realities of prostitution and challenging the demand for it. Furthermore, because the law recognises women in prostitution as victims of abuse, they have access to support services and resources such as accommodation, counselling and job training that enable them to exit prostitution. And the legislation also recognises the need to tackle conditions such as poverty that make women vulnerable to prostitution.

Achieving a government response to prostitution so comprehensive as this wasn't easy. Ekberg pointed out that 'we did this over a period of twenty years'. Over the years there were meetings and demonstrations to promote law change, and the campaign managed to forge strong links with Labour Party Women's Association, led by the future deputy prime minister. The 1994 Swedish elections were a major breakthrough for the campaign, as the number of women in the Swedish parliament rose from 27 per cent to 45 per cent, led by a Labour/left majority government.[26] Ekberg is clear about the significance of this: 'When you have a lot of women in parliament then you get issues like violence against women addressed.' (This is a crucial illustration of how different feminist issues interlink: Increasing women's representation in positions of power can have a beneficial knock-on effect on other problems relating to women's inequality.) The stage was then set for a final parliamentary campaign to introduce legislation that would criminalise demand.

The impact of this approach to prostitution has been staggering. Between 1999 and 2004 there was a 30–50 per cent drop in the number of women involved in street prostitution and the entry of 'new' women into prostitution had almost stopped.[27] The number of women as a whole involved in prostitution decreased from an estimated 2,500 to 1,500 by 2002. And while before the law came into force 13.6 per cent of men over eighteen years old had paid someone for sex acts, by 2008 that figure was 8 per cent. These changes are in stark contrast to countries that have chosen to fully legalise prostitution and recognise it as ordinary work. The Child and Woman Abuse Studies Unit in the UK compared Sweden's approach to those of the Australian state of Victoria and the Netherlands – places where prostitution is legal. They found that where prostitution is legalised, organised crime, including the trafficking of women into prostitution, 'flourishes' and there is a substantial expansion of both the legal and illegal prostitution markets.[28] Sweden, on the other hand, has the fewest trafficking victims in the EU. The Swedish National Rapporteur for Trafficking in Women has attributed this directly to the law criminalising demand – which acts as a trade barrier to traffickers. There has also been widespread support amongst the Swedish general public. Ekberg reports that 'consistently, the support for the law has been between 70–79 per cent'. What enabled this campaign to become so successful? 'It was the feminist principles that were written into the legislation – including not criminalising the victims . . . You need to have gender equality as the starting point.'

Undoubtedly the success of the Swedish approach to prostitution also owes much to the fact that grassroots activists, feminist organisations, support services, and legislators were all involved in delivering a solution. And it didn't simply rely on the introduction of one new law. As is clear from the many legal victories in the UK that are yet to translate into reality, legislation alone is not a guarantor of change. Men's use of women in prostitution is fuelled by everyday sexist cultures that legislation alone cannot reach. Therefore, the education campaigns designed to challenge those cultures have been central to the realisation of the Swedish law. The Swedes' approach to prostitution has subsequently been adopted in Iceland and Norway – where Ekberg was currently attending a prostitution conference when I spoke on the phone to her. Shortly after I initially wrote this chapter, a campaign was launched by women's rights organisations OBJECT and Eaves, calling for the 'Nordic model' of tackling demand for prostitution to be implemented in the UK. We are yet to see whether this campaign can mirror the successes of Nordic countries. And, while campaigns to end gender inequality like Eaves and OBJECT's can prove long and hard, Ekberg's work proves that change is possible. And she is resolute: 'It is up to us to never give up.'

Sweden's success is not an isolated case. Across the world there are women and men managing to effect revolutions in gender relations even under the harshest of conditions. And perhaps no greater example of what can be achieved in the face of adversity is offered than by Rwanda – a country that was decimated in 1994 when an estimated 800,000 people were killed and up to half a million women were systematically raped in three months of violence. Today, the country has the highest proportion of women parliamentarians in the world: as of September 2008 women hold 56 per cent of seats. This is hugely significant. International evidence shows that, as Gunilla Ekberg stated, the higher the numbers of women in parliament and other public-office positions, the more prominent women's issues become on the political agenda.[29] In the immediate aftermath of the Rwandan genocide women and girls made up 70 per cent of the population, and they were central to rebuilding society. The importance of women's role in governance of the country was recognised in the new constitution in 2003, which guarantees women 30 per cent of parliamentary seats (this is the figure reported by UNICEF to constitute the 'critical mass' for women's ability to effect change in male-dominated institutions). This constitutional guarantee is delivered through a quota system and innovative electoral structures. Ninety-five countries worldwide currently use some form of quotas in efforts to boost women's representation. And of the twenty-two countries that have reached a proportion of 30 per cent or more women in national assemblies, eighteen of them use quotas in some form.

While UNICEF report that it is still too early to fully assess the impact of women's representation in Rwanda,[30] crucial gains have been made – including a law guaranteeing women's right to inherit land and a law tackling gender-based violence. Women in Rwanda have also played a crucial role in the country's economic recovery. As Agnes Matilda Kalibata, Rwanda's minister of state in charge of agriculture, has stated: 'Bringing women out of the home and fields has been essential to our rebuilding. In that process, Rwanda has changed for ever . . . We are becoming a nation that understands that there are huge financial benefits to equality.'[31] Rwanda is leading the world in women's political representation and demonstrates what can be achieved if the will is there.

Every individual woman and girl who has shared her

experience in this book has testified to the illusory nature of gender equality today. But they have also demonstrated the enduring strength and courage of women to keep going about their day-to-day lives and to speak out against injustices – despite the centuries of laws, ideologies and cultures that have designated them second-class citizens. While the challenges still facing us may be great, the beauty of feminism is that it is inherently hopeful. It is based on the notion that change can happen, that women don't have to be defined by their appearance, that boys and girls needn't be shackled by femininity and masculinity, that equality in the workplace is achievable, that rape and prostitution are not inevitable, and that everyone benefits when women control their own bodies. Today, these notions go unrealised. Tomorrow is up to us.

Resources

UK Feminista

UK Feminista is a new organisation that has been established to coincide with the launch of *The Equality Illusion*. Its aim is to inspire and support feminist activism across Britain – enabling everyone to become involved in the movement for gender equality and to do something about the issues raised in this book. The organisation's website provides a one-stop shop for activism, and includes a wealth of information and practical resources.
www.ukfeminista.org.uk

Recommended reading

Bordo, S. (2003), *Unbearable Weight: Feminism, Western Culture and the Body*, University of California Press

Cameron, D. (2007), *The Myth of Mars and Venus: Do Men and Women Really Speak Different Languages?*, Oxford University Press

De Beauvoir, S. (1997 [1949]), *The Second Sex*, Vintage Classics

Dines, G., Jensen, R. and Russo, A. (1998), *Pornography: The Production and Consumption of Inequality*, Routledge

Faludi, S. (1992), *Backlash: The Undeclared War Against Women*, Chatto and Windus

Greer, G. (2006 [1970]), *The Female Eunuch*, HarperPerennial

Gupta, R. (ed.) (2003), *From Homebreakers to Jailbreakers: Southall Black Sisters*, Zed Books

Jeffreys, S. (1997), *The Idea of Prostitution*, Spinfex

Jeffreys, S. (2005), *Beauty and Misogyny: Harmful Cultural Practices in the West*, Routledge

Jeffreys, S. (2009), *The Industrial Vagina: The Political Economy of the Global Sex Trade*, Routledge

Jensen, R. (2007), *Getting Off: Pornography and the End of Masculinity*, South End Press

Katz, J. (2006), *The Macho Paradox: Why Some Men Hurt Women and How All Men Can Help*, Sourcebooks

Levy, A. (2005), *Female Chauvinist Pigs: Women and the Rise of Raunch Culture*, Pocket Books

McDonagh, E. and Pappano, L. (2008), *Playing with the Boys: Why Separate Is not Equal in Sports*, Oxford University Press

Miles, R. (1989), *The Women's History of the World*, Paladin

Stark, C. and Whisnant, R. (eds) (2004), *Not for Sale: Feminists Resisting Prostitution and Pornography*, Spinfex

Stoltenberg, J. (1989), *Refusing to Be a Man*, Fontana

Wolf, N. (1990), *The Beauty Myth*, Chatto and Windus

Feminist organisations and websites

The following list includes all the feminist organisations and websites featured in this book, together with a number of others that I hope will prove useful.

Abortion Rights
'We are campaigning to defend and extend women's rights and access to safe, legal abortion.'
18 Ashwin Street, London E8 3DL
020 7923 9792
www.abortionrights.org.uk

Afghan Women's Resource Centre
'Developing practical, empowering projects in the community for more than 26 years'
www.womankind.org.uk

beat
'beat is the leading UK charity for people with eating disorders and their families'
103 Prince of Wales Road, Norwich NR1 1DW
01603 619090
www.b-eat.co.uk

Birmingham Fems
'The Birmingham Feminists (or Bham Fems) are a grass-roots community organisation . . . dedicated to supporting women's rights at a local, national and global level.'
www.bruminist.com

Byron Hurt
'Byron Hurt is an anti-sexist activist who provides cutting-edge male leadership, expert analysis, keynote addresses, and workshop facilitation in the field of sexual and gender violence prevention and education.'
God Bless the Child Productions, Inc., PO Box 5463, Plainfield, NJ 07061, USA
www.bhurt.com

Carnival of Feminists
'The Carnival aims to build the profile of feminist blogging, to direct extra traffic to all participating bloggers, but particularly newer bloggers, and to build networks among feminist bloggers around the world.'
www.feministcarnival.blogspot.com

Cath Elliott – Too Much to Say for Myself
Cath Elliott is a feminist and a trade union activist.
www.toomuchtosayformyself.wordpress.com

Eaves Housing for Women
'Eaves is a London-based charity that provides high-quality housing and support to vulnerable women. We also carry out research, advocacy and campaigning to prevent all forms of violence against women.'
Unit 2.03, Canterbury Court, 1–3 Brixton Road, London SW9 6DE
020 7735 2062
www.eaves4women.co.uk

Equality and Human Rights Commission
'Our job is to promote equality and human rights, and to create a fairer Britain. We do this by providing advice and guidance, working to implement an effective legislative framework and raising awareness of your rights.'
3 More London, Riverside Tooley Street, London SE1 2RG
020 3117 0235
www.equalityhumanrights.com

F-Word
'The F-Word is an online magazine dedicated to talking about and sharing ideas on contemporary UK feminism.'
www.thefword.org.uk

Fawcett Society
'Fawcett campaigns for equality between women and men in the UK on pay, pensions, poverty, justice and politics.'
1–3 Berry Street, London EC1V 0AA
020 7253 2598
www.fawcettsociety.org.uk

Forum for African Women Educationalists
'Ensuring that girls and women are an integral part of the intellectual and technical resource base needed for the development and prosperity of Uganda and Africa.'
Uganda Chapter: PO Box 24117, Kampala; Plot 328, Bukoto, Kampala
+256-414-236863
www.faweu.or.ug

FORWARD

'The Foundation for Women's Health, Research and Development (FORWARD) is an international non-governmental organisation that works to advance and protect the sexual and reproductive health and human rights of African girls and women.'
Unit 4, 765–767 Harrow Road, London NW10 5NY
020 8960 4000
www.forwarduk.org.uk

GAP (Girls Are Proud)

'The GAP Project is a unique support service for sex workers in the North East.'
07983 427395
www.tynesidecyrenians.co.uk

Guerrilla Girls

'We're feminist masked avengers in the tradition of anonymous do-gooders like Robin Hood, Wonder Woman and Batman. How do we expose sexism, racism and corruption in politics, art, film and pop culture? With facts, humor and outrageous visuals.'
www.guerrillagirls.com

Iranian and Kurdish Women's Rights Organisation

'IKWRO can help you to escape violence within the family or forced marriage, with claiming benefits and making asylum claims, with language skills and other training, and by providing translation and interpreting services.'
PO Box 62651, London EC1P 1JP
0207 920 6460
www.ikwro.org.uk

London Feminist Network
The London Feminist Network (LFN) is a women-only networking and campaigning organisation. LFN organises the annual Reclaim The Night March and an annual conference called Feminism in London.
www.ldnfeministnetwork.ik.com
www.fil.btik.com

Marie Stopes International
'Marie Stopes International is the UK's leading provider of sexual and reproductive healthcare services.'
020 7636 6200
www.mariestopes.org.uk

MenEngage
'MenEngage is a global alliance of NGOs and UN agencies that seeks to engage boys and men to achieve gender equality.'
www.menengage.org

Million Women Rise
'Million Women Rise is a coalition of individual women and representatives from the Women's Voluntary and Community Sector who have come together to organise an annual national demonstration against male violence which coincides with International Women's Day in March each year.'
c/o WRC, Ground Floor East, 33–41 Dallington St East, London EC1V 0BB
www.millionwomenrise.com

Nottinghamshire Domestic Violence Forum
'NDVF *has been working on domestic violence issues*
since 1989. NDVF acts as a central reference and resource
point for organisations in the City and County of
Nottingamshire and works closely with Women's Aid and
other key organisations.'
0115 9623 237
www.ndvf.co.uk

NUS Women's Campaign
The women's campaign of the National Union of
Students.
Centro 3, Mandela Street, Camden, London NW1 0DU
www.officeronline.co.uk/women

OBJECT
'OBJECT *challenges "sex object culture" – the increased*
sexual objectification of women in the media and popular
culture, for example through lads' mags, advertising or
lap-dancing clubs.'
PO Box 50373, London W4 3ZP
www.object.org.uk

Prostitution Research & Education
'*Conducts research on prostitution, pornography and traf-*
ficking, and offers education and consultation to
researchers, survivors, the public and policymakers.'
PO Box 16254, San Francisco CA 94116-0254 USA
www.prostitutionresearch.com

Rape Crisis
'Rape Crisis (England and Wales) provides co-ordination for the national network of Rape Crisis Centres across England and Wales. Rape Crisis Centres provide a range of specialist services for women and girls that have been raped or experienced another form of sexual violence – whether as adults or as children.'
c/o WRSAC, PO Box 39, Bodmin, Cornwall PL31 1XF
www.rapecrisis.org.uk

Rights of Women
'Rights of Women works to attain justice and equality by informing, educating and empowering women on their legal rights.'
52–54 Featherstone Street, London EC1Y 8RT
020 7251 6575
www.rightsofwomen.org.uk

Sheffield Fems
'We are a group of feminists, who meet every week to campaign, hold discussions and provide a friendly space to raise issues that we feel strongly about.'
www.sheffieldfems.wordpress.com

Sheila McKechnie Foundation
'The Sheila McKechnie Foundation was established in 2005 to help develop a new generation of campaigners who are tackling the root causes of injustice.'
The Resource Centre, 356 Holloway Road, London N7 6PA
www.smk.org.uk

Southall Black Sisters

'Our aims are to highlight and challenge violence against women; empower them to gain more control over their lives; live without fear of violence; and assert their human rights to justice, equality and freedom.'

21 Avenue Road, Southall, Middlesex UB1 3BL

020 8571 9595

www.southallblacksisters.org.uk

Stonewall

'Stonewall works to achieve equality and justice for lesbians, gay men and bisexual people.'

Tower Building, York Road, London SE1 7NX

020 7593 1850

www.stonewall.org.uk

Stop Porn Culture!

'StopPornCulture! is dedicated to challenging the pornography industry and an increasingly pornographic pop culture.'

www.stoppornculture.org

UNIFEM

'UNIFEM is the women's fund at the United Nations, dedicated to advancing women's rights and achieving gender equality.'

304 East 45th Street, 15th Floor, New York, NY 10017, USA

+1 212 906-6400

www.unifem.org

Warwick Anti-Sexism Society

'WASS is all about bringing men and women together to combat sexist attitudes and practices in our society.'

http://www.warwicksu.com/societies/warwickanti-sexism/

White Ribbon Campaign UK
*'The WRC is the largest effort in the world of men work-
ing to end men's violence against women.'*
Birchcliffe Centre, Birchcliffe Road, Hebden Bridge, West
Yorkshire HX7 8DG
01422 844675
www.whiteribboncampaign.co.uk

WOMANKIND Worldwide
*'We work closely with 37 partner community groups in 15
developing countries. All our projects are connected to
enabling women to understand their legal rights. And to
use these rights to benefit their daily lives.'*
2nd Floor, Development House, 56–64 Leonard Street,
London EC2A 4LT
020 7549 0360
www.womankind.org.uk

Women's Aid
*'Women's Aid is the key national charity working to end
domestic violence against women and children. We support a network of over 500 domestic and sexual violence
services across the UK.'*
PO BOX 391, Bristol BS99 7WS
0117 944 44 11
www.womensaid.org.uk

The Women's Library
*'The Women's Library is a cultural centre housing the
most extensive collection of women's history in the UK.'*
London Metropolitan University, 25 Old Castle Street,
London E1 7NT
020 7320 2222
www.londonmet.ac.uk/thewomenslibrary

Women's Resource Centre
'The Women's Resource Centre supports women's organisations to be more effective and sustainable. We provide training, resources and support to women's organisations and we campaign and lobby on key issues for the sector.'
Ground Floor East, 33–41 Dallington St, London EC1V 0BB
020 7324 3030
www.wrc.org.uk

Women's Sport and Fitness Foundation
'The Women's Sport and Fitness Foundation is the charity that campaigns to make physical activity an integral part of life for women and girls in the UK.'
3rd Floor, Victoria House, Bloomsbury Square, London WC1B 4SE
020 7273 1740
www.wsff.org.uk

Women's Support Project
'The Women's Support Project is a voluntary organisation, which works against violence against women and children. We work on a broad range of issues including domestic violence, rape and sexual assault, child sexual abuse and incest.'
0141 552 2221
www.womenssupportproject.co.uk

WomenWatch
'WomenWatch is the central gateway to information and resources on the promotion of gender equality and the empowerment of women throughout the United Nations system.'
www.un.org/womenwatch

Working Families
'Working Families helps children, working parents and carers and their employers find a better balance between responsibilities at home and work.'
1–3 Berry Street, London EC1V oAA
020 7253 7243
www.workingfamilies.org.uk

XY Online
'XY is a website focused on men, masculinities, and gender politics. XY is a space for the exploration of issues of gender and sexuality, the daily issues of men's and women's lives, and practical discussion of personal and social change.'
www.xyonline.net

YWCA
'YWCA is the leading charity working with the most disadvantaged young women in England and Wales.'
Clarendon House, 52 Cornmarket Street, Oxford OX1 3EJ
01865 304200
www.ywca-gb.org.uk

Notes

Introduction: An Alarm Call

1 'I have nothing in common with feminists. They never seem to think that one might enjoy men', Doris Lessing interviewed in the *Observer*, 9 September 2001.

2 '"Women have never had it so good at work," Says M&S Chief', *Observer*, 31 May 2009.

3 'Still Time to Discover Feminism', *New Statesman*, 20 March 2006.

4 Richard H. Robbins, *Global Problems and the Culture of Capitalism* (Allyn and Bacon, 1999), p. 354.

5 'A Record High for Women in Parliament in 2008', Inter-Parliamentary Union press release, 5 March 2009.

6 'The State of the World's Children 2007. Women and Children: The Double Dividend of Gender Equality', report, United Nations Children's Fund, 2006.

7 'Family Planning Is so Easy, Yet so Little Is Invested in It', *Guardian*, 1 April 2009.

8 'A Record High for Women in Parliament in 2008'.

9 'Sex and Power 2008', report, Equality and Human Rights Commission, 2008.

10 'The State of the World's Children 2007'.

11 See www.standagainstpoverty.org (accessed October 2008).

12 See www.makepovertyhistory.org (accessed October 2008).

13 See www.live8live.com (accessed October 2008).

14 'Because I Am a Girl: The State of the World's Girls (2007)', report, Plan UK, 2007.

15 'Gender Equality at the Heart of Development: Why the Role of Women Is Crucial to Ending World Poverty', report, Department for International Development, 2007.

16 'Debt and Women', Jubilee Debt Campaign briefing, 2007.

17 'The State of the World's Children 2007'.

18 'State of the World Population 2005. The Promise of Equality: Gender Equity, Reproductive Health and the Millennium Development Goals', United Nations Population Fund, 2005.

19 Ibid.

20 'Changing the Climate: Why Women's Perspectives Matter', report, Women's Environment & Development Organisation, 2007.

21 'Gender Perspectives on Climate Change', written statement by Lorena Aguilar for the Emerging Issues Panel at the United Nations Commission on the Status of Women, 52nd session, 25 February to 7 March 2008.

22 'Speaking Out: Promoting Women as Decision-Makers Worldwide', report, WOMANKIND Worldwide, 2008.

23 E. Neumayer and T. Plumper, 'The Gendered Nature of Natural Disasters: The Impact of Catastrophic Events on the Gender Gap in Life Expectancy, 1981–2002', *Annals of the Association of American Geographers*, 97(3) (2007): 551–66.

24 Naomi Klein, *No Logo* (Flamingo, 2001).

06:56 | Mirror, Mirror on the Wall

1 Figures from the UK charity beat (beating eating disorders) website, www.b-eat.co.uk.

2 J. K. Bosson, E. C. Pinel and J. K. Thompson, 'The Affective Consequences of Minimizing Women's Body Image Concerns', *Psychology of Women Quarterly*, 32 (2008): 257–66.

3 D. H. John and V. Ebbeck, 'Gender-Differentiated Associations among Objectified Body Consciousness, Self-Conceptions and Physical Activity', *Sex Roles*, 59 (2008): 623–32.

4 'Beyond Stereotypes: Rebuilding the Foundation of Beauty Beliefs', findings of the 2005 Dove Global Study, Unilever, 2006.

5 'The Real Truth about Beauty: A Global Report', findings of the Global Study on Women, Beauty and Well-Being, Unilever, 2004.

6 S. Bordo, *Unbearable Weight: Feminism, Western Culture and the Body* (University of California Press, 2003).

7 A. Dworkin, *Woman Hating* (E. P. Dutton, 1974), p. 112.

8 N. Wolf, *The Beauty Myth* (Vintage, 1990), p. 10.

9 N. Walter, *The New Feminism* (Little, Brown, 1998), p. 4.

10 J. Baumgardner and A. Richards, 'The Number One Question about Feminism', *Feminist Studies*, 29(2) (2003): 448–52.

11 Wolf, *The Beauty Myth*, p. 272.

12 S. Jeffreys, *Beauty and Misogyny: Harmful Cultural Practices in the West* (Routledge, 2005), p. 24.

13 'Betraying the Student Body?', *Guardian*, 5 December 2008.

14 'Beauty Industry Failing Minority Ethnic Women', *Guardian*, 15 November 2007.

15 'Why We're All Beautiful Now', *Observer*, 9 January 2005.

16 H. Klein and K. S. Shiffman, 'Messages about Physical Attractiveness in Animated Cartoons', *Body Image*, 3 (2006): 353–63.

17 'Self-Esteem: Girls Shout Out! Under Ten and under Pressure?', *Girlguiding UK*, 2007.

18 'Report of the APA Task Force on the Sexualization of Girls', American Psychological Association, 2007.

19 M. K. Gordon, 'Media Contributions to African-American Girls' Focus on Beauty and Appearance: Exploring the Consequences of Sexual Objectification', *Psychology of Women Quarterly*, 32 (2008): 245–56.

20 G. B. Forbes and D. A. Frederick, 'The UCLA Body Project II: Breast and Body Dissatisfaction among African, Asian, European, and Hispanic American College Women', *Sex Roles*, 58 (2008): 449–57.

21 G. B. Forbes et al., 'Sexism, Hostility toward Women, and Endorsement of Beauty Ideals and Practices: Are Beauty Ideals Associated with Oppressive Beliefs?', *Sex Roles*, 56 (2007): 265–73.

22 'Bank Tells Staff: "Don't forget the lipstick, girls"', *Independent on Sunday*, 1 February 2009.

23 'Female Accountants Sent on Course to Learn How To Dress Appropriately', *Daily Telegraph*, 3 November 2008.

24 'Report of the APA Task Force on the Sexualization of Girls'.

25 S. Grabe, J. S. Hyde and S. M. Lindberg, 'Body Objectification and Depression in Adolescents: The Role of Gender, Shame, and Rumination', *Psychology of Women Quarterly*, 31 (2007): 164–75.

26 M. Tiggemann and M. Boundy, 'Effect of Environment and Appearance Compliment on College Women's Self-Objectification, Mood, Body Shame, and Cognitive Performance', *Psychology of Women Quarterly*, 32 (2008): 399–405.

27 A. M. Brausch and J. J. Muehlenkamp, 'Body Image and Suicidal Ideation in Adolescents', *Body Image*, 4 (2007): 207–12.

28 'Beyond Stereotypes'.

29 B. L. Fredrickson et al., 'That Swimsuit Becomes You: Sex Differences in Self-Objectification, Restrained Eating, and Math Performance', *Journal of Personality and Social Psychology*, 75(1) (1998): 269–84.

30 B. Harper and M. Tiggemann, 'The Effect of Thin Ideal Media Images on Women's Self-Objectification, Mood, and Body Image', *Sex Roles*, 58 (2008): 649–57.

31 A. R. Malkin, K. Wornian and J. C. Chrisler, 'Women and Weight: Gendered Messages on Magazine Covers', *Sex Roles*, 40 (1999): 647–55.

32 E. J. Strahan, S. J. Spencer and M. P. Zanna, 'Don't Take Another Bite: How Sociocultural Norms for Appearance Affect Women's Eating Behaviour', *Body Image*, 4 (2007): 331–42.

33 'Has Fashion Got Its House in Order?', report for beat's inquiry into the fashion industry, 2007.

34 'Body Image Study Reveals Genders' Anxiety Gap', *Guardian*, 10 May 2001.

35 Bordo, *Unbearable Weight*.

36 *Stopgap* (Fawcett Society magazine), Summer 2007.

37 *Diet Clinic*, BBC TV, 21 May 2009.

38 'The Diet Business: Banking on Failure', BBC News Online, 5 February 2003.

39 Harper and Tiggemann, 'The Effect of Thin Ideal Media Images on Women's Self-Objectification, Mood, and Body Image'.

40 Y. Yamamiya et al., 'Women's Exposure to Thin-and-Beautiful Media Images: Body Image Effects of Media-Ideal Internalization and Impact-Reduction Interventions', *Body Image*, 2 (2005): 74–80.

41 B. T. Bell, R. Lawton and H. Dittmar, 'The Impact of Thin Models in Music Videos on Adolescent Girls' Body Dissatisfaction', *Body Image*, 4 (2007): 137–45; D. A. Hargreaves and M. Tiggemann, 'Idealized Media Images and Adolescent Body Image: "Comparing" Boys and Girls', *Body Image*, 1 (2004): 351–61.

42 Ibid.

43 A. E. Becker et al., 'Eating Behaviours and Attitudes Following Prolonged Exposure to Television among Ethnic Fijian Adolescent Girls', *British Journal of Psychology*, 180 (2002): 509–14.

44 '"Models are too skinny for my size 10 styles", Says Fashion Designer', *Guardian*, 25 October 2008.

45 '*Vogue* Editor Says Fashion Photos Retouched to Make Models Look Fatter', *Guardian*, 13 June 2009.

46 K. L. Tucker et al., 'Examining "Fat Talk" Experimentally in a Female Dyad: How Are Women Influenced by Another Woman's Body Presentation Style?', *Body Image*, 4 (2007): 157–64.

47 J. S. Mills and J. L. Miller, 'Experimental Effects of

Receiving Negative Weight-Related Feedback: A Weight Guessing Study', *Body Image*, 4 (2007): 309–16.

48 The Alliance for Eating Disorders Awareness, www.eatingdisorderinfo.org

49 Figure from beat website.

50 Bordo, *Unbearable Weight*.

51 'Report of the APA Task Force on the Sexualization of Girls'.

52 Bordo, *Unbearable Weight*.

53 B. J. McGee et al., 'Perfectionistic Self-Presentation, Body Image, and Eating Disorder Symptoms', *Body Image*, 2 (2005): 29–40.

54 D. B. Sarwer and C. E. Crerand, 'Body Image and Cosmetic Medical Treatments', *Body Image*, 1 (2004): 99–111.

55 'Brits Demand a High Daily Dose of Cosmetic Surgery', Mintel press release, December 2007.

56 C. Chambers, *Sex, Culture, and Justice: The Limits of Choice* (Penn State Press, 2008).

57 'Over 32,400 Cosmetic Surgery Procedures in the UK in 2007' British Association of Aesthetic Plastic Surgeons press release, February 2008.

58 *Grazia*, 8 December 2008.

59 Sarwer and Crerand, 'Body Image and Cosmetic Medical Treatments'.

60 S. Tait, 'Television and the Domestication of Cosmetic Surgery', *Feminist Media Studies*, 7(2) (2007): 119–35.

61 'Surgeons Denounce Booby Prize', British Association of Aesthetic Plastic Surgeons press release, August 2007.

62 Forbes and Frederick, 'The UCLA Body Project II'.

63 Press releases, American Society for Aesthetic Plastic Surgery and the British Association of Aesthetic Plastic Surgeons, 2009.

64 National Clearinghouse of Plastic Surgery Statistics: 2008 Report of the 2007 Statistics, American Society of Plastic Surgeons.

65 Jeffreys, *Beauty and Misogyny*.

66 Reported in 'Sidelines', *Guardian*, 30 May 2007.

67 L. M. Liao and S. M. Creighton, 'Requests for Cosmetic Genitoplasty: How Should Healthcare Providers Respond?', *British Medical Journal*, 334 (2007): 1090–2.

68 'Female Genital Mutilation', Fact Sheet No. 241, World Health Organisation, May 2008.

69 See www.beautifulfigure.com (accessed September 2009).

70 See www.surgicare.co.uk (accessed September 2009).

71 'The Real Truth about Beauty: A Global Report'.

72 D. and E. Henderson-King, 'Acceptance of Cosmetic Surgery: Scale Development and Validation', *Body Image*, 2 (2005): 137–49.

73 *Extreme Makeover*, season 2, episode 6 (first broadcast October 2003).

74 See www.thehospitalgroup.org/cosmetic-surgery/patient-stories.php.

08:40 | Hands Up for a Gendered Education

1 Cited in 'Safe Schools: Every Girl's Right. Stop Violence Against Women', Amnesty International, 2008.

2 A. J. Ormerod et al., 'Critical Climate: Relations Among Sexual Harassment, Climate, and Outcomes for High School Girls and Boys', *Psychology of Women Quarterly*, 32 (2008): 113–25.

3 J. E. Gruber and S. Fineran, 'Comparing the Impact of Bullying and Sexual Harassment Victimisation on the Mental and Physical Health of Adolescents, *Sex Roles*, 59 (2008): 1–13.

4 Ormerod et al., 'Critical Climate'.

5 'Feminised Curriculum "has thrown boy out with bathwater"', *Guardian*, 13 June 2006.

6 'Hit or Miss? Women's Rights and the Millennium Development Goals', ActionAid, 2008.

7 Ibid.

8 Irmin Durand, Forum for African Women Educationalists, personal correspondence, February 2009.

9 'Safe Schools: Every Girl's Right'.

10 'British Tourist in Aids Fear after Rape Ordeal', *Daily Mail* (online edition), www.dailymail.co.uk/news/article-148017/ (accessed September 2009).

11 H. Aydt and W. A. Corsaro, 'Differences in Children's Construction of Gender Across Culture: An Interpretive Approach', *American Behavioral Scientist*, 46 (2003): 1306–25.

12 D. E. Boyle et al., 'Gender at Play: Fourth-Grade Girls and Boys on the Playground', *American Behavioral Scientist*, 46 (2003): 1326–45.

13 V. A. Green et al., 'The Variability and Flexibility of Gender-Typed Toy Play: A Close Look at Children's Behavioural Responses to Counterstereotypic Models', *Sex Roles*, 51 (2004): 371–86.

14 Aydt and Corsaro, 'Differences in Children's Construction of Gender Across Culture'.

15 A. B. M. Teixeira et al., 'Exploring Modes of Communication among Pupils in Brazil: Gender Issues in Academic Performance', *Gender and Education*, 20(4) (2008): 387–98.

16 Aydt and Corsaro, 'Differences in Children's Construction of Gender Across Culture'.

17 C. Skelton and B. Francis, 'Introduction: Boys and Girls in the Primary Classroom', in Skelton and Francis, *Boys and Girls in the Primary Classroom* (McGraw-Hill, 2003), pp. 3–26.

18 E. W. Morris, '"Ladies" or "Loudies"? Perceptions and Experiences of Black Girls in Classrooms', *Youth & Society*, 38(4) (2007): 490–515.

19 Aydt and Corsaro, 'Differences in Children's Construction of Gender Across Culture'.

20 National Science Foundation website: www.nsf.gov/statistics/wmpd/sex.cfm (accessed February 2009).

21 Remarks at NBER Conference on Diversifying the Science & Engineering Workforce, Lawrence H. Summers, Cambridge,

MA, 14 January 2005.

22 A. van de Gaer et al., 'Mathematics Participation and Mathematics Achievement Across Secondary School: The Role of Gender', *Sex Roles*, 59 (2008): 568–85.

23 V. Bonnot and J.-C. Croizet, 'Stereotype Internalisation and Women's Math Performance: The Role of Interference in Working Memory', *Journal of Experimental Social Psychology*, 43 (2007): 857–66.

24 Van de Gaer et al., 'Mathematics Participation and Mathematics Achievement Across Secondary School'.

25 'Boys Not Better Than Girls at Maths, Study Finds', *Guardian*, 30 May 2008.

26 T. M. Ortner and M. Sieverding, 'Where Are the Gender Differences? Male Priming Boosts Spatial Skills in Women', *Sex Roles*, 59 (2008): 274–81.

27 'Chemistry Sets Could Become Best-Selling Toys', *Telegraph*, 28 January 2009.

28 'Playing Fair?', *Guardian*, 16 December 2008.

29 C. J. Ferguson et al., 'Gender, Video Game Playing Habits and Visual Memory Tasks', *Sex Roles*, 58 (2008): 279–86.

30 'Girls Choosing Camera Lenses over Microscopes', *Guardian*, 3 October 2008.

31 'Free to Choose: Tackling Gender Barriers to Better Jobs. EOC's Investigation into Workplace Segregation and Apprenticeships', report, Equal Opportunities Commission, 2005.

32 Excerpts from comments made by Bernard McGuirk, Sid Rosenberg, Lou Ruffino, and Don Imus on Imus's MSNBC radio show, *Imus in the Morning*, 4 April 2007; www.youtube.com/watch?v=bmF8iIeOVEo (accessed February 2009).

33 'It's Time: Future Forecasts for Women's Participation in Sport and Exercise', report, Women's Sport and Fitness Foundation, 2007.

34 'Women in Sport: The State of Play 2006', report, UK Sport, 2006.

35 'It's Time: Future Forecasts for Women's Participation in Sport and Exercise'.

36 S. Shakib, 'Female Basketball Participation: Negotiating the Conflation of Peer Status and Gender Status from Childhood through Puberty', *American Behavioral Scientist*, 46 (2003): 1405–22.

37 'It's Time: Future Forecasts for Women's Participation in Sport and Exercise'.

38 C. Paechter, 'Reconceptualising the Gendered Body: Learning and Constructing Masculinities and Femininities in School', *Gender and Education*, 18(2) (2006): 121–35.

39 E. McDonagh and L. Pappano, *Playing with the Boys: Why Separate Is not Equal in Sports* (Oxford University Press, 2008).

40 'Women in Sport: The State of Play 2006'.

41 J. R. Angelini, 'How Did the Sport Make You Feel? Looking at the Three Dimensions of Emotion through a Gendered Lens', *Sex Roles*, 58 (2008): 127–35.

42 H. M. Parker and J. S. Fink, 'The Effect of Sport Commentator Framing on Viewer Attitudes', *Sex Roles*, 58 (2007): 116–26.

43 'The Star Next Door', *Observer*, 23 November 2008.

44 *Independent*, 8 August 2008.

45 'Safe Schools: Every Girl's Right'.

46 K. H. Robinson, 'Reinforcing Hegemonic Masculinities through Sexual Harassment: Issues of Identity, Power and Popularity in Secondary Schools', *Gender and Education*, 17(1) (2005): 19–37.

47 C. Bagley et al., 'Sexual Assault in School, Mental Health and Suicidal Behaviours in Adolescent Women in Canada', *Adolescence*, 32(126) (1997): 361–6.

48 Gruber and Fineran, 'Comparing the Impact of Bullying and Sexual Harassment'.

49 E. J. Meyer, 'Gendered Harassment in Secondary Schools: Understanding Teachers' (Non) Interventions', *Gender and Education*, 20(6) (2008): 555–70.

09:21 | Sexism and the City

1 'Shaping a Fairer Future', report, Women and Work Commission, February 2006.

2 The Equalities Review was commissioned to investigate the causes of discrimination and inequality in UK society. The final report, 'Fairness and Freedom: The Final Report of the Equalities Review', was published in February 2007.

3 'You're Fired', *Guardian*, 23 April 2008.

4 'Sir Alan Sugar: "Our children need enterprise"', *Daily Telegraph*, 9 February 2008.

5 Employment Law Advisory Service survey of 1,100 company bosses and personnel managers across the UK, April 2008.

6 'Greater Expectations, Summary Final Report. EOC's Investigation into Pregnancy Discrimination', Equal Opportunities Commission, 2005.

7 'Feminist Finds Herself Silently Agreeing that Family Rights Could Be Harming Women's Careers', *Daily Mail*, 15 July 2008.

8 Ibid.

9 Cited in 'Selfish Adults Damage Children', BBC News, 2 February 2009

10 Cited in 'Kids in Crisis? Women Must Be to Blame', *Guardian*, 3 February 2009.

11 G. Ellison et al., 'Work and Care: A Study of Modern Parents', YouGov report for the Equality and Human Rights Commission, 2009.

12 K. Bellamy and K. Rake, 'Money, Money, Money: Is It Still a Rich Man's World? An Audit of Women's Economic Welfare in Britain Today', The Fawcett Society, 2005.

13 'The Equal Sharing of Responsibilities Between Women and Men, Including Caregiving in the Context of HIV/AIDS', 52nd session of the Commission on the Status of Women, Issues Paper, 27 February 2008.

14 R. Hausmann, L. D. Tyson and S. Zahidi, 'The Global Gender Gap Report 2008', World Economic Forum.

15 B. Baker and S. S. Lightle, 'Cracks in the Glass Ceiling: An

Analysis of Gender Equity in the Federal Government Auditing Career Field', *Journal of Government Financial Management*, 50(3) (2001): 18–26.

16 Alice H. Eagly and Linda L. Carli, 'Women and the Labyrinth of Leadership', *Harvard Business Review*, September 2007.

17 'The Female FTSE Report 2008', International Centre for Women Business Leaders, Cranfield University School of Management, 2008.

18 'The Power Vacuum in the Boardroom', *Guardian*, 9 January 2009.

19 Catalyst, December 2008.

20 'Lifts and Ladders: Resolving Ethnic Minority Women's Exclusion from Power', report, Fawcett Society, 2009.

21 'A Record High for Women in Parliament in 2008'.

22 'Women MPs to the Fore in Healing of Rwanda', *Independent on Sunday*, 17 September 2008.

23 'The Glass Ceiling Isn't Broken, In Fact It's Getting Thicker', *Observer*, February 2008.

24 Eagly and Carli, 'Women and the Labyrinth of Leadership'.

25 Eurostat, summer 2007.

26 'Enter the Timelords: Transforming Work to Meet the Future', final report of the Equal Opportunity Commission's investigation into the Transformation of Work, June 2007, available at www.equalityhumanrights.com.

27 Cited in Eagly and Carli, 'Women and the Labyrinth of Leadership'.

28 'Different Cultures, Similar Perceptions: Stereotyping of Western European Business Leaders', Catalyst, 2007.

29 'Mining Gets Dirty with Sexist Rant at Anglo's Carroll', *Guardian*, 9 July 2009.

30 '2007 Annual Survey of Hours and Earnings', Office of National Statistics, 7 November 2007.

31 'Not Having It All: How Motherhood Reduces Women's Pay and Employment Prospects', report, Fawcett Society, 2009.

32 See http://news.bbc.co.uk/1/hi/magazine/8048707.stm

(accessed July 2009).

33 'Salary, Gender and the Social Cost of Haggling', *Washington Post*, July 2007.

34 'Landmark Victory for Women in Fight for Equal Pay', *Independent*, 4 April 1997.

35 D. Grimshaw and J. Rubery, *Undervaluing Women's Work* (University of Manchester Press/Equal Opportunities Commission, 2007).

36 'Not Having It All: How Motherhood Reduces Women's Pay And Employment Prospects'.

37 Leticia Veruete-McKay, 'Patterns of Low Pay in London', Current Issues Note 14, GLA Economics, Living Wage Unit, Greater London Authority, 2007.

38 'Fawcett Launches New Campaign: "Keeping Mum"', Fawcett Society press release, May 2008.

39 'It's not the Cadilla Tailfins, It's the Clarity – That's Why We Love Mad Men', *Guardian*, 8 April 2009.

40 Cited in M. Hunt, S. Fielden Davidson and H. Hoel, 'Sexual Harassment in the Workplace: A Literature Review', Working Paper Series No. 59, Equal Opportunities Commission, 2007.

41 L. Meyers, 'In Brief: Sexual Harassers Target Women Who Violate Gender Norms', *Monitor on Psychology*, 38(5) (May 2007): 12.

42 'Sexual Harassment Okay as It Ensures Humans Breed, Russian Judge Rules', *Daily Telegraph*, 29 July 2008.

43 Hunt, Davidson and Hoel, 'Sexual Harassment in the Workplace'.

18:27 | Tough Love

1 'Domestic Violence: Frequently Asked Questions', Factsheet 2009, Women's Aid.

2 UNIFEM, 'Violence Against Women – Facts and Figures', www.saynotoviolence.org.

3 'It's In Our Hands: Stop Violence Against Women', report,

Amnesty International, 2004.

4 E. Povey et al., 'Home Office Statistical Bulletin: Crime in England and Wales 2006/07', Home Office, 2008.

5 'Domestic Violence: Frequently Asked Questions'.

6 'Factsheet: Domestic Violence', Government Equalities Office.

7 P. K. Lundberg-Love and S. Marmion (eds), *Intimate Violence Against Women: When Spouses, Partners, or Lovers Attack* (Praeger, 2006).

8 'Women and the Criminal Justice System: The Facts', briefing, Fawcett Society, 2008.

9 'What He Did Seems Inhuman', *Guardian*, 2 April 2008.

10 'Domestic Violence: Frequently Asked Questions'.

11 T. Allen et al., 'Patterns of Injuries: Accident or Abuse', *Violence Against Women*, 13 (2007): 802–16.

12 M. B. Mechanic et al., 'Mental Health Consequences of Intimate Partner Abuse: A Multidimensional Assessment of Four Different Forms of Abuse', *Violence Against Women*, 14 (2008): 634–54.

13 UNIFEM, 'Violence Against Women', for the US figure; Sylvia Walby, 'The Cost of Domestic Violence: Research Summary', Women and Equality Unit, 2004, for the UK.

14 'It's In Our Hands: Stop Violence Against Women'.

15 S. Warner, *Understanding the Effects of Child Sexual Abuse: Feminist Revolutions in Theory, Research and Practice* (Routledge, 2008).

16 'Just Representation? Press Reporting and the Reality of Rape', report, Eaves, February 2008.

17 UNIFEM, 'Violence Against Women'.

18 'It's In Our Hands: Stop Violence Against Women'.

19 H. Littleton et al., 'Beyond the Campus: Unacknowledged Rape among Low-Income Women', *Violence Against Women*, 14 (2008): 269–86.

20 'Drug Facilitated Sexual Assault', report, Advisory Council on the Misuse of Drugs, 2007.

21 H. Littleton and C. E. Henderson, 'If She Is Not a Victim,

Does that Mean She Was not Traumatized? Evaluation of Predictors of PTSD Symptomatology among College Rape Victims', *Violence Against Women*, 15(2) (2009): 148–67.

22 J. R. Temple et al., 'Differing Effects of Partner and Nonpartner Sexual Assault on Women's Mental Health', *Violence Against Women*, 13(3) (2007): 285–97.

23 Littleton and Henderson, 'If She Is Not a Victim, Does that Mean She Was not Traumatized?'

24 A. Rao, 'The Politics of Gender and Culture in International Human Rights Discourse', in J. Peters and A. Wolper (eds), *Women's Rights, Human Rights: International Feminist Perspectives* (Routledge, 1995).

25 'Eliminating Female Genital Mutilation: An Interagency Statement', World Health Organisation, 2008, for the world figure; 'Engendering Justice – from Policy to Practice: Final Report of the Commission on Women and the Criminal Justice System', Fawcett Society, 2009, for the UK figure.

26 'Because I Am a Girl: The State of the World's Girls (2007)', report, Plan UK, 2007.

27 UNIFEM, 'Violence Against Women'.

28 'A Veil Drawn over Brutal Crimes', *Guardian*, 3 October 2003.

29 Jeffreys, *Beauty and Misogyny*, p. 28.

30 'Eliminating Female Genital Mutilation'.

31 'Asda T-shirt "Incitement to Rape"', BBC News Online, 5 April 2007.

32 *Daily Mirror*, 24 June 2004.

33 Cited in C. Kilmartin and J. Allison, *Men's Violence Against Women: Theory, Research, and Activism* (Psychology Press, 2007).

34 J. L. Mullaney, 'Telling It Like a Man: Masculinities and Battering Men's Accounts of Their Violence', *Men and Masculinities*, 10(2) (2007): 222–47.

35 D. Y. Borochowitz, 'The Taming of the Shrew: Batterers' Constructions of Their Wives' Narratives', *Violence Against Women*, 14(10) (2008): 1166–80.

36 Kilmartin and Allison, *Men's Violence Against Women*.

37 L. M. Pazzani, 'The Factors Affecting Sexual Assaults Committed by Strangers and Acquaintances', *Violence Against Women*, 13(7) (2007): 717–49.

38 'Violence Against Women Opinion Polling', Home Office, February 2009.

39 N. M. Capezza and X. B. Arriaga, 'Why Do People Blame Victims of Abuse? The Role of Stereotypes of Women on Perceptions of Blame', *Sex Roles*, 59 (2008): 839–50.

40 'Teenage Girls Stand by Their Man', *New York Times*, 19 March 2009.

41 'Dame Helen Rape Remark Criticised', BBC News Online, 1 September 2008.

42 'On Rape and Personal Responsibility', *Guardian*, 12 August 2008.

43 K. M. Chapleau et al., 'How Ambivalent Sexism Toward Women and Men Support Rape Myth Acceptance', *Sex Roles*, 57 (2007): 131–6.

44 'Violence Against Women Crime Report, 2007–2008', Crown Prosecution Service.

45 'Engendering Justice – from Policy to Practice: Final Report of the Commission on Women and the Criminal Justice System', Fawcett Society, 2009.

46 'Rape: The Facts', Fawcett Society, 2008.

47 'Police Targets "Meant Car Crime Was Given Higher Priority Than Rape"', *Guardian*, 17 March 2009.

48 'Rape: The Facts', briefing, Fawcett Society, 2008.

49 'Justice for Rape Victims', briefing, Fawcett Society, 2008.

50 R. Franiuk et al., 'Prevalence and Effects of Rape Myths in Print Journalism: The Kobe Bryant Case', *Violence Against Women*, 14(3) (2008): 287–309.

51 R. Franiuk et al., 'Prevalence of Rape Myths in Headlines and Their Effects on Attitudes Toward Rape', *Sex Roles*, 58 (2008): 790–801.

52 'Legal Threat to Councils over Rape Victims', *Guardian*, 30 January 2009.

53 'Realising Rights, Fulfilling Obligations: A Template for an Integrated Strategy on Violence Against Women for the UK', report, End Violence Against Women, 2008.

54 'No Recourse, No Safety: The Government's Failure to Protect Women from Violence', report, Amnesty International UK & Southall Black Sisters, 2008.

20:30 | The Booty Myth

1 'Hugh Hefner Insists that Playboy Liberated Women', Softpedia, 7 December 2005.

2 Douglas Fox, 'Why Sex Workers Need the IUSW', 18 May 2009, http://littlebitcheaper.blogspot.com/2009/05/why-sex-workers-need-iusw.html.

3 M. Farley, '"Bad for the Body, Bad for the Heart": Prostitution Harms Women Even if Legalised or Decriminalised', *Violence Against Women*, 10(10) (2004): 1087–1125.

4 'Jessica Valenti: Full Frontal Feminism', *The Nation*, 28 September 2007.

5 M. Karp and D. Stoller, *The Bust Guide to the New Girl Order* (Penguin, 1999): 82.

6 'Feminism is a Failure, and Other Myths', AlterNet, 8 July 2009.

7 See: www.itv.com/Drama/contemporary/TheSecretDiaryofaCallGirl/Castinterviews/.

8 'We Don't Sell Sex for a Living', *Northern Echo*, 7 August 2006.

9 GMB press release, 7 December 2008.

10 'Paying the Price: A Consultation Paper on Prostitution', Home Office, 2004.

11 J. Bindel and H. Atkins, 'Big Brothel: A Survey of the Off-Street Sex Industry in London', The POPPY Project, 2008.

12 S. Jeffreys, *The Industrial Vagina: The Political Economy of the Global Sex Trade* (Routledge, 2009).

13 'Paying the Price: A Consultation Paper on Prostitution'.

14 M. Farley, J. Lynne and A. J. Cotton, 'Prostitution in Vancouver: Violence and the Colonization of First Nations Women', *Transcultural Psychiatry*, 42(2) (2005): 242–71.

15 M. Farley, 'Prostitution and the Invisibility of Harm', *Women & Therapy*, 26(3/4) (2003): 247–80.

16 Farley, '"Bad for the Body, Bad for the Heart"'.

17 Ibid.

18 Farley, Lynne and Cotton, 'Prostitution in Vancouver'.

19 L. DeRiviere, 'A Human Capital Methodology for Estimating the Lifelong Personal Costs of Young Women Leaving the Sex Trade', *Feminist Economics*, 12(3) (2006): 367–402.

20 'Challenging Men's Demand for Prostitution in Scotland: A Research Report Based on Interviews with 110 Men Who Bought Women in Prostitution', Women's Support Project, 2008.

21 A. Levy, *Female Chauvinist Pigs: Women and the Rise of Raunch Culture* (Pocket Books, 2005): 39–40.

22 'Stop Porn Culture', http://stoppornculture.org.

23 'Jowell Finds Support over Criticism of Desmond', *Independent*, 1 June 2002.

24 R. Wosnitzer and A. J. Bridges, 'Aggression and Sexual Behavior in Best-Selling Pornography: A Content Analysis Update', paper presented at the annual meeting of the International Communication Association, San Francisco, CA, 2007.

25 G. Dines, 'The White Man's Burden: Gonzo Pornography and the Construction of Black Masculinity', *Yale Journal of Law and Feminism*, 18(1) (2006): 283–97.

26 Jeffreys, *The Industrial Vagina*, p. 77.

27 G. Dines and R. Jensen, 'Pornography Is a Left Issue', http://users.rcn.com/gaildines/articles.htm.

28 Robert Jensen, interview with the author, April 2009.

29 Jensen, *Getting Off: Pornography and the End of Masculinity* (South End Press, 2007), p. 76.

30 M. Flood, 'Men, Sex, and Homosociality: How Bonds

between Men Shape their Sexual Relations with Women', *Men and Masculinities*, 10(3) (2007): 339–59.

31 C. Itzin et al., 'The Evidence of Harm to Adults Relating to Exposure to Extreme Pornographic Material: A Rapid Evidence Assessment (REA)', Ministry of Justice Series 11/07, September 2007.

32 Jeffreys, *The Industrial Vagina*.

33 J. K. Wesley, 'Growing Up Sexualised: Issues of Power and Violence in the Lives of Female Exotic Dancers', *Violence Against Women*, 8(10) (2002): 1182–1207.

34 'Confessions of a Teenage Stripper', Pacific News service, 27 January 2004, available at http://news.pacificnews.org/

35 Jennifer Danns, 'Generation Sex', unpublished BA dissertation, University of Liverpool, 2008.

36 'Profitable Exploits: Lap Dancing in the UK', Child and Woman Abuse Studies Unit, London Metropolitan University for Glasgow City Council, 2004.

37 'Challenging Men's Demand for Prostitution in Scotland'.

38 M. Coy et al., 'It's Just Like Going to the Supermarket: Men Buying Sex in East London', Child and Woman Abuse Studies Unit for Safe Exit at Toynbee Hall, 2007.

39 K. Holsopple, 'Strip Club Testimony', Freedom and Justice Center for Prostitution Resources, A Program of the Volunteers of America of Minnesota, 1998.

40 K. Frank, '"Just Trying to Relax": Masculinizing Practices and Strip Club Regulars', *Journal of Sex Research*, 40(1) (2003): 61–75.

41 Royal Town Planning Institute, Gender and Spatial Planning: Good Practice Note 7, 10 December 2007.

42 'Licensing of Strip Clubs', London Borough of Tower Hamlets, 2008.

43 L. A. Morgan and K. A. Martin, 'Taking Women Professionals out of the Office: The Case of Women in Sales', *Gender and Society*, 20(1) (2006): 108–28.

44 'Tesco Condemned for Selling Pole Dancing Toy', *Daily Mail*, 24 October 2006.

45 'Magazine ABCs: Lads' Mags Take Circulation Hit', *Press Gazette*, 12 February 2009.
46 Coy et al., 'It's Just Like Going to the Supermarket'.
47 J. M. Stankiewicz and F. Rosselli, 'Women as Sex Objects and Victims in Print Advertisements', *Sex Roles*, 58 (2008): 579–89.
48 E. Monk-Turner et al., 'Who Is Gazing at Whom? A Look at How Sex Is Used in Magazine Advertisements', *Journal of Gender Studies*, 17(3) (2008): 201–9.
49 See www.ryanair.com/site/EN/news.php?yr=08&month=jun&story=gen-en-200608.
50 See www.blogsouthwest.com/blog/raising-bar-si-one.
51 Christine Nicholson, 'Women as Sex Objects', *Scientific American*, 17 February 2009.
52 'Report of the APA Task Force on the Sexualization of Girls', American Psychological Association, 2007.
53 'Row Erupts Over School Pole Dancing Demonstration', Press Association, 29 January 2009.
54 '"Sexy" Children's Underwear Withdrawn', BBC News Online, 26 March 2003.
55 'Naked Ambition Rubs Off on Teen Girls', *Manchester Evening News*, 6 June 2005.

22:57 | Bedroom Politics

1 'Raising the Bar: What Next for the Early Childhood Education and Care Workforce?', report, Daycare Trust, 2008.
2 'Surviving Pregnancy and Childbirth: An International Human Right', report, Centre for Reproductive Rights, 2005.
3 'Family Planning: The Unfinished Agenda', report, World Health Organisation, 2003.
4 S. Blaffer Hrdy, *Mother Nature: Natural Selection and the Female of the Species* (Chatto & Windus, 1999), p. 90.
5 S. Jeffreys, *Anticlimax: A Feminist Perspective on the Sexual Revolution* (The Women's Press, 1990).

6 Ibid.

7 J. Katz and V. Tirone, 'Women's Sexual Compliance with Male Dating Partners: Associations with Investment in Ideal Womanhood and Romantic Well-Being', *Sex Roles*, 60 (2009): 347–56.

8 L. Y. Bay-Cheng and R. K. Eliseo-Arras, 'The Making of Unwanted Sex: Gendered and Neoliberal Norms in College Women's Unwanted Sexual Experiences', *Journal of Sex Research*, 45(4) (2008): 386–97.

9 Katz and Tirone, 'Women's Sexual Compliance with Male Dating Partners'.

10 A. K. Kiefer et al., 'How Women's Nonconscious Association of Sex with Submission Relates to Their Subjective Sexual Arousability and Ability to Reach Orgasm', *Sex Roles*, 55 (2006): 83–94.

11 V. R. Schick, A. N. Zucker and L. Y. Bay-Cheng, 'Safer, Better Sex Through Feminism: The Role of Feminist Ideology in Women's Sexual Well-Being', *Psychology of Women Quarterly*, 32 (2008): 225–32.

12 ZOO, 13–19 March 2009.

13 J. M. Albright, 'Sex in America Online: An Exploration of Sex, Marital Status, and Sexual Identity in Internet Sex Seeking and Its Impacts', *Journal of Sex Research*, 45(2) (2008): 175–86.

14 'Bristol Palin Campaigns for Teenage Abstinence', *Telegraph*, 7 May 2009.

15 Editorial, 'Reducing Unintended Pregnancy in the United States', *Contraception*, 77 (2008): 1–5.

16 J. Santelli et al., 'Abstinence and Abstinence-Only Education: A Review of U.S. Policies and Programs', *Journal of Adolescent Health*, 38 (2006): 72–81.

17 Ibid., p. 73.

18 J. Kay and A. Jackson, 'Sex, Lies & Stereotypes: How Abstinence-Only Programs Harm Women and Girls', report, Legal Momentum, 2008.

19 'The Pursuit of Teen Girl Purity', *Time*, 17 July 2008.

20 'Dancing the Night Away, With a Higher Purpose', *New York Times*, 19 May 2008.

21 Santelli et al., 'Abstinence and Abstinence-Only Education'.

22 'Obama to Scrap Funding for Abstinence-Only Programmes', *Guardian*, 8 May 2009.

23 'Sex Education for Five-Year-Olds to Be Made Compulsory in Schools', *Guardian*, 27 April 2009.

24 'Faith Schools Free to Preach Against Homosexuality', *Guardian*, 28 April 2009.

25 See www.humanism.org.uk.

26 Figures issued by the Department for Children, Schools and Families, January 2007: www.dcsf.gov.uk/rsgateway/DB/SFR/s000744/index.shtml.

27 D. Chambers, 'Peer Regulation of Teenage Sexual Identities', *Gender and Education*, 16(3) (2004): 397–415.

28 'Porn: The New Sex Education', *Guardian*, 30 March 2009.

29 A. Frankel and D. A. Curtis, 'What's in a Purse? Maybe a Woman's Reputation', *Sex Roles*, 59 (2008): 615–22.

30 J. Pearson, 'Personal Control, Self-Efficacy in Sexual Negotiation, and Contraceptive Risk among Adolescents: The Role of Gender', *Sex Roles*, 54 (2006): 615–25.

31 L. L. Heise, 'Freedom Close to Home: The Impact of Violence Against Women on Reproductive Rights', in J. Peters and A. Wolper (eds), *Women's Rights, Human Rights: International Feminist Perspectives* (Routledge, 1995), pp. 238–55.

32 C. M. Williams et al., 'Intimate Partner Violence and Women's Contraceptive Use', *Violence Against Women*, 14(12) (2008): 1382–96.

33 See Abortion Rights website, www.abortionrights.org.uk.

34 'Shock Tactics', *Guardian*, 25 November 2008.

35 D. Dickenson, 'Ownership, Property and Women's Bodies', in H. Widdows et al. (eds), *Women's Reproductive Rights* (Macmillan, 2005), pp. 188–98.

36 'Time to Speak Up', *Guardian*, 27 October 2006.

37 'Choking on the Global Gag Rule', *Guardian*, 26 January 2009.

38 Ibid.

39 'The World's Abortion Laws', Centre for Reproductive Rights, 2008.

40 C. Kenny, 'Abortion – A Reproductive Right', in H. Widdows et al. (eds), *Women's Reproductive Rights* (Macmillan, 2005), pp. 17–32.

41 'Rape Row Sparks Excommunications', BBC News Online, 5 March 2009.

42 See www.msnbc.msn.com/id/21255186/.

43 M. Goldberg, *The Means of Reproduction: Sex, Power, and the Future of the World* (Penguin, 2009).

44 'What if Roe Fell?', Center for Reproductive Rights, 2007.

45 'Abortion Worldwide: Twelve Years of Reform', Center for Reproductive Rights, 2007.

46 'A Murderous Wake-Up Call', *Guardian*, 2 June 2009.

47 'Family Planning Is So Easy, Yet So Little Is Invested in It', *Guardian*, 1 April 2009.

48 R. Ingham et al., 'Reasons for Second Trimester Abortions in England and Wales', *Reproductive Health Matters*, 16(31), Supplement, (2008): 18–29.

49 'Shock Tactics', *Guardian*, 25 November 2008.

50 Life, 'Review of the Year 2007/2008': www.lifecharity.org.uk/support/annualreport.

51 See www.lifecharity.org.uk/education/lifebeforebirth.

52 S. W. G. Derbyshire, 'Can Fetuses Feel Pain?', *British Medical Journal*, 332 (2006): 909–12.

53 See www.lifecharity.org.uk/faq.

54 'Reasons for Second Trimester Abortions in England and Wales'.

55 V. E. Charles et al., 'Abortion and Long-Term Mental Health Outcomes: A Systematic Review of the Evidence', *Contraception*, 78 (2008): 436–50.

56 Editorial, 'You Say "Regret" and I Say "Relief": A Need to Break the Polemic about Abortion', *Contraception*, 78 (2008): 87–9.

00:00 | A New Day

1 J. Valenti, *Full Frontal Feminism: A Young Woman's Guide to Why Feminism Matters* (Seal Press, 2007), p. 175.

2 See www.thesmokinggun.com/archive/091505 1hooters1.html (accessed June 2009).

3 'A Growing Tide Update: The Need to Reform Licensing of Lap Dancing Clubs', *Object*, December 2008.

4 See www.therocketclub.com.

5 See www.womankind.org.uk.

6 J. J. Pettman, 'Global Politics and Transnational Feminisms', in L. Ricciutelli, A. Miles and M. McFadden (eds), *Feminist Politics, Activism and Vision: Local and Global Challenges* (Zed Books, 2005), pp. 49–63.

7 'Taking Stock Update: Afghan Women and Girls Seven Years On', report, WOMANKIND Worldwide, 2008.

8 '"Teacher, Can We Leave Now?" "No."', *New York Times*, 18 July 2009.

9 'Taliban Kill Top Afghan Woman', *Guardian*, 26 September 2006.

10 'Education Under Attack', briefing, UNESCO, 2007.

11 'Afghanistan Passes "Barbaric" Law Diminishing Women's Rights', *Guardian*, 14 August 2009.

12 'Prostitution Q & A', Women's National Commission Sexual Violence Policy Monitoring Sub-group, February 2008.

13 Julie Bindel, 'No Escape? An Investigation into London's Service Provision for Women Involved in the Commercial Sex Industry', The POPPY Project, 2006.

14 'It's Abuse and a Life of Hell', *Guardian*, 29 February 2008.

15 'Donkeys in Clover – But Charity Leaders Call for a Rethink', *Guardian*, 26 April 2008.

16 'The Crisis in Rape Crisis', Women's Resource Centre & Rape Crisis (England and Wales), 2008.

17 'Women and the Criminal Justice System: The Facts'.

18 Mill to Joseph Giles, 24 August 1871, cited in R. Reeves, *John Stuart Mill: Victorian Firebrand* (Atlantic Books, 2007), p. 414.

19 Ibid., p. 448.

20 M. Flood, 'Men's Collective Struggles for Gender Justice: The Case of Anti-Violence Activism', in M., Kimmel, J. Hearn and R. W. Connell (eds), *The Handbook of Studies on Men and Masculinities* (Sage, 2003), pp. 458–66.

21 See www.stonewall.org.uk/what_we_do/research_and_policy/2843.asp.

22 See www.stonewall.org.uk/education_for_all/research/2731.asp.

23 D. Chambers, E. Tincknell and J. Van Loon, 'Peer Regulation of Teenage Sexual Identities', *Gender and Education*, 16(3) (2004): 397–415.

24 'Hip-Hop: Beyond Beats & Rhymes, A Resource Guide for Community Organisers and Educators', www.bhurt.com.

25 'Not Quite Jam and Jerusalem: Women's Institute Ladies Toured the World in Search of the Perfect Brothel', *Mail on Sunday*, 29 July 2008.

26 'Abolishing Prostitution: The Swedish Solution. An Interview with Gunilla Ekberg', *Rain and Thunder: A Radical Feminist Journal of Discussion and Activism*, 41 (2008); available online at http://nopornnorthampton.org/files/28534-27078/RT_Interview_with_Gunilla_Ekberg.pdf.

27 G. Ekberg, 'The Swedish Law that Prohibits the Purchase of Sexual Services: Best Practices for Prevention of Prostitution and Trafficking in Human Beings', *Violence Against Women*, 10(10) (2004): 1187–1218.

28 'A Critical Examination of Responses to Prostitution in Four Countries: Victoria, Australia; Ireland; the Netherlands; and Sweden', Child and Woman Abuse Studies Unit for the Routes Out Partnership Board, 2003.

29 See www.unifem.org.

30 'Rwanda: The Impact of Women Legislators on Policy Outcomes Affecting Children and Families', report, UNICEF, 2006.

31 'Women Rise in Rwanda's Economic Revival', *Washington Post*, 16 May 2008.

Index